With the Compliments of

PRO CHAUFFEUR SERVICES

In a very historic year for our country

1994

Thank you for your support

Magnificent
South Africa

Magnificent
South Africa

Contents

10. INTRODUCTION
Overview of the land, its history, peoples and economy

34. WITWATERSRAND – HEART OF GOLD
Johannesburg, Soweto, Pretoria, Sun City

50. EASTERN TRANSVAAL – BUSHVELD AND BERG
Kruger National Park and the Lowveld private reserves

66. MOUNTAINS OF THE DRAGON
Scenic highlands and mountain retreats

84. SUBTROPICAL KWAZULU-NATAL
Golden sands, battlegrounds and game parks

102. XHOSA COUNTRY
The Eastern Cape's 'settler' region, Ciskei and Transkei

114. THE GARDEN ROUTE
South Africa's enchanting coastal Eden

128. BOUNDLESS SPACES
Flowering deserts and horizons that stretch forever

144. FAIREST CAPE AND WINELANDS
Cape Town, the Peninsula and the Winelands

INDEX

FRONTISPIECE: THE MAGNIFICENT ROTUNDA *at Lost City's Palace.*
TITLE PAGE: THE LONELY SEA AND SKY. *South Africa's coastline
extends 3 000 kilometres from the desolate Orange River Mouth
in the west to the Mozambique border in the east.*
OPPOSITE: GRAND MOUNTAINS, *snow-capped in winter, fringe
the fertile Ceres basin in the Western Cape.*

FOREWORD

The year 1994 will always be regarded as a turning point in the history of South Africa. This was the year of constitutional change and the re-entry of South Africa into the community of nations. Although these new challenges created fresh expectations, the land stayed the same – as magnificent and as diverse as ever.

ABOVE: THE EASTERN TRANSVAAL'S *lovely Lisbon Falls.*
RIGHT: THE CITRUS SWALLOWTAIL *butterfly.*
OPPOSITE: FAREWELL TO ISOLATION – *jubilant fans cheer the Kaiser Chiefs soccer team in its match against Cairo's Zamalek club.*

The southern tip of Africa is still a place where the infinite variety of the sub-continent is fused into a potpourri of natural and cultural marvels. From the Cape Peninsula, with its looming Table Mountain, to the stately baobabs of the Transvaal bushveld, this is truly a land of amazing diversity. As new international doors open to South Africa, the challenge will be to manage this diversity in a sustainable manner, yet to utilize it in such a way that will create optimum living conditions for all its inhabitants.

The environmental emphasis of the new government of national unity will be on quality of life, with shelter, energy, domestic water supplies and sanitation heading the list of priorities. The provision of these amenities will automatically promote conservation efforts through the abatement of pollution.

Present attempts to maintain the country's diverse wildlife and the unique opportunities it offers for ecotourism will, of course, continue. We cannot afford to lose one single species, whether it is the migratory and endangered blue swallow or the black rhino. Botanical gardens will have to be protected jealously as well as extended, and we will have to guard against the temptation of over-utilization or over-development of the environment in general.

It should also be borne in mind that South Africa's extraordinary variety is not our heritage alone. Not only do we frequently share migratory species with neighbouring countries, but we also hold in trust the diversity of our savannahs, the richness of our oceans and the expertise of our scientists for the entire world. For these and other reasons we can expect to enter into global alliances to counter international environmental problems such as global warming, depletion of the ozone layer and poverty.

South Africa faces a challenging future. By honouring international commitments and maintaining the excellence of past environmental milestones, South Africa can remain a leader in Africa and, indeed, the world.

It is vital that we constantly strive to conserve those elements which together make South Africa a truly magnificent land.

DR DAWIE DE VILLIERS
MINISTER FOR ENVIRONMENTAL AFFAIRS AND TOURISM

South Africa: the rainbow nation

'South Africa is richly endowed

with great men and women in its

political, cultural, religious and

economic life. When they become

free, they will show the world why

this is a land of hope'. Chester Crocker, 1988

The Republic of South Africa stretches 2 000 kilometres from Kipling's great and grey-green Limpopo south to blustery Cape Agulhas, southernmost tip of the African continent, and 1 500 kilometres from the bleak Atlantic seaboard in the west to the lushly subtropical Indian Ocean shores of KwaZulu-Natal in the east. A big country by any standards, and a varied one too, its 1 220 430 square kilometres cover high central plateau and game-rich bushveld, forested upland, dry semidesert and fertile coastal terrace that, together, embrace a bewildering number of different ethnic groups, cultures, creeds and languages.

This human diversity is the product of a turbulent and often tragic history that goes back millennia, to the

Stone Age hunter-gatherers of the sunlit plains and the Bantu-speaking migrants who came from the north to supplant them. In modern times, the story has been one of European conquest and colonization and, latterly, of an oppressed people's increasingly effective resistance to a monumentally unjust political system. Indeed, in all the decades since the first white settlers arrived at the Cape – in 1652 – there have been few years that were not blighted by confrontation and violent conflict, much of it race inspired.

But in the early 1990s, in an extraordinary (some say even miraculous) reversal of trends, leaders of the various opposing groups came together to bridge the yawning divide and, in May 1994, to inaugurate a new era. And today, for the first time in centuries, South Africa is at peace with itself, revealed to the world – as these pages show – not as a battleground but a country of endless fascination and great beauty.

Left: Vibrant colours and geometric patterns grace Ndebele homesteads.
Right: Traditional Craftwork in a Tsonga village.

The nature of the land

One has to go far, far back into the mists of time in order to understand the geophysical origins of South Africa – to when the African continent was locked into a single mass of land, called Pangaea, which once made up a third of the surface of the planet.

About 200 million years ago, Pangaea split up and a vast piece of land – consisting collectively of what is today Africa, Australia, South America, Antarctica and India – drifted off to form a new southern continental mass named Gondwana. Some 40 million years later Africa split off from the supercontinent, thus becoming a continent in its own right.

The splitting off of the African continent from Gondwana, and its subsequent shift across the face of the earth, caused enormous stresses within this land mass and these stresses contributed towards the creation of South Africa's Great Escarpment – a vast semicircle of mountain ranges that separates the interior plateau from the lower coastal areas – the so-called marginal zone.

The Great Escarpment of South Africa is one of the single most important factors affecting the country's weather as it serves to deprive much of the vast inland plateau of the sea-given rains that water the country's southern and eastern coastal areas. As a direct result of the Great Escarpment, South Africa is a predominantly dry country, with only 10 per cent of the land surface receiving more than 750 millimetres of rain a year.

However, South Africa's geography and climate is a lot more complex than a mere division of the country into a wet coastal area and a dry interior region lying behind the Great Escarpment. The country's surface terrain includes desert areas and subtropical forests, barren sand dunes and fertile agricultural soils; there are both winter and summer rainfall areas, and the country is periodically subjected to devastating floods and equally destructive droughts, winter snows in the upland areas and searing summer heats.

TOP: SOME OF THE RUGGED *and dramatically beautiful mountains of the southern coastal rampart.* RIGHT: THE LOVELY GEORGE LILY, *one of the myriad plants of the winter rainfall region.*

A combination of South Africa's varied geography and climate have served to create no less than seven vegetation types.

Desert

Although desert is a feature of much of Namibia, it only strictly occurs in the north-western, Kalahari section of South Africa. In this desert environment, plant cover is minimal and stunted. However, deep-rooted trees are found along dry watercourses and the sandy flats and gravel plains support sparse succulents and lichen cover. After rain there is often a scattering of ephemeral grasses.

Succulent Karoo

This semidesert ecosystem occurs along the West Coast from Lambert's Bay northwards, and inland to Springbok and Calvinia. The rainfall here is between 50 and 200 millimetres per year and the flora is dominated by a rich variety of hardy perennial succulent and small-leaved shrubs. Recurring droughts, coupled with overstocking with sheep and goats, have caused considerable ecological degradation in recent years.

Nama-Karoo

The great semidesert of South Africa's central plateau extends over the greater part of the Cape Provinces and north-westwards to Mariental and Rehoboth in Namibia. Rainfall is erratic and averages between 125 and 375 millimetres a year. The vegetation comprises perennial succulents and low scrub bushes with small drought-resistant leaves and spreading root-systems. Once sweet grasses were also a major component of the Nama-Karoo vegetation type but selective grazing by an overabundance of sheep has gradually led to the dominance of less-palatable scrubby vegetation.

Grassland

This plant community dominates the interior uplands and rolling plains of the Transvaal, Lesotho, the Eastern Cape and inland Natal, with altitudes ranging from 1 200 to 2 100 metres. The highveld grasses are short and the terrain supports few indigenous trees, partly due to frost, drought and fire during the winter months. In the lower-lying areas, however, the grasses are taller and of a more truly temperate type. Bad agricultural practices have caused Nama-Karoo vegetation to expand into the south-eastern grasslands.

Fynbos

The Mediterranean climate of the south-west and southern Cape, with predominantly winter rainfall (between 400 and 2 000 millimetres) and hot, dry summers has led to the development of a unique array of plant species known as fynbos. Although forest remnants survive in the wetter kloofs, fynbos is essentially a fire-adapted heathland consisting of a remarkably rich array of distinctive plants such as proteas and ericas.

Forest

South Africa is not generously endowed with extensive natural forests – although its man-made forest plantations are among the largest in the world. Many indigenous forest patches fell prey to the axe and the saw as white settlement expanded in the 18th and 19th centuries. However, small forested areas do still occur in the year-round rainfall areas of the coastal zone and in the wetter parts of the Eastern Transvaal. The largest surviving natural forest is the 180 by 6 kilometre strip between George and Humansdorp in the southern Cape. This stretch of woodland is strictly protected and is famous for its iron-woods, stinkwoods and yellowwoods. Evergreen subtropical species, such as palms, grow along the hot and humid Natal coast, where the swampier lagoons and estuaries also support mangroves.

Savannah

Known in South Africa as bushveld, this vegetation is characteristic of the northern regions of the country although it does extend down the east coast as far as Port Elizabeth. Bushveld vegetation is varied, ranging from the dry, dense bush of the Transvaal Lowveld to the open parkland of parts of the Northern Transvaal where the grassland is studded with umbrella-thorn, marula, mopane and baobab trees.

TOP: SCATTERS OF COSMOS *decorate the grasslands of the southern Highveld. The terrain sustains few indigenous trees.*

ABOVE: EXQUISITE PATCHES *of natural forest grace the well-watered lower slopes of the Drakensberg.*

Coast of contrasts

TOP: INDIAN OCEAN ROLLERS *pound the coast at Storms River Mouth in the Eastern Cape.*
ABOVE: A CLOWN FISH *at rest off Natal's seaboard.*

The South African coastline consists of a rough 3 000-kilometre semicircle that is washed by two of the world's great oceans – the Atlantic along the country's West Coast and south-western tip, and the Indian along the south and east coasts. It is a shoreline of dramatic contrasts ranging from long white beaches to sheer rocky cliffs.

From a mariner's point of view, the South African coast has always been accorded the utmost respect. The formidable winds and currents often cause huge seas. To date, no less than 3 000 shipwrecks have occurred along the country's seashore – an average of one for every kilometre of coastline.

The country's coastal margin is well defined, being separated from the interior of the subcontinent by the almost continuous band of mountains known as the Great Escarpment. This coastal margin consists of three coastal zones: the arid West Coast, the temperate south-east coast and the warm subtropical east coast – each of these being very distinctive in terms of their vegetation and faunal composition.

The whole of South Africa's West Coast abuts the Atlantic Ocean and the cold, north-flowing Benguela Current bestows this stretch of shoreline with a combination of oceanographic and weather phenomena that make it the country's most important commercial fishing region. It is also a major source of West Coast rock lobster (*Jasus lalandii*), which thrive in thick forests of kelp found along much of the seaboard.

At intervals along the West Coast's windswept length there are remote harbours and fishing hamlets, protected lagoons, seal and seabird colonies, and the occasional skeletons of beached seals and whales. It is a harsh environment with an intemperate climate, and most people are unmoved by its debatable charms. However, for others, the West Coast's starkly sculpted landscapes, often draped in ectoplasmic mists, are an ongoing source of poetic and artistic inspiration.

Merging of the oceans

Although it is the view of oceanographers that the Atlantic and Indian oceans meet at Cape Agulhas, there is no immediate change here from cold to warm water. Instead, a gradual transitional zone of temperate water occurs from the coastal resort of Hermanus for more than 1 000 kilometres eastwards to Port St Johns. Warm, subtropical conditions are only reliably found further north along the east coast proper – from Port St Johns to Maputaland and beyond. Here one finds an aquatic world of crystal waters and coral reefs that stands in radical contrast to the grey, bone-chilling Atlantic waters of the West Coast.

It is along the stretch of Indian Ocean coastline that South Africa's abundant bathing, watersport and sailing activities are concentrated. These warmer waters also attract thousands of fishermen who cast in their lines in the hope of landing one of the many subtropical species brought into South African waters by the warm, south-flowing Mozambique and Agulhas currents.

It is also along this stretch of coastline that the majority of the country's 343 estuaries are to be found. In fact, within the single 745-kilometre stretch from Cape Padrone, east of Port Elizabeth, to Mtunzini, south of St Lucia, there are no less than 225 estuaries, together providing an exceptionally wide range of specialized marine habitats.

Conservation has become a top priority along South Africa's coastline and, in order to safeguard its myriad inhabitants effectively, a total of 12 marine and adjacent onshore conservation areas are now officially protected. In each case, the marine boundaries are at least 12 nautical miles offshore, with the exception of the De Hoop coast between Cape Agulhas and Mossel Bay, where the reserve area projects even further seawards to include a section of the ecologically and commercially important Agulhas Bank. Largest of the marine reserves is the 84 000-hectare strip within the Greater St Lucia Wetland Park in northern KwaZulu-Natal.

All in all, these conservation areas protect some of the most significant marine and adjacent terrestrial ecosystems along the coast, taking in varying stretches of shoreline from just half a kilometre at the Great Fish River Mouth Bird Sanctuary to the extensive 65-kilometre shore frontage of the Tsitsikamma National Park. Migrating southern right and humpback whales, which come into local waters to mate and calve each year, are also protected. Recent legislation safeguards these whales from 'harassment' and it is an offence to come within 300 metres of one of these giant mammals.

Whale watching during the winter months is an increasingly popular pastime along the western and southern seaboards. Of the many viewing points dotted along the coast from St Helena Bay to Plettenberg Bay, the most rewarding is undoubtedly the coastal resort town of Hermanus, now considered by many to be one of the best sites for whale watching in the world. Here, from the rocky cliffs at the edge of the town, it is possible to watch whales cavorting with their newly born calves less than a hundred metres away.

ABOVE: WEATHERWORN *fishing craft at Kalk Bay, near Cape Town.*
LEFT: EARLY MORNING ANGLERS *try their luck on the shores of KwaZulu-Natal.*

Majestic mountains

South Africa has many natural treasures but its wealth of mountainous terrain must certainly rank as one of its greatest. Mountain ranges form a fundamental part of the geography of the country, stretching as they do in an almost continuous loop from the Soutpansberg in the north-eastern corner of the country, down to the Drakensberg of Natal, south-west through the folded mountains of the Cape, and up to the Cedarberg and Bokkeveldberg of Namaqualand.

Much of South Africa's mountain region collectively makes up what is known as the Great Escarpment, the great rocky divide that separates the high-lying interior plateau of the country from the lower-lying areas that stretch from the Great Escarpment down to the coastline in the south and east.

To the east of the country, the dominant part of the Great Escarpment is known as the Great Drakensberg Escarpment. It rises in the far north-eastern Transvaal and flanks the eastern seaboard for hundreds of kilometres. The towering buttresses and soaring pinnacles of this rampart have been sculpted by millennia of erosion – accelerated in the last 160 million years when the eastern landmass of Gondwana tore itself away from Africa.

The distinctive peaks of the lofty Drakensberg range – which separate Natal from the landlocked country of Lesotho – are remnants of more recent lava flows, being up to 1,5 kilometres thick in some places. Here the Escarpment consists essentially of a one-sided mountain – rather like a retaining wall – that serves to separate the verdant green hills of Natal from the interior plateau of the country.

Raptors and ice rats

The Drakensberg is an area of predominantly high, lonely places. Here all is silent but for the wingbeats and cries of birds of prey, and noises that betray the passage of antelope, mountain tortoises and tiny ice rats. However, the lower-lying parts of the Drakensberg constitute one of the country's most popular recreational areas, with holiday-makers flocking there on weekends and during holidays to enjoy the region's wonderful walks, climbs, riding trails and trout fishing.

The southern tail of the Drakensberg Escarpment extends down towards a series of different ranges that run the entire length of the eastern and southern Cape. Here are to be found some of the most geologically interesting of South Africa's mountains – the folded ranges of the southern Cape, which were thrust out of the earth by the accretion of continental plates 250 to 270 million years ago. In the process, they were folded, tilted and twisted into tortured, often near-vertical planes. The phenomenon of folding rock is most theatrically displayed in the extraordinary contortions of Meiringspoort, a narrow river gorge winding through the Swartberg range on the brink of the Great Karoo.

Another geologically interesting mountain in this area is the Kompasberg. Consisting of a sandstone base topped with sharply tilted

BELOW: THE AMPHITHEATRE, *the most striking component of the Drakensberg's Mont-aux-Sources formation, viewed from the upper Tugela River.*

dolerite, it towers over the little Karoo hamlet of Nieu-Bethesda, 2 504 metres above sea level. Its near neighbours – Spandaukop and Valley Mountain – stand sentinel over the bleakly magnificent 'Valley of Desolation', a panoramic moonscape of semiarid Karoo plains framed in jagged dolerite crags.

Farther to the south-west, the hills of the Nuweveldberg and Komsberg poke their stubby, doleritic heads out of the vast, flat plains of the Karoo. Somewhat stunted, and destined never to grow into 'real' mountains, their view to the sea is blocked by their older southern siblings, which march in two parallel rows from west to east and separate the Little and Great Karoo from the coast. These are the Witteberg, Swartberg, Langeberg and the Outeniqua range – all folded mountains of Table Mountain sandstone.

At the most wasterly end of the Cape's folded coastal rampart is the flat-topped mas-

sif of Table Mountain itself – unquestionably South Africa's most famous landmark. The product of aeons of erosion, Table Mountain represents the last, resistant fragment of a once-extensive blanket of quartzitic sandstone that once covered a large part of the southern Cape. While other segments of this belt were folding and buckling under the stress of tectonic forces, Table Mountain stood firm on its granite plinth. Although hard to imagine, Table Mountain's huge mass is in fact an eroded shadow of its former self.

One of the most notable upland areas to the north of Cape Town is the Cedarberg. Named after its once prolific cedar forests, the Cedarberg is home to numerous, rare endemic varieties of fynbos, and also provides sanctuary to the wide-ranging mountain leopard. It is also enormously popular among hikers and campers, offering as it does many interesting trails to explore.

Flowers in the dust

Although South Africa is a predominantly dry country, vegetation is able to thrive in some of the unlikeliest places. This is especially true in the semiarid West Coast area of Namaqualand and the north-western Cape where the indigenous plants have produced fascinating strategies in order to ensure their survival.

From as little as 50 kilometres north of Cape Town, climatic conditions change dramatically under the influence of the chill Benguela current where, in the grip of the South Atlantic high pressure system, forceful, downward winds impede the rise of water vapour from the sea and inhibit rainfall. This clash of elemental wills creates a lot of 'steam' – a dense coastal fog that moves laterally landward off the sea. The result is a lengthy stretch of coastal desert, many of whose plants have only the fog – aside from their own clever survival strategies – to thank for their existence.

Some have adapted to meet the challenges of extreme heat and drought by means of plump, moisture-retentive stems and leaves (succulents), or by means of bulbs, corms

and tubers that lie buried beneath the surface (geophytes). Then there are the region's swiftly flowering ephemerals, which avoid drought altogether by remaining dormant in seed form until the rains come. They then germinate rapidly, grow, flower, and again survive the long dry summer in the form of seed. In their short but vivid life they produce brilliant, spontaneous flower shows for hundreds of kilometres from just north of Cape Town up through to Namaqualand.

The spring flower season stretches from mid-August to late September and October, and during this time the region is transformed into a sea of knee-high flowers. Eager visitors arrive in coachloads to witness this multicoloured spectacle. The flowers open earliest in the south and their blossoming then advances northward in a colourful procession which finally transforms the coastal 'desert' and arid inte-

ABOVE: THE CEDARBERG'S *Wolfberg Arch*.
BELOW: ONE OF NAMAQUALAND'S *exquisite, but hardy, babiana plants.*

rior into a many-splendoured garden. Spring flower shows are held along the length and breadth of the region, with village hotels, country homes and restaurants cashing in for the duration of the season. During these spring months, a Flower Hotline is in operation to advise tourists on the best areas for wildflower viewing.

Come early summer, when the flowers have wilted, the landscape reverts to its cover of dwarf shrubs and sturdy succulents. These include the large family of mesembryanthemaceae (more than 2 000 species have been counted), fleshy crassulas and the cleverly disguised stone flowers, or Lithops. These plants will also have had a short season of assertive flowering after the brief but welcome spring rain, in compensation for months of dreary camouflage.

Floral kaleidoscope

When not carpeted with a tapestry of colour, Namaqualand's main geographical areas display distinctive regional flora. For example, the Knersvlakte, with its white quartz pebbles and extremely saline soils, is the land of dazzling varieties of Mesembryanthemaceae.

Slightly farther north, in the red and white sands of the Sandveld, low coastal vegetation – such as *Zygophyllum cordifolium*, *Drosanthemum*, *Euphorbia karroensis* and *Othonna sedifolia* – is found in the loose white coastal sand, with shrubby vygies (*Othonna cylindrica*, *Lampranthus suavissimus* and *Caphalophyllum spongiosum*) growing farther inland. It is the rocky hills, or Namaqualand 'klipkoppe', even farther north that are considered the 'true' Namaqualand. Here, along a low escarpment about 50 kilometres wide, the rainfall varies between 100 and 200 millimetres a year, and supports a variety of low shrubs including *Eriocephalus ericoides*, *Didelta spinosa*, *Zygophyllum meyeri* and varieties of Mesembryanthemaceae.

The Richtersveld, Namaqualand's mysterious northernmost wilderness, hosts an exceptional variety of succulents. The area usually has less than 50 millimetres of water a year, and the vegetation is generally less than 50 centimetres high.

Inland, where the Succulent Karoo vegetation area gives way to that of the Nama-Karoo, a variety of *Euphorbias* punctuate the landscape with a stark graphic quality. These include the somewhat human-looking 'half-mens' tree, *Pachypodium namaquanum*, which rears its head above the stony ground, facing forever into the blazing sun. Various aloes seem to stab the air with their defensive fleshy spears, while the kokerboom or quiver tree (*Aloe dichotoma*) – which can grow to a towering 12 metres – dominates the desert from vantage points on stony hillcrests. This tree's outlines are frequently all but obliterated by large communal nests built by the sociable weaver birds for whom the kokerboom is a favoured habitat. Top-heavy with weighty dormitories, these trees sometimes break under the burden of their hospitality.

From the arid north-west it is a short hop to the red dune sands of the Kalahari in the extreme north-west of the country. Here are located the sweet grasses (*Stipagrostis* and *Aristada*) that have ensured their survival by means of huge seed output that germinates quickly after rain, and extensive surface root networks. Various acacias are also found here, including the cruelly barbed camel thorn (*Acacia erioloba*) which provides valuable shade, and nutritious fodder from its leaves, seed pods and gum.

Buried treasure

Nara melons (*Acanthosicyos horrida*) – the so-called 'water flasks' of the desert – lie partly concealed in the sand, and are keenly sought by Bushmen and gemsbok alike.

The gemsbok kick up trails of sand looking for the juicy melons, while the Bushmen, after having located these melons, judiciously bury them in the sand for later retrieval in emergencies. The Bushmen also store water in ostrich egg shells. The caches, interred deep below the ground, in often featureless countryside, are relocated at a later date with uncanny accuracy.

The nara melon has adapted to the hot, dry environment by replacing its leaves with dry-looking, brittle spikes. The Kalahari is also home to the occasional, scattered silver bush-willow (*Combretum psidioides*) and the life-giving shepherd's tree, or 'witgat' (*Boscia albitrunca*), which provides food and medicine for man and beast, and is held in near-reverence by tribal people who have endowed it with magical properties.

BELOW: THE GLORY OF NAMAQUALAND *in springtime. The floral show usually lasts for less than a month.*
BOTTOM: PINK BRUNSVIGIA – *near Nieuwoudtville.*

The wild kingdom

There's little to equal the sheer adrenalin charge of seeing wild animals in their natural habitat, and Africa is indisputably the best place to do it. Although South Africa's game was seriously depleted by early white hunter-settlers, strict conservation measures have halted the wholesale and wanton destruction of earlier decades and resulted in the preservation and expansion of the country's wild heritage.

The richness of this heritage is underlined by the fact that South Africa, which occupies a mere one per cent of the earth's land surface, is home to no less than six per cent (227 species) of the world's total number of mammals – not to mention a huge diversity of birds, plants, fish, flowers and reptiles.

Most of the country's 17 national parks and its many well-appointed private reserves boast one or more of the famous 'Big Five' – buffalo, leopard, lion, rhino, and elephant – but it is within the sanctuary of the 20 000-square kilometre world-renowned Kruger Park that visitors can be certain of seeing the greatest number of big game animals.

The Kalahari's wildlife wealth

Besides the Kruger, other major national reserves include the Kalahari Gemsbok National Park in the far north-western Cape, which has large herds of gemsbok (as its name suggests), as well as being the home of lion, cheetah, red hartebeest, blue wilde-

ABOVE: THE WILD DOG, *also known as the Cape hunting dog, is one of the country's most endangered mammal species. For long regarded as a pest, the animal is now strictly protected.*

ABOVE: A REGAL LION, *one of some 1 500 resident in the Kruger National Park.*
BELOW: THE SPRINGBOK, *which once roamed the high plains in its millions, is now largely confined to reserves and game farms.*

beest, small antelope, leopard, eland, spotted and brown hyaena and about 200 bird species, among them a fine array of raptors.

The Karoo National Park near Beaufort West has indigenous mountain reedbuck, grey rhebok, grey duiker, klipspringer and caracal, with introduced populations of Cape mountain zebra, gemsbok, red hartebeest, black wildebeest and springbok. Kudu and black-backed jackal have spontaneously entered the park and there are at least 160 bird species to be seen, as well as a variety of reptiles, geckoes and lizards.

KwaZulu-Natal's Hluhluwe Game Reserve and its neighbour, Umfolozi (the two in fact were recently combined), offer a large variety of big game and exceptional birdlife, including many different raptors. Once the exclusive hunting ground of the Zulu kings, Hluhluwe has been a game sanctuary for almost a century. Umfolozi is home to the world's greatest concentration of white rhino – about 900 of them – and is renowned for pioneering a revolutionary drug-darting technique that enabled these animals to be placed in sanctuaries throughout the world.

Maputaland's Ndumu reserve provides breeding grounds for vast numbers of aquatic birds in its network of flood plains. The reserve's concentration of birds, many of

which are tropical ones at the southern limit of their range, is far greater than in the Kruger Park, and the variety of species is very nearly as extensive.

In addition to the birds, fish and insects that thrive here, there are also hippo, crocodile, impala, nyala, white and black rhino, buffalo, giraffe and smaller creatures such as water mongoose, vlei rat, fruit bat, pangolin and forest dormouse. Farther south, in the shadow of the Lebombo Mountains, the Mkuzi reserve is home to an impressive list of bird species and an abundant variety of fauna that includes antelope, carnivores, giraffe and the African python.

As fascinating as it is different from the Kruger Park, the vast St Lucia complex of forest, lake, estuarine, marine and terrestrial reserves provides a host of specialized habitats for a variety of animals as diverse as Nile crocodiles and pink-backed pelicans.

Visiting the country's reserves

Game-viewing in South Africa is generally best in the cooler, winter months (June to August) when grass is short and water more plentiful. Some visitors prefer early summer (November and December) when wildebeest, impala and other species give birth and great numbers of migrant birds are present.

There is a clear code of conduct for visitors to all South Africa's game parks. This code includes basic safety precautions such as not sleeping on the open ground, not getting out of vehicles in unprotected areas, not straying into off-limits sections and not going out unaccompanied after dark. Another important prohibition is that of feeding animals: baboons, and even hyaena and elephant, can quickly become dependent on human handouts. As a result, they may develop scavenging habits and even turn on humans when food is not forthcoming.

Animals to see

Africa's biggest land mammal, the elephant, is probably the most beloved of all big game. Voracious eaters, these usually gentle giants ingest up to 250 kilograms of grass and 200 litres of water a day – a time-consuming business which means that they spend most of their day browsing to maintain their 3 000 to 5 000 kilogram weight. Their eating habits are, however, destructive – an elephant will tip over a tree to get at a succulent root, or ringbark others, such as the baobab, for a nibble of juicy bark.

Another heavyweight of the African bush is the hippo, which tips the scales at about 1 500 kilograms. Also vegetarian, an adult hippo will eat about 180 kilograms of grass a day. The hippo has a very thin epidermis over an extremely thick underlayer (dermis), which is sun-sensitive and easily damaged. For this reason the animal remains submerged for the greater part of its life, usually migrating (and facing real danger from dehydration when it does so) only when water is scarce. The hippo is an important link in the ecosystem that it inhabits; fish feed off the algae on its skin and its faeces serve to nourish plants and other organisms in the water.

Another resident of the waters is the crocodile, which although preferring fish, will greedily consume water tortoises, antelope and other game that come to the water's edge. The crocodile is one of the most dangerous predators in the world and is believed to cause more deaths in Africa each year than any other creature.

Ways of the lion

The Eastern Transvaal Lowveld is the world's undisputed lion kingdom. The lion is a powerful carnivore, capable of killing animals twice its size and dragging them back to the lair where the male always feeds first. It is highly sociable and lives in prides of up to 30 members. Although it spends much of its time sleeping and grooming, once roused to action, a lion can fell a much bigger opponent with one lazy swipe of a massive paw, and on the run can cover 100 metres in a mere four seconds.

Of particular interest are the legendary white lions of Timbavati. The first recorded white lion was discovered as far back as 1927, but it was not until 1976 – when an all-white male was born at Tshokwane, rapidly followed by another three born in the private Timbavati reserve – that world interest was aroused. Since then there have been many more (the whiteness being caused by a recessive gene) and these are eagerly sought as rarities and as photographic subjects by

visitors. However, when mature, the coats of these white lions become slightly darker.

Lion frequently prey on giraffe, especially at waterholes where the giraffe, bending awkwardly to reach the water, with forelegs splayed wide, are particularly vulnerable. It is not uncommon to see them drinking in strict rota, one at a time, while the others stand watch. The adult giraffe bull stands about five metres tall and represents food for a week for up to 20 lions.

Less visually impressive than the lion, but an equally relentless predator, is the spotted hyaena. One of the most distinctive aspects of this ungainly looking animal is its long-drawn-out whooping call and hysterical giggles, which have served to unnerve many a game-reserve visitor during the night. Hyaena hunt in packs, and often muscle in on kills made by lion and leopard.

Another notable predator is the wild dog – southern Africa's most endangered carnivore. Wild dogs comprise a small population of between 3 000 and 5 000 animals in sub-Saharan Africa. The Kruger Park – with 360 wild dogs counted in the last census – is one of only three reserves where they are found.

TOP: GIRAFFE, TALLEST MEMBERS *of the mammal kingdom, are a familiar sight in KwaZulu-Natal's reserves.*
ABOVE: A GRACEFUL KUDU *and her offspring in the Kruger Park's Skukuza area.*

Birdlife in South Africa

ABOVE: A SOLITARY *yellowbilled stork.*
BELOW: A HOOPOE HOVERS *to feed her chick.*

South Africa has a rich and varied avifauna with close on 900 species. They range in size from the ostrich, standing 2 metres tall and with an average weight of 70 kilograms, to the diminutive penduline tit 10 centimetres in length and weighing a mere 8 grams. Both have interesting and quite different breeding strategies, the ostrich laying its eggs in a simple scrape in the sand and the penduline tit constructing a complex enclosed nest with a spout entrance that can be closed. Between these two extremes is a range of species of bewildering variety that attracts birdwatchers from around the world.

The coastline and offshore waters of South Africa, rich in nutrients, attract species ranging from albatrosses and petrels that breed on subantarctic islands, or even Antarctica itself, to the jackass penguin, the only penguin that breeds on the African continent. In order to see some of the deep-sea species, seabird enthusiasts are forced to charter a boat and travel about 40 kilometres out to sea.

An endemic species is one confined to a particular region, or even limited habitat, and there are close on 100 endemic birds in South Africa. Most of the central and western regions are arid and it is here that many endemics occur, particularly among groups such as korhaans and larks, but the sociable weaver, which constructs a huge communal nest, also merits mention. The Cape Floral Kingdom of the Western Cape Province is characterized by fynbos of which our beautiful ericas and proteas form an integral part.

It is home to several endemics such as the Cape sugarbird, orange-breasted sunbird, Cape rockjumper, Cape siskin, protea canary and the skulking Victorin's warbler.

There are almost 70 species of diurnal birds of prey, ranging from the most powerful – the rapacious crowned eagle – to the smallest – the pygmy falcon that nests in the chamber of a sociable weaver's nest. Additionally there are 12 species of owl. For raptor enthusiasts South Africa is a treasure-trove in which endemics such as the Cape vulture and black harrier are a particular attraction.

It is impossible in a brief account to highlight the many bird groups found in South Africa, but those that merit special mention for their colour or variety, or both, include the kingfishers, bee-eaters, hornbills, barbets, woodpeckers (including the endemic terrestrial ground woodpecker), larks, flycatchers, shrikes, starlings, sunbirds and weavers.

For the visitor who wants to achieve a good list of birds, it is essential to set aside enough time to sample as many habitats as possible. A visit to the bushveld environment of an area such as the Kruger National Park will yield species such as hornbills, rollers, shrikes and starlings, but it would be necessary to visit Cape Town to see Cape sugarbirds, the Karoo for certain korhaans and larks, and the Kalahari for sociable weavers and pygmy falcons.

In conclusion one thing is certain: wherever visitors find themselves in South Africa, they will awake to the songs of new species and will have a good birdwatching day.

ABOVE: THE GOLIATH HERON – *found singly or in pairs in the quieter riverine and wetland areas.*

Pointers to the past

Man's presence in Africa goes back to the most ancient of days. Indeed it is evident from archaeological finds, notably around Tanzania's Olduvai Gorge and in the fossil-rich caves of the Transvaal and Northern Cape, that the continent was the very birthplace of humankind.

Millions of years later – from about 30 000 years ago – the southern subcontinent was home to the ancestors of the modern San, or Bushmen, scattered bands of Stone Age hunter-gatherers who roamed the great sunlit plains in search of sustenance and solitude and, over the millennia, evolved a unique and remarkable culture. These gentle people, whose vivid artistry adorns thousands of caverns and other rocky sites from the Drakensberg in the east to the desolate Atlantic coast in the west, hardly knew the meaning of enmity or greed: they believed profoundly in the oneness of nature and in the need to share its bounty with all living things.

Eventually, though, more aggressive folk – people who owned cattle and were acutely conscious of and prepared to fight for their territorial rights – appeared on the scene.

The first to arrive were the Khoikhoi (also known as Hottentots), who were of San (Bushmen) stock but lived in well-organized tribal groupings and developed a capacity for group warfare. For the most part they settled the western, west-central and southern regions of the subcontinent.

Later came the Bantu-speaking or 'black' peoples, the first of whom began to filter southwards across the Limpopo River around AD 200 in a slow migration that gathered momentum over the centuries. By the mid-1600s the Sotho, Tsonga and others had spread across much of the great interior plateau, and the Nguni had moved down and along the Indian Ocean seaboard, their spearhead – the Xhosa or southern Nguni – becoming firmly entrenched in what is now the Eastern Cape.

By that time, too, European seafarers had charted much of Africa's shoreline. Not too long after the Xhosa had occupied their new

ABOVE LEFT: THE NATIONAL ASSEMBLY DEBATING chamber in Cape Town's parliamentary buildings. The first national parliament, elected by white voters, convened in 1910.
ABOVE: THE INNER YARD of the Castle of Good Hope in Cape Town, the country's oldest occupied building. After its completion in 1676 it served as both the headquarters of the military establishment and the colonial governor's official residence.

ABOVE: BARTHOLOMEW DIAS RAISES a cross, or padrão, on the island of St Croix in Algoa Bay in 1488, before sailing on to chart the first sea lane to India. The bayshore is now fringed by the city of Port Elizabeth. The painting is by the noted Victorian artist CD Bell.

lands, a small party of Dutch pioneers made their cautious way down the Atlantic coast. Their destination: a well-watered bay set beneath the moody grandeur of Table Mountain, 500 kilometres to the west.

Explorers and settlers

Several countries shared in the discoveries that brought southern Africa to the tardy attention of the few powerful European nations – states that, collectively, regarded themselves as the civilized world of the 15th, 16th and 17th centuries.

Although there were elements of religious zeal and individual ambition, the greatest spurs to exploration and discovery were profit and power. Profit was made respectable by the grant of a royal charter, and the quest for power was viewed as patriotism. And out of simple trade there grew successive empires – foreign lands easily and arbitrarily annexed to the crowns of Portugal, Spain, the Netherlands and Great Britain.

Portuguese sailors and merchants, seeking an ocean trade-route to the East, had made a landfall on the shores of the southern Cape in 1488. They encountered small groups of Hottentot pastoralists. Nothing then was known or even suspected of the inhabitants of the great interior regions. Later, Portuguese survivors of shipwrecks were to encounter the Nguni of what is today the Eastern Cape and KwaZulu-Natal.

In 1510 a Portuguese attack on a Hottentot kraal at Table Bay was beaten off with the loss of 58 of the seafaring visitors, including the Viceroy of Portuguese India and a number of noblemen. Thereafter the Portuguese were wary of landing on these remote and hostile southern shores and tended, instead, to steer for Angola or Mozambique. But their place was soon taken by the Dutch, then starting to gain confidence and repute as international traders. It was to service the fleets of their chartered East India Company that they decided to establish a station at the Cape of Good Hope. This they did in 1652.

The Cape outpost

The Dutch were forbidden by their masters, the Dutch East India Company, to enslave or otherwise ill-treat the indigenous people. The

company's directors in Amsterdam – 'the Lords Seventeen' – hoped their representatives would barter cattle and other foodstuffs from the local inhabitants, so it was essential to show friendly intent. The newcomers had no plans whatsoever to found a colony and, indeed, the first commander of the station, Johan van Riebeeck, went to some trouble to mark its limits, even planting a hedge of bitter almonds as a boundary.

Within a few years, though, burghers were allowed to settle beyond this flimsy barrier, and farms were 'granted' by the Company, which thereby tacitly assumed the rights of landowner supreme. Company servants became settlers, and the seeds of a colony were sewn, to be nurtured in 1688 by the arrival of groups of French Huguenots fleeing religious persecution in their own country.

And in *their* own country, the Hottentots found themselves treated increasingly as intruders. The impact of European settlement destroyed the social and economic structure of those clans who lived at and around Table Bay. For the most part the destruction was not deliberate, nor was it achieved with guns (though two minor wars were fought), but it had a ripple effect that caused unease and distress over an ever-widening area. Clans rivalled and eventually fought one another to secure the material benefits of Dutch trade. In the event precious few benefits materialized: the rivalry brought little but their own ruin and a growing dependence on the Dutch, who delighted in the low prices that were an inevitable consequence of chaos. Clans and even families were split as some members aligned themselves with the Dutch and others moved to the interior and an uncertain welcome at the hands of trading competitors.

With Hottentot fortunes in serious and irreversible decline, the settlement spread, albeit only slowly, under Dutch rule. Overextended and corrupt, the Dutch East India Company, too, suffered total eclipse at about the time – in the 1790s – that European affairs dictated that Britain should occupy the Cape. It was a relatively short occupation, but the British were back again in 1806 – this time determined to stay. A few years later the Cape of Good Hope – its internal boundaries only loosely defined – formally became a British colony. As the vanguard of the white settlers moved farther and farther from the seat of government in Cape Town, so the frontiers of the colony, and its laws, were adjusted to ensnare them anew; as the border was progressively shifted eastward, yet more land became the property of the British Crown, to be sold or 'loaned' to settlers – even though, in many instances, it had been occupied and used by Xhosa or other pastoralists and graziers. In 1820 the first of several thousand British (and later, German) immigrants were placed on allotments along the eastern frontier, partly in the hope that their numbers alone would help to quell resistance by the resident Xhosa.

African and European concepts of property ownership differed. In common with many of the continent's indigenous cultures, the Xhosa regarded land as the possession of the people, the chiefs having the right only to allocate its use, not to sell it. Conflict over territorial rights was thus virtually inevitable, and several 'frontier wars' of varying severity and duration were fought. Units of the British Army and men of the so-called 'Hottentot' or 'coloured' Cape Corps took a prominent part in the military campaigns. So too did some of the settlers, though they were accused of showing more interest in cattle-raiding than in fighting. Peace – an uneasy one – finally settled on the Eastern Cape in 1878.

The origins of Afrikanerdom

By 1820, the year the British settlers arrived on the shores of Algoa Bay (today's Port Elizabeth), a new power had appeared on the scene in faraway Natal – the militaristic and expansionist kingdom of the Zulu under their great leader Shaka.

Shaka had allowed a handful of British subjects to settle at Port Natal (now Durban), but had he lived he would undoubtedly have opposed large-scale settlement by emigrant Cape Dutch, or Boer, families in the late 1830s, wanderers who called themselves Voortrekkers and who had left the Cape with their worldly goods on their oxwagons, their flocks and herds driven alongside, soon after the emancipation of slaves. This mass movement came to be known as the Great Trek, and it had many causes. Boer homesteaders in the Cape's eastern frontier region had suffered grievous losses in their never-ending battle for land against the Xhosa – a struggle

in which, it was perceived, they were rarely helped and indeed often hindered by the British colonial government. British missionaries and political liberals, conscious of the status and rights of the black peoples, were constantly interfering in the affairs of the independent-minded Boer communities.

British lawmakers had led the Dutch-speaking frontiersmen to believe that blacks would be placed on the same legal footing as 'Christians', and this, together with the financial loss suffered by slave-owners, had proved the last straw.

Some Voortrekkers went to Natal, where they clashed with Shaka's assassin and successor, Dingane. In 1838 Boer and Zulu fought the Battle of Blood River in which, it was generally believed among the white invaders, God Himself had given them victory.

A few years later Britain annexed Natal, and the Boers loaded up their wagons yet again, this time to join their northern compatriots on the highveld of the Transvaal, where clans of indigenous peoples who opposed them were being defeated and dispossessed.

Vacillating British policies enabled the Boers to form their own independent republics – the Transvaal (later known as the South African Republic) in 1852, the Orange Free State two years later. Britain, however, ensured that these small, badly run and impecunious states had no easy access to any seaport other than through a British colony. As part of this power-play Britain went to war against the Zulu kingdom and, after a humiliating start, destroyed King Cetshwayo's Zulu army at the Battle of Ulundi in 1879.

In the meantime, a degree of prosperity had finally come to the Cape Colony with the discovery of diamonds, around Kimberley in the arid northern regions, in the late 1860s.

Gold and Union

Throughout the subcontinent, especially in the fever-stricken lowveld of the Eastern Transvaal, men pursued gold and rumours of gold. They struck it rich, briefly, at Pilgrim's Rest and Barberton, but the great, epoch-making strike was made on the high-lying Witwatersrand in 1886. This was reef gold, extending deep below the earth's surface and requiring vast amounts of capital for its successful exploitation. Kimberley supplied

BELOW: THE IMPOSING VOORTREKKER MONUMENT just outside Pretoria. The structure – begun in 1938, the centenary of the Great Trek, and completed in 1949 – comprises a 40-metre-high central block ringed by 64 granite oxwagons. Its Hall of Heroes features a frieze of 27 marble panels depicting the Trek's main events; its lower hall a cenotaph and everlasting flame.

ABOVE: SOUTH AFRICANS IN CHEERFUL *mood during the run-up to the first fully democratic national elections, held in April 1994.*
BELOW: THE NEW NATIONAL FLAG *flutters at the gates of Parliament, beside an equestrian statue of Louis Botha, first prime minister of the Union of South Africa.*

much of the funding for the gold mines, mostly indirectly through European financiers who had already invested in diamonds.

A new type of settler now streamed into the Transvaal. This was the *Uitlander* (outsider, or foreigner), despised by President Paul Kruger and his republican government (which nonetheless taxed him heavily). The newcomers, the Boers argued, cared nothing for the Transvaal or the Boer way of life and wanted only to make money. British politicians and highly placed officials, on the other hand, believed that, since the Uitlander contributed so much to the Transvaal treasury, he should at least be entitled to the vote.

These differences created serious tension between Britain and the republics, and Anglo-Boer relations reached a new low when a plan, dreamed up by arch-Imperialist and financier Cecil Rhodes, went spectacularly astray with the failed invasion of the Transvaal by a mounted force under Rhodes's friend LS Jameson. Fullscale war followed in October 1899, and it took the forces of the British Empire nearly three years – until May 1902 – to overcome the military resistance of the two small, landlocked Boer states.

In 1910 the former republics were united with the colonies of the Cape of Good Hope and Natal in the Union of South Africa, which was granted dominion (or self-governing) status within the British Empire. The right to vote, though, was almost exclusively reserved for white males.

The creation of the Union of South Africa, from the colonies and states that had been at war less than a decade earlier, was hailed as a miracle of reconciliation – as indeed it was.

But it was far from complete reconciliation, and far from a complete union. The hardline Afrikaner Boer, defeated in battle, was determined to regain his lost independence, while blacks had almost no say at all in national affairs. Only in the Cape did some non-whites have any political power.

In 1912 blacks formed the South African Native National Congress, which was to become the African National Congress (ANC), a movement dedicated, at least for the first half-century, to peaceful opposition to a manifestly unjust system. The next year, 1913, saw the unobstructed passage of an act of parliament that created 'white' areas and 'black' areas throughout the country. The

framework for future development along grim apartheid lines had been clearly drawn.

Then, in 1914, came war with imperial Germany and, within South Africa, a short-lived 'armed protest' staged by groups of anti-British Boers, a rebellion swiftly crushed by the 'enlightened' Afrikaner leadership of Louis Botha and Jan Smuts. Both men had fought brilliantly against the British forces during the Anglo-Boer War but were now 'Empire men', dedicated to reconciliation between the two white races.

South African volunteers served in West and East Africa, Egypt, Palestine, France and Flanders. German South-West Africa (now Namibia) was conquered by South African troops in 1915, and the former German colony became a mandated territory under South African control. With the exception of the 'coloured' Cape Corps, black South Africans were permitted to join only non-combat units such as the South African Native Labour Contingent.

Black hopes that war service might win some political privilege were dashed by an Act of 1923 that provided for 'native locations' beyond city limits, allowing blacks into white areas only for the purposes of employment. This, in fact, was just one of a number of discriminatory statutes enacted by successive Union governments during the between-wars years to create a formidable arsenal of laws designed to exclude the African people entirely from the political, social and economic mainstream.

South African volunteers of all races also served in the many theatres of the Second World War, a period during which the prime minister, General Smuts, enjoyed international acclaim but steadily shed popularity at home.

The wilderness years

In 1948 Smuts lost the parliamentary election to the National Party, which had the declared intent of returning South Africa to republican status on a tide of Afrikaner nationalism. Apartheid – 'apartness' or 'separateness' – was about to be introduced into almost every sphere of private and public life. The overall policy was to create a number of 'homelands', which critics scathingly referred to as Bantustans. It was argued that all black people could be allocated to a particular group and, therefore, to a particular area which, in time, would be granted a form of 'independence' by South Africa. Eventually, all blacks would be citizens of one or other of these states and there would thus be no black South Africans. Within 'white' South Africa, the policy – officially called 'separate development' – was rigorously enforced. Entire communities, almost exclusively black or 'coloured', were removed from newly proclaimed white 'group areas' and re-settled.

Despite the growing burdens of 'grand apartheid' – a hugely expensive and ultimately unworkable system – South Africa appeared to prosper, even after withdrawing from the British Commonwealth as an independent republic in 1961. But appearances were deceptive. The shooting of blacks by police at Sharpeville in 1960, during a campaign against the pass laws, had already provoked critical world attention. Gradually the country withdrew even further into isolation as sporting, trade and diplomatic links snapped under the pressures of international condemnation. Crushingly expensive military operations in Angola and Namibia sapped national resources, and further damage was done by the devastating economic crisis following on President PW Botha's aggressive 'Rubicon' speech in 1985 – a much-heralded address that failed to deliver the expected message of reform and hope.

The pressures were beginning to tell. In 1984 a new constitution had created a three-chamber parliament in which 'coloureds' and Indians were granted some say in their own affairs but from which, significantly, blacks were excluded.

Indeed the reforms served only to fan the flames of unrest, and violence often engulfed the townships during the 1980s. The protracted struggle for liberation, it seemed, was approaching its climax.

The seeds of protest

The distant roots of resistance to white dominance can be traced back more than three centuries: in 1655, for instance, the Hottentots of Table Bay protested against the Dutch occupation of their lands. Other forms of opposition included raids and counter-raids in the Eastern Cape that resulted in nine frontier wars fought over a hundred-year span.

Resistance to white dominance during the 20th century remained peaceful for the most part, especially in the earlier decades. For much of the time too, the liberation movement, spearheaded by the African National Congress, lacked cohesion, its strength undermined by imprisonment and defections. The most sensational of the arrests, trials and convictions occurred in the 1960s when Nelson Mandela was among the many sentenced to long jail terms.

The withdrawal of colonial powers from Africa, a process that began in the late 1950s, progressively heightened local expectations of democracy and, indirectly, provided vast numbers of cheap but effective modern weapons for the 'armed struggle'. Civil disturbance became a familiar feature of the South African scene, the most significant outbreak occurring in 1976, when hundreds of Soweto students rebelled in the wake of high-handed government insistence that Afrikaans be the medium of instruction in black schools. The upheaval was matched in its intensity and effect in 1984, when sustained nation-wide opposition to the new constitution evolved into the irresistable 'rolling mass action' of the later 1980s.

The new South Africa

The peak of activity within the liberation movement coincided with the accession to the presidency of FW de Klerk who, in February 1990, surprised both South Africa and the wider world with his dramatic announcement of a wide-ranging reform package leading to full democracy.

Long-banned organizations were legalized, and a mass of apartheid legislation disappeared from the statute books. In particular, the world's imagination was captured by the release from prison, after 27 years, of the African National Congress's Nelson Mandela.

After several gruelling series of negotiations over a four-year period – a time of sustained mass action, political violence and, occasionally, of assassination – South Africans of all races went to the polls at the end of April 1994 to elect a government of national unity, together with nine provincial administrations, in terms of an interim constitution. Ten days later Nelson Mandela became the first president of a democratic South Africa.

BELOW: THE PEACEMAKERS. *President Nelson Mandela and his predecessor, FW de Klerk, were the key figures in the protracted negotiation process that inaugurated the new South Africa.*

These are the people

ABOVE: YOUNG AFRICAN GIRLS, *smeared with white clay, celebrate their initiation into womanhood. Western culture has largely supplanted time-honoured tradition in the increasingly detribalized urban areas, but the ways of old Africa are still stongly entrenched among many rural people.*
BELOW: THE FACE *of the townships.*

South Africa is home to about 40 million people. Their dwellings range through the spectrum – multi-storeyed electronic marvels, simple shelters of sticks and skins, Victorianized urban terraces, traditional homes of mud and thatch and transitional styles in planks and plastic sheeting. The tales of their lives and of their families, their backgrounds and origins are as varied as the styles of their kraals and homes, and their roots extend to almost all parts of the world.

The written history begins with the Portuguese maritime explorers of the late 15th century, who were really more interested in finding a sea-route to the East than in chronicling the people of the subcontinent. Thus the inhabitants of Mossel Bay, on the Cape's south coast, were simply recorded as being similar to those seen earlier, along the west coast in present-day Namibia.

These, undoubtedly, were the Khoikhoi, whom early visitors referred to as Hottentots. Victims of the pressures exerted by Western ways and capitalism, as well as of smallpox, they no longer survive as a distinctive race.

The closely related San people, or Bushmen, do survive, and so do the enigmatic paintings that their ancestors left on the rocks of countless caves and shelters across the country. When hard pressed by the weight of successive migrations, the Bushmen simply withdrew farther and farther into dry and inhospitable country, beyond the reach and predatory ambitions of others.

One version of South African history used to claim that, at the time the Cape was being settled by the Dutch – in the mid-17th century – so the Bantu-speaking peoples were arriving in the Northern Transvaal from somewhere near the equatorial regions. It was from these starting points that they gradually approached one another, white and black, finally meeting, and confronting each other, somewhere in the Eastern Cape.

Black tradition – and the archaeologists and anthropologists – tell another story, supported in part by the accounts of 16th-century Portuguese survivors of ships wrecked off the south-eastern coast: the Nguni were in occupation of the Eastern Cape region well before the colonists made their appearance.

The African people of the subcontinent are not a single or homogeneous group, but are made up of a great many separate ethnic divisions, each with its own language and culture. Many of the southern languages reflect early association with the Hottentots and Bushmen – most notably through the click sound in the speech of the Xhosa, who were in the closest and most prolonged contact with these peoples.

Although traditional village groupings, based on kinship, are still to be found in the remoter rural areas, accelerating urbanization is fast blurring lines that were formerly distinctive. But traditions survive even in the adversity of peri-urban squatter settlements. Here, in many cases, the young man about to be initiated into manhood still takes himself off, away from family and friends, and lives apart in his own small lodge as custom decrees. It may be built of plastic and sited beside a busy highway, but it is a part of tradition that cannot be lightly discarded.

One of the four main African groups is the Nguni, which includes those people who speak Xhosa, Zulu, Swazi and Sindebele. These languages are mutually understandable although there are a great number of semantic differences. The Xhosa are traditionally associated with the Ciskei and Transkei of the Eastern Cape Province. The Zulu-speaking population – and Zulu is the home language of far more South Africans than any other tongue – is associated with northern Natal and the KwaZulu 'homeland'. The Zulu royal line survives: King Goodwill Zwelethini Bhekezulu is descended from the noted 19th-century warrior-kings.

Another kingdom, and a sovereign independent country, is that of Swaziland. Swazi-speaking South Africans live mostly in the KaNgwane region in the north-east. The Ndebele of the Transvaal comprise a northern and a southern group and, as a people, are known to the casual visitor for the colourful geometric decorations they paint on the walls of their homes. The area known as Gazankulu in the north-eastern Transvaal is settled principally by the Tsonga and Shangaan people, many of whom live also in Zimbabwe and Mozambique. They have a wonderfully rich folklore and are traditionally highly regarded as raconteurs and tellers of tales.

The Sotho-Tswana (the latter are sometimes referred to as the West Sotho) have occupied the area round Mmabatho and Mafikeng since about the time of the Norman invasion of Britain – the 11th century.

The South Sotho group are the people of the Kingdom of Lesotho and of the South African region of QwaQwa, a former 'homeland' in the eastern Orange Free State.

Many Venda people (VhaVenda) live in the far north-eastern Transvaal, along the Soutpansberg Mountains and between that range and the Limpopo River, which forms the border with Zimbabwe. Much of the land of the Venda is forested, and the green and shadowy depths provide a suitable setting for the tales of mystery that enliven the local folklore.

The territory around Cape Town – the south-western Cape – is the part of South Africa longest settled by Europeans, and the region to which came the first of the many and varied peoples whose descendants make up the modern Cape's kaleidoscopic social fabric. Few of the ancestors came voluntarily.

There were slaves from Angola and Delagoa Bay, from Madagascar and far beyond – from the fabled coasts of India and the East Indian islands. There were exiles too, saints and princes and politicians who, discomfiting to the Dutch in their eastern possessions, were sent to distant Africa to live out the rest of their lives. There was one, Sheik Yusuf, who is credited with founding Islam at the Cape and, thus, throughout South Africa. Minarets with their star and crescent are to be seen in many towns, but nowhere in such numbers as in Cape Town. Here, the mosques are concentrated among the modest houses that line the steep, cobbled streets of Bo-Kaap, or the 'Malay Quarter' as the slopes of Signal Hill are sometimes known.

The longest pedigrees

The scourge of the slave trade was outlawed by the British in 1807, soon after they occupied the Cape, although the actual ownership of slaves remained legal and many continued in bondage for another three decades. Their descendants are among South Africans with the longest of local pedigrees, and curiously classical names bestowed centuries ago, when it was not universally considered inhumane for one person to 'own' another, have survived as family names.

Then there were Indians who came to Natal. Not known as slaves but as indentured labourers, they arrived on the sugar plantations from about the middle of the 19th century. Their descendants add their own colourful blend of the exotic and indigenous to make another facet of the many-sided South African personality.

Of the people of Europe, the Dutch settled here first (from 1652), followed by the French Huguenots. Later came the English, who were military occupiers as well as large-scale settlers, and then Germans recruited by the English. Portuguese have also settled in South Africa, most from Madeira and the former Portuguese colonies of Angola and Mozambique. Of the European social 'colonies' of South Africa, that of Portugal is by far the largest. Many national associations, of these and other lands of origin, still preserve many of the traditions and festivals of an 'old country' amid the confusion, and excitement, of a new land in the making.

ABOVE: JOHANNESBURG'S STREETS *reflect the new freedom.* BELOW: MUSLIM WOMEN DURING *one of their rare mosque appearances. This one is in Cape Town's famed District Six.*

Sporting South Africa

ABOVE RIGHT: ENGLAND'S RUGBY TEAM *humiliated the South African national squad at Loftus Versveld, Pretoria, in the first of the 1994 tests.*
ABOVE: A DEFEAT AVENGED – *the South Africans won the second test, played at Cape Town's Newlands ground, by a convincing 27 points to 9.*
RIGHT: A STAR MIDDLE-DISTANCE *athlete burns the track at the African Games, held in Durban.*

Sport is an integral and highly valued part of South African community life, and has the distinction of being the first major sphere in which the artificial barriers of apartheid were breached.

But for decades, like the communities themselves, South African sport was sadly fragmented. From the 1960s onwards, segregation brought increasing isolation from world competition; tour plans were abandoned, the country excluded from the Olympics, the World Cup and practically every other international event, individual sportsmen (with some exceptions, notably in the golfing and boxing professions) cold-shouldered by the world's sporting bodies.

In 1991, however, South Africa's 21 years in the wilderness came to an end with the acceptance of the country's new, non-racial credentials by the International Olympic Committee. Participation in the 1992 Barcelona Games marked the official return to world sport. Full international acceptance was dependent in part on unificiation of the various controlling bodies that, for many years, had operated on opposite sides of a racial divide. To the delight of sportlovers at home and abroad, the desired unity was achieved.

Indigenous to South Africa is a class of rather unsophisticated and essentially friendly competition known as 'boeresport'. Its practice – in a village-green atmosphere in which grown men run three-legged races, have pillow fights and engage in eccentric equestrian events – may seem quaint or even downright puzzling to the visitor, but it has its place and its history. It developed from the games played during long treks by oxwagon, or on the rare occasions when families from remote farms met on seaside holidays and at gatherings before *Nagmaal*, the communion service of the Dutch Reformed Church.

The game of jukskei, although also indigenous and originally played with yoke-pins, is much like the American pastime of horse-shoe pitching and, unlike boeresport, does have its strict rules and regulations. But the crowd-pullers remain the conventional spectator sports – soccer, rugby, cricket, boxing, and, increasingly, road and track athletics – though curiously enough, angling is reckoned to be the sport with the greatest number of active participants.

The open doors

The return to international sport in 1992 was marked by an almost frantically busy round of competitions. New Zealand and Australian rugby teams toured the country, providing South Africa with its first official test matches in almost a decade, and the South African rugby team played in both France and England. A South African cricket team was cheered in the streets of Calcutta by a crowd estimated at 200 000 people whose country's leaders, during the years of apartheid, had assiduously shunned sporting contact with South Africa (itself home to a sizeable Indian community). To nobody's surprise, South Africa lost the first two internationals but won the third in grand style. India, generous hosts and opponents, shared the delight. At cricket's World Cup contest in Australia, South Africa reached the semi-finals, their courageous performance after years in limbo earning the side the name 'Springbacks'.

Other previously 'unthinkable' events were a tour of the West Indies, and a visit by the Indian team to South Africa.

Soccer is perhaps the pioneer non-racial South African sport and, at professional level, has a vast and knowledgeable following (the country boasts over 12 000 soccer clubs and well over a million active participants). The return from the wilderness saw South Africa readmitted to the International Soccer Federation as well as to the Confederation of African Football. In their first season's foray, the national team played several matches in Africa with, to say the least, mixed fortunes. Much, it was clear, remained to be learned about sporting life at the top.

Penalties of isolation

But if the proportion of victories garnered by the new South African sides and individual sportspeople has been relatively modest, the greatest triumph has been simply to be in contention once again. Because of the lack of international competition, a great many talents failed to achieve their potential. For the sportlovers of South Africa, it has been a sad and frustrating time, and its end, and the new beginning, are widely applauded.

The springbok, long associated with South African sport (and with South Africa's armed forces in wartime), made its first sports-related appearance in the 1890s when a British-made bicycle, modified for racing in Cape Town, was named 'The Springbuck'. Appropriately, South Africa's first world champion was a cyclist, Lourens Meintjies, who rode to victory at the World's Fair in Chicago in 1893. It is uncertain whether the springbok will survive as the national sporting emblem, but many South Africans of all races have emulated Meintjies and achieved world championship status in sports as diverse as boxing, grand prix and motorcycle racing, surfing, bowls, athletics and shooting, while there are many other sports in which South Africans have excelled at world level.

Tapping the talent

Although isolation is a thing of the past and the doors are now open, a great deal needs to be done – and is being done – to provide South Africans with equal opportunities to compete at the highest level. In particular, this means investing heavily – in terms of both facilities and expertise – in the so-called 'black' townships where, as performances have already shown, a stunning wealth of talent lies waiting to be tapped.

BELOW: SOCCER HERO 'DOCTOR' KUMALO *weaves his way into the penalty area.*
BOTTOM: SOUTH AFRICAN CRICKETERS *compete with the world's best. The game is fast gaining popularity among the traditionally soccer-addicted youngsters of the townships.*

The economy

South Africa is classed as a developing country but its economy, shaped by generations of political and social segregation (or apartheid), is an awkward compound of the First and Third worlds.

On the one hand a large percentage of its 40-million population lives below the breadline, lacking jobs and most of the amenities of a decent life. On the other the country has vast natural resources; its dynamic industrial and commercial sectors employ advanced technologies, and they sustain a highly skilled managerial class.

It is this imbalance that the country's first democratic government, elected in May 1994, seeks to redress as its first priority.

Wealth of a nation

Beneath the country's surface lies an immense quantity and variety of minerals.

The ancient Swazian and Randian geological formations of the Highveld contain the world's richest repositories of gold, whose discovery a little more than a century ago propelled the country into the industrial age. Diamonds are found in huge numbers in the alluvial gravels of the Namaqualand coastal region in the far west, in the kimberlite 'pipes' of the Northern Cape and at Cullinan near Pretoria. Locked into the gigantic (500 by 240 square kilometres) Bushveld Igneous Complex of volcanic strata of the north-west and Northern Transvaal are the earth's largest deposits of platinum group metals as well as massive reserves of high-grade chromium and nickel. Also prominent among the 60 or so minerals mined are manganese, asbestos, phosphates, coal (about 58 billion workable tons of it), vanadium, fluorspar and andalusite. Oil and natural gas have been charted off the southern coast.

The platform for growth

The country's highly developed infrastructure is the envy of Africa and a powerful aid in attracting overseas investment.

The various regions, cities and suburbs are linked by 240 000 kilometres of roads, 100 000 kilometres of which are tarred. The national routes, stretches of which are comparable to Germany's renowned autobahns, are used by over five million vehicles. The rail network comprises 36 000 kilometres of track, much of which is electrified; efficient suburban railways service Pretoria-Witwatersrand, the Cape Peninsula and the Durban-Pinetown conurbation. South African Airways, the national carrier, and some two dozen other airlines connect the country's three international airports with points the world over; domestic services link the country's major and many of its minor centres.

The principal harbours are at Durban (one of the southern hemisphere's biggest and busiest), Cape Town, Port Elizabeth, East London (the only river-port), Richards Bay on the northern KwaZulu-Natal coast (the leading outlet for bulk commodities), Mossel Bay to the east of Cape Town and Saldanha Bay on the semiarid western seaboard.

South Africa is a net exporter of energy; Eskom, by far the largest supplier of electricity,

BELOW: ONE OF SOUTH AFRICA'S *modern coal-fired power stations. The national utility, Eskom, has a turnover larger than the gross domestic products of most other African countries.*

operates 19 giant coal-fired plants together with two hydroelectric, two pump-storage, one nuclear and three gas-turbine stations. The utility generates around 60 per cent of all power produced on the continent of Africa.

Coal and petroleum gas are also used, extensively, in the manufacture of synthetic fuels: Sasol, founded as a state enterprise in the 1950s but now a listed public company, runs three massive plants that, together, represent the world's most productive (though subsidized) large-scale oil-from-coal operation.

Telecommunications and broadcasting services are comparable to those of the most advanced industrialized countries.

Leading producers

The largest contributors to the Gross Domestic Product are manufacturing industry (about 22 per cent), financial services (15 per cent; Johannesburg has the world's ninth biggest stock exchange; the banking and insurance sectors are highly developed), mining (13 per cent), commerce (11 per cent), informal sector (9,5 per cent), transport and communications (9,1 per cent), agriculture, forestry and fishing (5,8 per cent), and electricity, gas and water installations (5 per cent).

These figures illustrate the radical transformation from an agrarian- to a mining-based economy a century ago to one driven, in recent years, by manufacturing industry.

Agriculture: South Africa's soils are for the most part poor; just 12 per cent of the land is suitable for arable farming; rainfall is seasonal and often erratic; droughts have been a depressing feature for much of the 20th century. Nevertheless, agricultural production has doubled since the 1960s and in most years the country remains a net exporter of food – unusual in the African, even in the world, context, and something of a tribute to the local farmers and water engineers.

Climatic diversity accommodates a huge variety of crops ranging from dryland harvests like tobacco to the subtropical fruits of KwaZulu-Natal and the Eastern Transvaal. Large-scale irrigation schemes, notably along the Orange River and in the Eastern Cape's Sundays River Valley, have enriched large tracts of previously ungenerous terrain.

The country's principal crops are maize, sugar cane, wheat, lucerne, sunflower seeds, groundnuts, tobacco, grain sorghum, cotton, winter cereals, fruit (deciduous, citrus and subtropical), wine and table grapes, and vegetables. The national herd comprises some 12 million head of cattle; around 28 million sheep graze the great plains of the Karoo, Orange Free State and parts of the Eastern Cape. Wool is a valuable export product. The enormous pine plantations of the Eastern Transvaal and the rich trawling grounds of the Cape west and south (Agulhas Bank) coasts sustain thriving forestry, fishing and fish processing industries.

Most of the bigger and better farms are owned by whites; the African people were for decades confined to crowded and mostly poorly endowed 'homelands'; many communities were overtly dispossessed of their traditional lands, and the thorny question of land redistribution looms large among the issues debated in the political arena.

Mining: The deep mines to the east and west of Johannesburg and around Welkom in the Orange Free State produce about 600 tons of gold a year – a third of the world's total output. But production costs have escalated in recent years, the price has failed to keep pace and, although gold is still the single most valuable export commodity, it no longer enjoys a pre-eminent place in the economy. Among other major mineral exports are coal (100 mines produce nearly 200 million tons a year), diamonds, copper, manganese, asbestos, uranium (a by-product of gold), vermiculite and phosphates (for the manufacture of fertilizers).

Industry: South Africa is virtually self-sufficient in manufactured products, although its factories, long accustomed to a high degree of protection through tariffs, quotas and subsidies, are now having to adjust to the demands of international competition. Many are finding the exercise painful. Manufacturing industry has export potential, is able to absorb more job-seekers than any other sector and, consequently, holds the key to the economic future.

Among the bigger subsectors are metal industries (steel and

ABOVE: POURING GOLD *at the West Driefontein mine. South Africa produces about a third of the world's total output of the yellow metal.*
BELOW: GOLDEN RICHES *also flow from the sunflower, grown extensively for its oil-seed in the country's northern regions.*

BELOW: ONE OF CLIFTON'S FOUR *fashionable beaches, just to the west of Cape Town city. Tourism is set to rank high among South Africa's leading money-spinners.*

BOTTOM: HOUT BAY'S CHARMING *harbour, on the Cape Peninsula's western seaboard. The fishing industry has been damaged by the over-exploitation of resources, but still contributes substantially to the national exchequer.*

aluminium figure prominently); construction materials; transport and equipment (notably vehicle assembly); chemicals and pharmaceuticals; fresh and processed foods (around 60 per cent of the national output is exported), and clothing, footwear and textiles.

'The informal economy': Over half of South Africa's economically active citizens are classed as unemployed or under-employed: years of recession, a Third World-type population explosion (about 3 per cent a year) and massive migration to the cities have created whole armies of jobless people and a socio-economic problem of critical proportions.

As a consequence, the past decade has seen the evolution of a flourishing 'informal economy' – the euphemism for a myriad micro-enterprises ranging from backyard industries and one-man craft services through hawking and market trading to shebeens (township pubs) and taxis. Apart from generating work opportunities and income, these tiny businesses are helping develop much-needed skills and managerial expertise.

No firm financial statistics are available (for sound reasons: the informal economy is neither regulated nor taxed), but it is reckoned that around 30 per cent of the country's total domestic income derives from this sector.

Tourism: South Africa, long isolated from the international mainstream, is on its way to becoming one of the world's prime tourist destinations. The country has a great deal going for it: sophisticated cities; stunning scenic splendour; big-game parks; and an excellent infrastructure of hotels, resorts, travel services, and communications.

Major tourist areas include the Eastern Transvaal's Escarpment (mountain) and Lowveld (wildlife); northern KwaZulu-Natal (lakes, game reserves); the spectacular Drakensberg; the subtropical Natal south coast; the southern seaboard's exquisite Garden Route; Cape Town, the Cape Peninsula and the neighbouring Winelands. Tourism is a vital component of the economic spectrum: it is estimated that every ten or so visitors create an additional local job, and of course what they spend represents instant and much-needed foreign earnings. The sector could well overtake mining, and even rival manufacturing industry, as a money-spinner.

Priorities and policies

Nearly half a century of institutionalized apartheid bequeathed, among other grim legacies, a grossly distorted economy, and there needs to be a significant redistribution of the national assets, a narrowing of the gap between rich and poor. The African National Congress's ambitious (perhaps too-ambitious)

reconstruction and development plan envisages a major investment of billions in:

Education – Ten years of free and compulsory schooling for all children; a pre-school reception year for five-year-olds; adult literacy programmes; education for the 'lost generation' of youths who spent much of the pre-liberation era on the streets; subsidized university and technical college education; massive expenditure on new schools, equipment and textbooks.

Health – Free health care for children under six; heavy investment in district health authorities, hospitals and clinics; the provision of basic nutritional requirements for all; supervised ante-natal care and child delivery for all mothers.

Housing – Over one million new houses within five years; the provision of water supplies (to every household), proper sanitation (one million families), electricity (2,5 million homes), and universal and affordable access to telephones. Urban hostels – huge, impersonal township warrens originally designed for migrant workers and for long the source of bitter conflict – are to be upgraded.

Jobs and social welfare – An extensive job creation programme; a living wage for all workers; compulsory six-months' paid maternity leave for working mothers; the equalization of pensions.

Cost of living – The reduction of income tax for those earning less than R48 000 a year; the easing of 'fiscal drag' within the tax system; the abolition of Value Added Tax on basic foods; price controls on bread.

Farms and mines – A fair redistribution of land resources (with appropriate compensation) and a reallocation of mineral rights.

The programme, which is subject to constant refinement, involves a vast amount of money, and revenue sources are limited.

One possible approach to funding – that which leans towards socialism and the command economy – would be to impose even higher taxes on companies and the wealthier individual, to nationalize major assets, to redistribute wealth by coercion. Such a policy has been largely discounted: it may have gone some way towards deflecting the immediate 'crisis of expectation' among millions of poor people but it would also, sooner rather than later, have forced the country into bankruptcy. Instead, stability and prosperity are to

be achieved by encouraging investment and stimulating growth in order to create jobs, generate wealth and raise revenue. Economic expansion will have to be export-driven, which means less government protection (this is demanded, in any case, by the terms of the World Trade Organisation – the former GATT – agreements) and a more efficient, more competitive private sector. The minimum growth rate needed to sustain forward movement is calculated at 5 per cent a year.

In sum, South Africa is retaining and refining what is known as a mixed economy: central government owns rather more of the national wealth and exerts a greater degree of control over the body economic than is found among the industrialized countries, but generally speaking market forces are given free play and, at base, unfettered and dynamic private enterprise is seen as the most important element in the development process.

TOP: CITY FRUIT STALL: *South Africa exports over half a million tons of deciduous fruit annually, mostly from the Western Cape. Huge citrus and subtropical crops are also harvested.*

ABOVE: 'BLACK TAXIS' *are leaders within the multi-billion rand informal economy.*

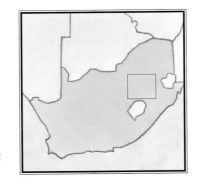

The discovery of the Witwatersrand's fabulous golden lode, just over a century ago, gave birth to the metropolis of Johannesburg – and transformed the Transvaal Highveld from a rural backwater into the powerhouse of Africa.

Heart of gold

Between them, Johannesburg, Pretoria and the so-called Vaal Triangle account for around six tenths of the total wealth generated in South Africa. They also form the heartland of the Transvaal, the most populous and by far the richest of the four provincial divisions established by a British Act of Parliament, the Act of Union, which came into effect in 1910. The provinces,

84 years later, were redefined once again into smaller areas to accommodate the regional demands of the new democratic order.

The Transvaal covers much of the Highveld, the rather bleak, largely treeless but well-grassed and generally fertile north-central plateau, whose pastures and farmlands sustain beef and dairy cattle, immense maize fields and fine crops of wheat, fruit,

groundnuts and sunflowers. To the Voortrekkers, this region of far horizons was the promised land: disenchanted with their British colonial overlords at the Cape, the hardy Dutch-speaking settlers began to arrive in large numbers at the end of the 1830s.

Within 15 years they managed to stamp their authority on the territories to the north of the Vaal River – and in large measure on the Ndebele, Tswana and Sotho peoples who occupied them. Pretoria, the seat of the Boer republican government, was later to become the administrative capital of South Africa.

The region, entirely rural until a century ago, was impelled into the modern era with the discovery of gold on the Witwatersrand near Pretoria in 1886 – an event which gave birth to Johannesburg. Since then a great many other minerals have been found in the area and are being profitably exploited, among them some of the world's biggest deposits of uranium and platinum, chromite, nickel, diamonds, asbestos, copper, manganese, vanadium, fluorspar, iron ore and coal.

Today Johannesburg is a densely packed, high-rise, sophisticated metropolis of about two million people. It is also the epicentre of a vaster conurbation that embraces Soweto, a city in its own right with a population of around three million; the elegant municipalities of Sandton and Randburg to the north; and the sprawl of mining, industrial and dormitory towns of the East and West Rand.

OPPOSITE: LOST CITY'S PALACE. *The magnificent towers and domes, adorned with animal sculptures, provide a palatial backdrop to The Royal Pool.*

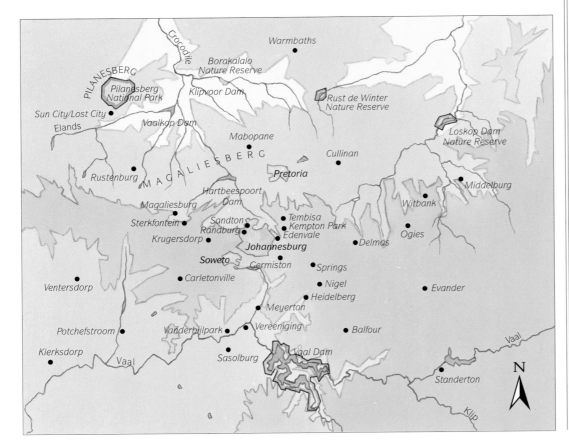

The alchemy of a city

The city of Johannesburg, known as Egoli by the early African miners, was

born in 1886 in a golden crucible, and the alchemy has continued ever since.

Almost as fast as one can flip a Krugerrand, luck here has time and time

again come up 'heads' for many fortune-seekers.

Johannesburg stands on a ridge of white quartzite, which gave rise to the name Witwatersrand. The ridge is a watershed: streams coursing down its northern slopes eventually drain into the Indian Ocean, those on the southern side reach the Atlantic.

The gold found in this area was deposited some 2 800 million years ago by rivers flowing into what was then an inland sea. After it was discovered, the metal burned its way into men's hearts and minds as implacably as the Highveld sunshine warmed the land which saw the birth of humankind.

Historic archaeological sites, and the remains of Stone Age and Iron Age settlements, are testimony to the attraction of this region over the centuries. Early communities looked to the sky for rain and sunshine to bless their cattle and crops, but it was the riches which lay beneath the earth that changed the heartbeat of the land forever.

From shacks to skyscrapers

The biggest gold rush in history began here in March 1886; tents and tin shacks were erected with such speed that wagon owners could return, thirsty and tired, after a day's work at the diggings and find themselves completely boxed in, unable to move their wagons except by dismantling them.

When mining magnate Cecil John Rhodes arrived from Kimberley in 1886, accommodation was so short that he had to share a room with three other men. Only four years later, Johannesburg had become a thriving town with sizeable and attractive buildings, street lighting, hansom cabs, hotels, theatres, nightspots and shops offering every kind of commodity. Soon after the turn of the century the embryonic city boasted 591 hotels and bars serving a population of well over 100 000.

Among the first popular attractions in Johannesburg – besides gold, of course – was a traffic light, erected at the intersection of Rissik and President streets: people came to town by oxwagon just to watch its changing colours. On that same corner the foundation stone of the post office was laid in 1897, ten years after the first motor car made its appearance in the dusty streets. The building remains one of the few gracious old structures that have managed to escape the march of time and modern property developers.

The changing skyline

Throughout the decades Johannesburg has continued to grow and change at a phenomenal rate, and today's residents sometimes experience the same feelings of bewilderment as the early wagoners: buildings are continuously imploded to make way for yet more skyscrapers, and the character of an entire neighbourhood can change almost beyond recognition in a matter of just a few years. The top floor of the 220-metre high Carlton Centre provides an impressive

ABOVE: JOHANNESBURG AT NIGHT. *The city is at the epicentre of sub-Saharan Africa's largest conurbation.*

THE FABULOUS REEF

Most of the Witwatersrand's early mines – those in and immediately around Johannesburg – have long since been worked out, leaving only their rusting headgear and their dumps to remined one of the rugged pion-eering days. Mining operations have moved outwards, to the smoke-hazed, hugely productive East and West Rand areas to either side of the city.

The mines tunnel into a giant gold-bearing 'saucer' that inclines an immense distance beneath the surface of the Highveld. The saucer's 'rim' describes a 500-kilometre arc from Evander in the east to a point beyond the young city of Welkom, deep in the Orange Free State.

South Africa's sixty-odd mines, many of which reach great depths (nearly four kilometres in one instance), produce around 600 tons of refined gold a year, roughly a third of the world's total output. The metal has retained its traditional position as the country's largest single export com-modity, but with rising production (and especially labour) costs and a sluggish bullion price, its relative importance has declined in recent years.

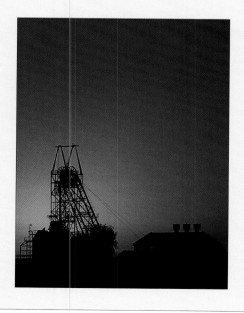

panoramic view over the city, its suburbs, mine dumps and parks and its street grid, fashioned after the style of the New York street system. Packed mini-buses – so-called 'black taxis' – rush up and down crowded streets; informal stalls, heaped with piles of golden oranges, watches and clothing, spill across the pavements, and newspaper sellers dance between the cars to serve customers.

Numerous five star and budget hotels cater for a growing number of tourists, while many fine shopping centres serve a population of millions. Restaurants reflect the multi-ethnic mix of the city, as do the 'muti' shops, offer-ing traditional African herbal medicines, which stand only a flick of a flywhisk away from huge, ultra-modern hospitals.

But perhaps what best expresses the ever-changing face of Johannesburg is the wrinkled reflection of an old mosque on the silvered, glass-clad walls of a neighbouring skyscraper: two symbols of the union of ancient beliefs and modern preoccupations in a city gearing up to fulfil the needs and meet the challenges of the new millennium.

ABOVE: ENTERTAINER MBONGENI NSEMA *and the cast of 'Township Fever'. Until recently much of African theatre reflected the harshness of life under apartheid, but it is now moving away from racial to more universal, often joyous themes. Especially notable are the exuberant musicals emerging from the townships.*
BELOW: A FUTURISTIC SEGMENT *of central Johannesburg's skyscape. Little of the old remains.*

Cosmopolitan kaleidoscope

When Johannesburg celebrated its centenary in 1986, its most enduring historic landmarks – the mine dumps – still stretched to the south of the Witwatersrand ridge in a 110-kilometre belt from Nigel in the east to Carletonville in the west.

The airborne dust from the golden dumps encouraged the city to grow northwards, where the ridge provided some protection, but in spite of acid-tolerant plants which grow over most of their surface, these enormous and unattractive mounds still dominate and disfigure the landscape.

Johannesburg was officially proclaimed a city only on 5 September 1928. The Boer government had originally hoped the *uitlander* miners and speculators would disappear once the gold ran out, but neither happened, and today the city is a cosmopolitan kaleidoscope of races. Some nationalities have tended to congregate in specific areas, giving an ethnic character to corners of some city suburbs with their speciality food shops, places of worship and colourful corner cafés.

One such example was Sophiatown, a black enclave well away from the huge 'official' black residential area of Soweto (an apartheid creation with a name contracted from South-Western Townships), which today is home to several million people.

Sophiatown, razed to the ground by 1960 to make place for the white suburb of Triomf, evolved its distinctive character, a personality fashioned by friendly, cheek-by-jowl living, its jazz clubs and shebeens (informal bars) and its warm, colourful atmosphere. For its part, Soweto survived and developed, albeit in haphazard and unattractive style. But today matchbox homes are softened by trees and small neat gardens, and some houses are as impressive as any in the northern suburbs.

'The Good, the Bad and the Ugly' is an appropriate name for the daily Face to Face tours which expose the visitor to the real, and fascinating, nature of Soweto.

Contrasts! Johannesburg is full of them. In another of its suburbs, the densely populated flatland of Hillbrow, night and day merge

LEFT: THE NEW SOUTH AFRICA: *The crowd at a Johannesburg 'human rainbow' concert.*
ABOVE: FEATHERY, LILAC-HUED JACARANDAS *bring springtime colour to the northern suburbs.*

buildings survive among the few authentic relics of Victoriana left untouched by modern developers. The old Indian fruit and vegetable market is another feature which has happily been preserved: it escaped destruction by being converted into the marvellous Market Theatre. Injunctions not to spit, or park vehicles on the platform, still hang on the auditorium walls, and on Saturday mornings the adjacent flea market (one of many in the city) offers a treasure trove of beautiful handicrafts. A splendid collection of more formal art can be viewed at the Johannesburg Art Gallery in Joubert Park, while early South Africa is celebrated in the Africana Museum and the privately owned Brenthurst Library.

Jan Smuts House, on the campus of the University of the Witwatersrand, houses Smuts' study, which was moved from the statesman's Doornkloof farm outside Pretoria and then painstakingly reassembled. Lining the walls are his 3 000 books, in their original order, and the desk looks as though it has been left unoccupied for only a moment.

ABOVE: JOHANNESBURG'S *Stock Exchange Building.*
BELOW: MIELIES (MAIZE CORN) *are roasted for the alfresco pavement trade.*

into a song of life which has a different beat on every corner, and is more difficult to pin down than a lively locust.

Zaïre's vibrant African culture and language have almost taken over Ponte's round apartment tower; while in the elegant, conservative, lofty-ceilinged Rand Club in mid-town Johannesburg, the bastion of the rich since the very early days of the city, businessmen conduct muted conversations from deep armchairs on thick pile carpets.

A dramatic, blue-glass building in downtown Johannesburg houses a division of Anglo-American, but in close-by Diagonal Street original

GOLD REEF CITY

The miners, traders, barmaids, doctors, entrepreneurs, mining magnates and pedlars who made up the rapidly growing population of early Johannesburg worked hard and played hard. They built tin huts, reed and mud houses and, some of them, even magnificent mansions.

The heady spirit of the early pioneering days has been brought to life at Gold Reef City. Tucked between mine dumps just south of Johannesburg, it is a charming replica of a turn-of-the-century mining community. On view are houses of miners and managers dating from 1900 to 1920; lower down the hill a reconstruction of the 1888-1890 settlement is proudly displayed. Visitors can also descend an operational shaft to see how gold is mined. After watching a pour of the molten metal, they are invited to

try to lift the heavy bar with one hand. 'If you can pick it up, you can keep it', encourages the smelt-house foreman.

A little steam train huffs and puffs around the perimeter of this living museum, which boasts 17 permanent exhibits, 31 shops, 21 bars and restaurants, three hotels, a farmyard and an amusement park.

LEFT: BOATMEN, YACHTSMEN AND PICNICKERS *relax at Emmarentia Dam, one of 600 parks and open spaces in and around Johannesburg.*
BELOW: GREY LOURIES *can be seen in many city parks.*

grassland and a sprinkling of acacia trees. On the horizon shimmered the soft purple outline of the Magaliesberg range, where six decades earlier a famous explorer and hunter, William Cornwallis Harris, had become the first white man to set eyes on the magnificent and stately sable antelope.

A sprinkling of those lovely Parktown homes still survives today, and a few have been declared national monuments. Dolobran is one of the most dramatic, but its extravagant Edwardian architecture and domed tower now look out on the traffic hurtling along a six-lane motorway. Northward is another example of that era. Designed by Sir Herbert Baker, it has a minstrel gallery overlooking a spectacular great hall.

Fashionable forays

The Parktown and Westcliff Heritage Trust conducts leisurely walking trails past many of these buildings. On Sundays it also runs Topless Tours, which are among the most fashionable outings in town. They are called 'Topless' because they entail a ride on an open double-decker bus which drives very slowly along the streets; a guide in period costume talks about the history of the area

From lions to limousines

It is hard to imagine that during the 1930s duck-shoots were held in what is today the crowded suburb of Craighall, or that Rosebank, now an elegant high-rise area five minutes from the city centre, was proclaimed in 1896 with advertisements describing 'attractive stands in the country'.

In 1885, in the area known today as Johannesburg, there was only one family for every nine kilometres. Three years later the population of the city had increased to such an extent that the church of Saint Mary's-the-Less in Park Street, Jeppestown, was bursting at the seams.

By 1904, almost 2 000 houses were going up each month, and today the urban sprawl has linked the rolling grasslands between Johannesburg and Pretoria, 60 kilometres to the north, with residential estates, hotels, theatres, cinemas, shopping complexes and light industrial parks.

In Parktown, where the mining magnates, or Randlords as they were called, moved to escape from noise and dust, lavish mansions originally looked across a countryside marked by rocky outcrops, sweeps of

ABOVE: DOLOBRAN: ONE OF THE MANSIONS *of the early magnates. Most were ornately elaborate affairs built in the Parktown area; few have survived.*
BELOW RIGHT: JOHANNESBURG'S ELLIS PARK STADIUM, *venue for soccer, rugby, and music festivals.*

and the larger-than-life personalities who played such an important part in Johannesburg's development. The tour ends with tea and scones at The Wilds, one of the many areas of lovely koppies (little hills) and emerald parks of the city, which, with great forethought, were set aside as recreational areas after the city was founded in 1886.

Oasis of leisure

Perhaps the most popular of these parks is the 80-hectare Zoo Lake; the artificial stretch of water, bordered by weeping willows and set in rolling lawns, is still a tranquil weekend picnic spot, and every month hosts an 'Artists Under The Sun' exhibition. It was given 'in trust for the inhabitants of Johannesburg for ever' by magnate Hermann Eckstein's company. The gift also included the nucleus of a zoological collection, which expanded over the years and has now become the Johannesburg Zoo. Popular attractions here include polar bears, which can be watched through glass windows happily swimming in their Arctic tank, and night tours, which

enable visitors to witness the lively nocturnal activities of owls, bushbabies and hyaenas.

At a later date, Eckstein's Corner House donated some land adjacent to Zoo Lake, on which the War Memorial and National Museum of Military History were built. The latter houses fascinating memorabilia such as the world's only surviving Messerschmitt Me 262 two-seater jet night-fighter.

Zoo Lake is in Saxonwold, an area originally planted with timber to provide pitprops for the mines. These plantations set a trend in the city: before they made their appearance there had been only the occasional indigenous tree; now exotics and local species line the streets and beautify the gardens. Certainly the grounds of the gracious Johannesburg Country Club have been splendidly enhanced by the huge old oaks.

Free-flying ducks homed in on Zoo Lake, as did many other species of bushveld birds. They built their nests in such havens as the Melrose Bird Sanctuary and Delta Park, and eventually took over suburban gardens. Even today kingfishers and herons gather to feed in ornamental ponds, and the raucous hadeda ibis, probing for crickets with its long,

curved bill, enjoys rich pickings on the manicured lawns. As for that bane of the hunter, the grey lourie, which gives its familiar 'kweh-h-h' or 'go-away' alarm call to alert the prey of impending danger, it now calls from the netting of the many private tennis courts which dot the northern suburbs of the city.

There are more private courts and swimming pools in the residential areas of Johannesburg than in any other city in Africa. Even in the early days, pioneers were determined to establish a pattern of gracious living: the first tennis court was laid out in 1886 by a Mrs Wolhuter, and the first cricket club opened the following year.

Today Johannesburg has extensive sports complexes, such as Wanderers and Ellis Park. They host international events that are televised worldwide. For the energetic, there is a 32-kilometre urban river trail. The trail follows the Braamfontein Spruit and links Johannesburg with its northernmost suburbs, forming the longest urban parkland in the world. Magnificent Lippizaner horses give displays every Sunday morning, and Africa's kings of the veld can be admired each day of the week in the Krugersdorp Lion Park.

A capital in transition

A soft, springtime haze of purple jacaranda blossoms; roads wide enough for a span of oxen to turn a covered wagon; gracious buildings: these are some of the distinctive features of Pretoria, the administrative capital of South Africa.

evening, receiving guests, acknowledging the greetings of passers-by, and answering the first telephone to be installed in Pretoria.

The city's citizens love parks, nature reserves, bird sanctuaries and fountains. One of the newest of these outdoor attractions is the Moreleta Spruit hiking trail. This will eventually complete a circular route as far as the Magaliesberg hills, but for the moment it offers a walk of sunlight and birdsong along many kilometres of open grassy plains, vleis (marshy areas) and thick woodland.

The more serious-minded visitor can follow another trail around the city: the Pretoria

P retoria is a modern city, its acknow-ledgment of the future symbolized by the 150 metre-tall headquarters of the Reserve Bank, with its walls of reflective glass. Among its four universities is Unisa, the largest correspondence university in the world. Founded in 1873, it admits over 122 000 students each year – students of dif-ferent nationalities and languages who study from home, whether that be in America, Aus-tralia, Asia, Europe or Africa. Also in Pretoria are the headquarters of Iscor, the giant iron and steel corporation, of the CSIR scientific research establishment, and of the largest brewery in the southern hemisphere.

The city was originally laid out in 1855, and grew in ambitious fashion: one of the longest urban thoroughfares in the world runs through its centre. This is Church Street, where the old and the new rub shoulders along its 26 kilometres. The midpoint of Church Street is dominated by Church Square, where some of the buildings have served successive governments since the days of the Zuid-Afrikaansche Republiek – the South African Republic constituted in 1860.

Farther along Church Street one finds the simply furnished house where President Paul Kruger lived from 1884 to 1900. He would sit on the covered verandah in the cool of the

ABOVE: PRETORIA'S UNION BUILDINGS, *the country's administrative headquarters.*
RIGHT: THIS BOER SOLDIER *is part of Pretoria's Kruger monument.*

Culture Route takes in 48 places of historical interest, all within easy walking distance of each other. Then there is the Pretoria Art Museum, which holds a superb collection of South African and international works. The Pierneef Museum displays many paintings by Jacob Pierneef, the early 20th-century artist who gave it its name, and who captured so magnificently the colours and shifting patterns of the South African countryside.

The gentle pinks, magentas and violets of Pierneef's mountainscapes are echoed by the city's jacarandas, which seem to cartwheel along the diverging spokes of the city's streets, creating undulating canopies of beauty. The best place to admire these trees during their short springtime flowering season is from the elevated gardens of the Union Buildings. The buildings, in an impressive design of dressed sandstone by Sir Herbert Baker, serve as offices for the departments of the State President and Foreign Affairs.

The towering granite walls of the Voortrekker Monument, encircled by a representation of 64 full-size wagons drawn into a stone laager of solid conviction, are another impressive landmark of the city, while the adjacent museum celebrates Voortrekker (early

TOP: PRETORIA'S STREETS, PARKS AND GARDENS *are graced by upwards of 70 000 jacaranda trees. Originally from South America, they burst into their lilac glory during the springtime months.*
ABOVE: THE ALL-CORRESPONDENCE UNIVERSITY OF SOUTH AFRICA, *largest of its kind in the world.*

THE PRETORIA ZOO

The National Zoological Garden of South Africa, established in 1899 in the heart of Pretoria, ranks among the top 10 of its kind in the world.

The Zoo is the largest in the country, covering 60 hectares, and in the early days visitors could view its attractions from an elevated position by enjoying one of the very popular camel rides. Today visitors can have a real bird's-eye view by boarding the cableway which stretches from the town end to higher ground on the northern side, or they may prefer to chug slowly past the camps on a tractor-train; there are donkey rides for children at weekends.

In keeping with worldwide trends, the Zoo now combines its entertainment function with considerable emphasis on conservation, education and research. It has been very successful in breeding local endangered species such as the cheetah, brown hyaena, roan antelope, wild dog and the riverine rabbit, and cooperation with authorized breeding programmes worldwide has led to similar achievements with such exotic animals as the giant eland, the Arabian oryx, the addax and the Père David's deer. To this end, the Zoo maintains game-breeding centres at Lichtenburg, in the western Transvaal, and Potgietersrus in the north.

Pretoria Zoo embraces some 140 mammal and 320 bird species, all living in family groups in enclosures designed to recreate their natural habitat. Among the rarest creatures kept in the zoo are the red forest buffalo, the Przewalski horse and the Waldrapp ibis. About 300 fish and 90 reptile (including crocodile, pictured), amphibian and invertebrate species are found in the aquarium and reptile park.

Education is an important part of the management philosophy. Displays encourage visitors to compare their body mass to that of an animal, or to measure the length of an arm against the wingspan of a bird. Children love imitating the brachiating movement of gibbons on the jungle gym. Night tours are also popular.

Visitors can picnic anywhere they like on the lawns, and braai (barbecue) facilities are available on the banks of the Apies River, which runs through the Zoo.

Afrikaner) lifestyle and culture. The Sammy Marks Museum honours the achievements of another early pioneer, Lithuanian-born Sammy Marks, who arrived at the diamond fields with only a canteen of cutlery to sell, and went on to become the Transvaal's first real industrialist. He developed coal mines, helped to found the giant Union Steel Corporation (now absorbed by Iscor) and used some of his new wealth to commission the statue of Paul Kruger which stands in the city's Church Square.

LEFT: HARTBEESPOORT DAM, *favourite weekend getaway for Johannesburgers.*
BELOW: HOT-AIR BALLOONS TAKE *the more intrepid kind of sightseer on cross-country trips.*

Reef rambles

More than six million people live within an hour's drive of the Magaliesberg, a

magnificent range of hills that draws all manner of visitors, from mountain

climbers and long-distance hikers to dinghy sailors and water-skiers.

The rocks of the Magaliesberg were first laid down 2 300 million years ago; today two main ridges of quartzite stand proud above the plains like surf-curled waves on a stationary ocean. In fact, ripple marks on some of the rock faces provide geological evidence of a time when they actually did form the shores of an inland sea.

This area was home to humankind's ancient ancestors. The world-famous *Australopithecus africanus* baby skull, thought to be about three million years old, was unearthed

some distance away from here, at Taung, in 1924; remains of an adult female (nicknamed 'Mrs Ples') were discovered 12 years later, in the dolomite Sterkfontein Caves, 25 kilometres south of the Magaliesberg.

Stone Age and Iron Age man also settled here, amid the rising hills, the sparkling streams, wooded kloofs, tumbling waterfalls and abundant game of the region.

In 1836 Captain William Cornwallis Harris wrote of 'a landscape actually covered with wild elephants'. Today the elephants have

gone, but leopards still lurk in the krantzes, and the majestic black eagle still soars on the thermals. More than 300 species of birds, 106 species of mammals, 130 species of trees and 100 species of grasses can be found in these mountains, as well as gorgeous butterflies, and a wealth of reptiles and insects. The hiking trails that wind through the hills offer an ever-changing panorama of natural beauty.

The Magaliesberg range curves in a shallow 'S' from west to east. The spacious Hartbeespoort Dam is roughly at its midpoint, and provides visitors with extensive fishing and boating facilities, a scenic cableway, an aquarium, and a snake and animal park.

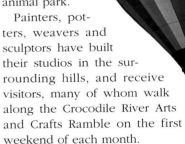

Painters, potters, weavers and sculptors have built their studios in the surrounding hills, and receive visitors, many of whom walk along the Crocodile River Arts and Crafts Ramble on the first weekend of each month.

Some of the studios serve refreshments – and their welcome is as refreshing as the cool, clear water which chatters over the weirs and stones of the river.

The Wag 'n bietjie (Tarry-a-while), in the Cullinan area, north-east of Pretoria, is a similar artists' route; tourists can also visit the famous mine which, in 1905, yielded the world's largest gem diamond – all of 3 106 carats – to enrich Sir Thomas Cullinan. The diamond was bought by the Transvaal government for presentation to King Edward VII, and some of the 105 brilliant stones cut from it are now part of the British crown jewels. Visitors wanting to capture some of the thrills of the early mining days can buy a bucket of gravel and sort through it in the hope of finding their own sparkler.

At Margaret Roberts' Herbal Centre near De Wildt, on the northern slopes of the Magaliesberg, the gardens are laid out in a patchwork of traditional styles: miniature, knot, fragrant, parterre, 16th-century, water, culinary and medical. The Little Herb Nursery offers a wide selection of plants for sale, as well as fragrant oils and potpourris. The miniature and charming Fairy Village laid out under the trees is exclusively for the use of the Little People who bless the herbs.

Nearby is the De Wildt Captive Breeding Centre for rare and endangered species, where carnivores such as the brown hyaena, the wild dog and the South American maned wolf are raised in camps laid out over the hillside. The centre's success with cheetah, including the rare king cheetah (a genetic variation with heavy black markings and larger spots), has been outstanding. There is also a vulture restaurant, which caters for the threatened birds: more than 100 are liable to drop in at the same time, having coasted on the thermals from their Skeerpoort colony near the Magaliesberg range.

Tours by train

Other visitors travel to the Magaliesberg by locomotive. On numerous weekends during the year, an authentic steam train (affectionately known as the Magaliesberg Express) leaves Johannesburg station to make the slow journey to Lover's Rock. Passengers alight at a disused station, now invaded by undergrowth, and wander down to the river to enjoy a picnic. At the end of the afternoon, the train gives a loud whistle to signal its imminent departure for the return journey.

Those who really want to get the area into perspective, so to speak, can take to the skies in mildly unusual style: by hot-air balloon or Junkers Ju 52 transport plane. The balloon glides silently over the hills, lakes and valleys

ABOVE: RETIEF'S KLOOF, *one of a myriad enchanting corners of the Magaliesberg, a low range of hills averaging a bare 300 metres above the surrounding flattish and fertile countryside.*
LEFT: HARTBEESPOORT DAM, *framed by its Magaliesberg backdrop, is just an hour's drive from Johannesburg.*

before setting down in a field for a champagne breakfast. The 1934 Junkers conducts hourly historic pleasure flights from Wonderboom Airport, taking off with a roar and making its way around a fascinating aerial circuit of the surrounding countryside.

At the western end of the Magaliesberg is the town of Rustenburg, bordered by an attractive 5 000-hectare nature reserve. To the north is the extinct volcanic crater of the Pilanesberg and its surrounding game park.

A taste of history can be enjoyed at the Phumangena uMuzi, an authentic Zulu kraal at the Heia Safari Ranch, where sangomas will throw the bones for you, and young Zulu maidens will dance the mzumba to the throb of drums. Alternatively, a three-hour drive from the Reef takes one to the Lotlamoreng Cultural Village, situated outside Mmabatho, a living museum of the traditional architecture, crafts, art, dance, music, customs and lifestyles preserved and practised by all the major black tribes of South Africa.

Ndebele art

More than any other decorative art in southern Africa, the colourful murals,

beadwork and metallic ornamentation of today's Ndebele people of the Northern

Transvaal graphically reveal a culture in rapid transition.

Some 400 years ago, the feminine fingers which first traced monochrome patterns of straight and wavy lines into wet clay or cow-dung belonged to the women of a community of Nguni-speaking people. Led by Chief Muzi, they had left the area of present-day Natal and Zululand to find a new home in the Transvaal, where in due course they became known as the maTebele (which means 'disappearers' or refugees).

Gradually the Ndebele women introduced colours to their art with the use of earth pigments and oxides. Ground-up stones yielded shades as varied as pink and violet. Black came from river mud or charcoal, and yel-

ABOVE: DISTINCTIVE GEOMETRICAL *Ndebele murals.*
BELOW: AN NDEBELE WOMAN *decorates her home.*

lows were produced by crushing sand and certain rocks. The tip of a tudze, a fibrous plant, made a good paintbrush, and chicken feathers were used to trace the finer lines.

Pleasing the spirits

The predominantly geometric art was created as both a statement of Ndebele identity, and as a means of enlisting the continued support and protection of the ancestors. The same motivation applied to Ndebele beadwork, which proclaimed status, feelings and events in subtle ways, not always obvious even to other members of the village. Often the use of a certain colour or pattern would need to be explained in words, before the silent language of the beads could send its message between two lovers, between families, or between communities.

Then, early in the 20th century, exposure to western society and culture – and particularly tourism – provided a major catalyst. For example, the small Ndebele Village at Botshabelo, eight kilometres outside Middelburg in the Transvaal, is a popular tourist attraction. But its gaily painted houses, and the beadwork *zillas* and *kowane* worn by the women, have little to do with the observance of ancestral traditions. These have altered largely in response to the demands of camera-toting visitors who hanker, it seems, after preservation of the old as a psycholo-gical comforter in a world skittering along in a process of hectic change.

Beads were initially ground from ostrich shell or seeds, but were supplanted by the colourful ready-made glass beads supplied by early traders. Then, with the introduction of the bright primary colours of plastic, imaginations ran riot.

The ready availability of commercial paints had a similar impact on Ndebele murals.

Today's artists usually maintain that there are no deep meanings in ubiquitous patterns like 'tyre-tracks' or 'razor blades'. They insist that these, along with cubist-style representations of houses, aeroplanes, staircases, lamp-standards and cars, are merely reflections of the world they see around them. Any mysticism detected is purely in the eye of the beholder. However, for the time being, the amazing enigma and beauty of their art continues to fascinate the western world.

Art on wheels

In 1991, Esther Mahlangu, one of the most renowned painters in the KwaNdebele village of Weltevrede, transformed a BMW 520-series into a stunning example of Ndebele art. The piece was commissioned to form part of an on-going, international travelling automotive exhibition, which now includes 15 cars decorated in completely disparate styles by different artists around the world. Esther Mahlangu has also painted the strikingly effective fire curtain of Johannesburg's Civic Theatre. She and her colleague, Francina Ndibande, are sophisticated artists who candidly admit to wearing traditional beadwork and to painting in modern Ndebele style because that is what the visitor wishes to see. Imagination and reality: the Ndebele know how to combine them to perfection.

TOP: NDEBELE FAMILY GROUP *in traditional costume.*
LEFT: NDEBELE ORNAMENTATION *uses a lot of metalwork.*
RIGHT: THE STRIKINGLY COLOURFUL *murals that grace these homesteads have no special meaning – they have been created simply to please the eye.*

TRADITIONAL HEALERS

For many centuries, traditional healers have been respected throughout the continent of Africa, but until comparatively recently their skills and knowledge have been ignored by modern medicine.

Now a new understanding and acceptance of these healers' methods has led to an informal but growing interchange, a trend encouraged by organizations such as the Dingaka Society and the National Steering Committee for Traditional Healers.

Future plans include the establishment of a legislatory and statutory body to create a better mutual understanding between practitioners of orthodox and traditional medicine. On the one hand, the worth of old ways will be recognized, and on the other, primary health care will be stimulated by exposure to conventional practices.

South Africa's traditional healers fall into three classes: herbalists, inyangas and sangomas. They have no association at all with what the westerner would refer to as witchcraft or black magic.

Herbalists, as the name implies, work with herbs, plants and trees that have healing properties, but which must be used correctly in order to derive the maximum benefit. Inyangas are diviners and psychologists, who interpret problems through the use of 42 special bones, or *dolos*, which have been gathered over time during their three-year, full-time training and are very personal to each inyanga. These are thrown in a random pattern onto a mat, and their message is divined during a period of intense concentration. Expert inyangas eventually become highly qualified specialists, and are then called mngomas.

Sangomas are healers who concentrate on the power of the mind. They are chosen by tribal ancestors, and realize they have been selected when they fall ill without any apparent cause. During their consultations they become possessed by tribal spirits, who help them to 'smell out' wrongdoers and to pinpoint the cause of evil influences.

Opulence in the veld

The pleasure oasis that is Sun City glitters under the African sun. Its sparkle and sophistication are like jewels clasped in an ancient bushveld setting, extending hospitality of a kind unrivalled in Africa.

On a farm north-west of Rustenburg the simple rustic home which the young Paul Kruger, later President, built for himself in 1841, is preserved as part of a 32-hectare museum. Not far away, sheltered in a long-extinct volcano, which is one of only two alkali craters in the world, lies the magnificent Sun City, an oasis of pleasure unequalled anywhere else in Africa.

Their proximity dramatically highlights the swift development of the Transvaal, for the luxury and sophistication of Sun City would have been beyond anyone's wildest dreams 150 years ago. When it opened in 1979, it established new standards of hotel accommodation and entertainment.

The resort has since expanded to include an amazing range of attractions. Showtime at Sun City is a glittering array of live entertainment, including international stars who perform in the 6 000-seater Superbowl in the Entertainment Centre. The gaming at the casino is equally remarkable, with multimillion rand slots, jackpots and tables for roulette, blackjack and punto banco. Sun City is a fantasy world of lakes, waterfalls and rushing streams, set amid magnificent gardens and forests which contrast with the encircling olive green and ochre slopes of the Pilanesberg Mountains. Four hotels offer accommodation which ranges from family-style comfort to supreme luxury.

The Lost City

The most fascinating aspect of Sun City is The Lost City and its remarkable Palace, a hotel which opened at the end of 1992.

Legend has it that a long time ago a people from the north wandered down Africa, bringing with them a rich heritage of art and architecture. They settled in a valley with clear mountain streams, where fruit and game were plentiful. Then a terrible earthquake destroyed their city and their fields and their watercourses, and forced them to flee. Over the centuries, vegetation gradually concealed The Lost City, and eventually all that remained of the metropolis was a legend.

The buried metropolis was then 'discovered' at Sun City and restored to its former

ABOVE: THE PALACE, *focal point of Sun City's new and extravagantly conceived 'Lost City' complex.*

ABOVE: SUN CITY, *one of the world's biggest and most opulent resorts, has four hotels, a glittering casino and entertainment centre, and beautifully landscaped grounds that embrace a man-made lake.*

TOP: BANKS OF SLOTS *can create instant millionaires.*
ABOVE: THE LOST CITY GOLF COURSE, *one of the two here designed by Gary Player.*
BELOW: THIS ELEPHANT *stands guard at the Palace.*

glory. The broken watercourses and dams were turned into the Valley of Waves, where perfect artificial surfing rollers now pulse across the Roaring Lagoon before ebbing away on a white sand beach. Water chutes plunge down from the Temple of Courage, and a Lazy River Ride winds slowly around an alfresco refreshment area.

The Palace overlooks the Valley of Waves, and dominates the sky-line with its majestic towers of imitation elephant tusks.

CONSERVATION IN THE PILANESBERG

The Pilanesberg National Park, which borders Sun City, covers 55 000 hectares of natural bush that serves as home to the Big Five: lion, elephant, rhino, buffalo and leopard.

Like the Sun City resort, it lies in a bowl encircled by concentric rings of volcanic hills 1 200 million years old, and its many natural amphitheatres provide excellent game-viewing opportunities.

Over 140 kilometres of tarred and dirt roads wind over the veld, up hills and through poorts (wide clefts) in the rock, to give access to an extraordinarily wide range of wildlife habitats.

The park is a meeting point of the Highveld and the Lowveld, so it is one of the few reserves where springbok and impala naturally cohabit. The mixed sourveld vegetation and huge variety of trees, interspersed with numerous water-holes, support over 8 000 head of game.

A large lake is home to hippos, croco-diles and such waterbirds as the long-necked cormorant and the dapper king-fisher. Descendants of that sable antelope spotted by Cornwallis Harris in the Magaliesberg in the 1830s, lower their impressive sweep of horns to drink at the lake's edge. A short-tempered rhino trots past with a surprisingly dainty gait, and stately giraffes keep a watchful eye open for unwelcome intruders.

Guests from the surrounding resorts of Sun City, Kwa Maritane and Bakubung can enjoy evening braais in the bush, and game drives are conducted morning and evening for those who choose not to use a private vehicle. There are also several tented camps within the park, and an attractive and welcome refreshment centre close to the lake provides an area where visitors are allowed to leave their cars.

Other national parks in Bophuthatswana include Borakalalo, where the 10-kilometre long Klipvoor Dam provides some superb fishing, and Botsalano near Mmabatho, which has 5 800 hectares of wooded and game-rich grassland.

A few hours north of Pretoria, in the Waterberg range, the Lapalala Wilderness offers its own kind of 'Out of Africa' experi-ence; a major conservation effort is under-way to save the endangered black rhino.

Once the reputed home of the ancient king, it now offers royal hospit-ality to all. So superb is the craftsmanship of its weathered archi-tecture, frescoes and carvings that the legend is totally believ-able, and The Lost City has be-come a world-renowned attraction. It is surrounded by 25 hec-tares of rare and beauti-ful gardens tumbling down the cliffside.

The gardens at the Cascades Hotel are also remarkable, with rushing streams and pools of exotic fish. They open out onto rolling lawns in front of the Sun City Hotel, and then sweep on down towards the family cabanas and the superb 750-metre long recreational lake of Waterworld.

This is where the fun goes literally sky-high, with every kind of watersport on offer, from parasailing to waterskiing. Other sports amenities include two championship golf courses (both designed by Gary Player), ten-nis and squash courts, five swimming pools in charming settings and horse-riding stables.

A paradise for the adventurer, the lover of nature and the seeker of beauty; a quixotic past that tells of golden strikes and fortunes made and lost, and a breathtaking display of wildlife ... this is the Eastern Transvaal.

Bushveld and Berg

Roughly 400 kilometres long by 150 wide, the region sprawls across the north-east corner of South Africa between Zimbabwe, Swaziland, Mozambique and the Great Escarpment, a massive mountain rampart that plunges 1 500 metres from the inland plateau to the coastal plain.

Stone Age Bushmen lived here, until they were supplanted by slow waves of Bantu-speaking migrants from the north. After these came the first Europeans, who touched the nearby coast nearly five centuries ago but were defeated by the hinterland's barriers of heat, hostility and sickness. It wasn't until the 1830s that white men arrived in considerable numbers from the interior, as hunters, traders, and trekkers seeking a way to the coast. These hardy pioneers, intent on living as far away as possible from the British colonial presence, established a mini-republic at Ohrigstad in the early 1840s, but the community was soon devastated by fever and it moved, lock, stock and barrel, to a healthier spot 50 kilometres to the north. The new settlement was named Lydenburg, which means the 'town of suffering' – though as it turned out the place flourished, and is now a substantial and attractive centre that serves as the informal capital of the Escarpment area.

And then, in 1870, gold was found.

The rush of diggers – they arrived from all corners of the world – opened up the region like a flower and for nearly twenty years its life revolved around the glossy yellow metal. The camps – Spitskop, Mac Mac and, most notably, Pilgrim's Rest – grew quickly to take on a veneer of permanence, if not always of respectability. Solid, iron-roofed houses replaced the tents at Pilgrim's Rest; traders and publicans set up shop; a school, a church, a newspaper made their appearance, and the Royal Hotel opened its hospitable doors to thirsty customers. Then the surface deposits ran out, and syndicates and companies were formed to sink shafts and tunnel adits into the hillsides in search of deeper gold, so ending the era of the lone pick-and-shovel digger. The last of the mines closed in the 1970s (though, if the gold price climbs high enough, one or two could reopen).

Long before then, however, the owners had seen the glitter fading and they diversified into forestry to create some of the world's largest and most beautiful plantations. Eucalyptus and, especially, *Pinus patula*, a tree species native to South America but perfectly suited to the Eastern Transvaal, now mantles much of the region's cool uplands.

The territory is rich in diversity, ranging from hot, wild, bushveld country to gentle foothills, green with orchards and timber, rising to the Escarpment, a cool world of echoing valleys cloaked in mist, laced by rivers and waterfalls and home to a treasure-house of forest, flowers and ferns.

Above all it is a region of wilderness. It is the home of the Kruger National Park, haven to the largest variety of wild creatures on earth, and to many smaller game reserves. It is abundantly rich, too, in its human diversity.

It is South Africa at its splendid best.

OPPOSITE: A SOLITARY TUSKER *explores the river-bed near the Kruger Park's Bateleur camp.*

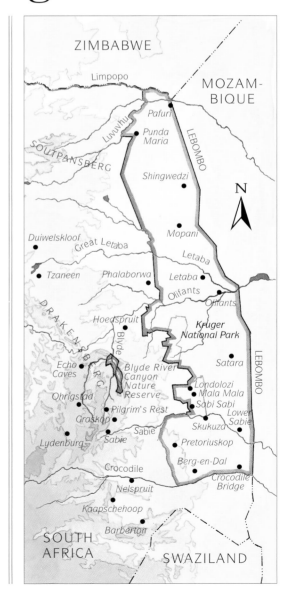

Designer safaris

Wild animals are big business today, and nowhere more so than among the

private safari enterprises of the Transvaal Lowveld, a region that boasts a

greater number and variety of wildlife than any similar sized area in Africa.

Until a few decades ago wildlife species venturing out of the vast expanses of the Kruger National Park and other sanctuaries were regarded as a nuisance – destroyers of crops, livestock and grazing, good for nothing except hunting and eating. Thanks to the soaring popularity of the Kruger and to the efforts of conservationists, this attitude changed dramatically over the decades following the Park's elevation to national status in 1926.

Lowveld ranchers discovered that wild animals prospered where domestic livestock dwindled, and game suddenly became a marketable asset – an attraction for tourists and trophy hunters, capable of generating more profit than ranching. Landowners, enthusiastic about the prospects and alarmed at the diminishing numbers of wild animals on their farms, erected game fences and began restocking. Today they buy white rhino, sable antelope, roan antelope, hartebeest and other prized species at wildlife auctions where millions of rands change hands. The Kruger National Park has become a major source of such animals, especially of elephants.

Private reserves

There are scores of smaller reserves in the Lowveld, all differing widely in character according to their environment. The biggest and best are located along the Kruger's western boundary, and are so well run that the park has dismantled its fences (originally erected to stop the spread of foot-and-mouth

ABOVE: LION SEEK SHELTER *from the midday heat. Fences that once separated the private reserves from the Kruger National Park have been dismantled and wildlife can now move freely over the wider region.*

TOP: LONDOLOZI'S SOCIABLE *dining and bar area.*
ABOVE: OUT-OF-AFRICA *décor at Mala Mala.*

HEDONISM ON WHEELS

The key that finally opened the Lowveld to the world was the railway, completed in 1894 to give Paul Kruger's Transvaal Republic access to the sea at Baía de Lourenço Marques (now Maputo, the capital of Mozambique).

Today the line is busy with freight, which regularly goes to and from the coast, but the initial wonder of the railroad is indelibly stamped on the region's character. For example, on the mountainsides near Kaapse Hoop and Hazyview, old wooden coaches have been converted to picturesque stop-over refuges for hikers. Halfway between Sabie and White River, a stationary 16-coach train, still known as the 'Shunter's Express', has become a colourful inn with dining, buffet, saloon, lounge and sleeping cars.

The old railway line has been put to especially imaginative use by two of the most opulent trains on earth: the Blue Train and the Rovos Rail. The Blue Train, once used exclusively on the Pretoria-Cape Town route, has long been renowned for its luxurious appointments, which include en suite private compartments, hot and cold and iced water on tap, air conditioning, and delicious meals. Now the train also runs from Pretoria through the bewildering twists and turns of the Escarpment and along verdant valleys to Nelspruit, from where passengers may visit the Kruger National Park.

The privately owned Rovos Rail takes hedonism several stages further. Its 'Pride of Africa' is drawn by old classic steam locomotives, and the lovingly restored vintage coaches – all teak, leather, brass and silver – provide the 46 passengers with a padded, pampered, luxurious environment. In Pretoria, Rovos Rail guests may stay in the line's five-star hotel, and in the Lowveld they can stop at one of the super-exclusive private game lodges. It is a safari on wheels, the ultimate in cosseted travel.

ABOVE: THE LONDOLOZI RESERVE, *owned and run by the Varty brothers, is world-famed for its leopards. Here, in a reversal of roles, a youngster grooms its mother.*

a hulking white rhino, an imperiously watchful lion, or an angry leopard twitching its tail.

Energetic guests are taken in small groups on easy walks, to see, smell and almost touch the animals and learn about their behaviour; they also discover the wonders of the prolific bird, insect and plant life of the veld.

Five and counting

Visitors usually encounter some, if not all, of the Big Five in a matter of hours, and occasionally also come across the elusive cheetahs, wild dogs and hyaenas; they can enjoy watching antelope frolicking and feeding, and can study sleeping owls from a distance of just a few metres.

As the sun lowers there is a pause for drinks, and the evening's magnificent dinner is enlivened by performances from African dancers. Nightcaps around the campfire are enjoyed to the eternal sounds of Africa – the roar of a big cat, the cackling of a hyaena, and the unending symphony of frogs and crickets. It is a unique experience, an elegant blend of the sophisticated and the primordial.

For people who cannot quite afford so rich a fare, there is a profusion of country inns, hotels, camps, resorts, self-catering chalets and guest farms, all without exception set in attractive surroundings. And after all, wherever you are in the Lowveld, the wilderness is never very far away.

---

disease) to allow its animals to move freely around the wider area – a tribute to the dedication and expertise of the private owners.

Some of these private safari venues cater for a jet-setting clientele who prefers to learn the ways of the wild in supreme comfort.

The oldest and arguably the best known of these designer safaris is the Mala Mala Game Reserve, which has three camps altogether, each providing a different kind of bush experience. Among other stylish destinations are the Londolozi, Sabi Sabi, Inyati, Ulusaba, Motswari and M'Bali camps, where guests are waited on hand and foot by numerous servants and plied with exotic drinks and imaginative cordon bleu cuisine; the service is impeccable and the accommodation merits a multi-star rating.

The daily calendar of these safaris is full and fascinating; most of it is taken up with game-viewing. Experienced rangers, together with trackers hugely skilled in bushcraft, conduct a handful of people into the bush in customized open vehicles. The jeeps have stepped bench seats to allow a clear view of the constant passing parade of animals, which can include

ABOVE LEFT: THE KRUGER'S *1 500 lion occur through-out the park but tend to congregate in the south-central grasslands, feeding ground for the herds of herbivores on which they prey.*
ABOVE: THE DWARF MONGOOSE, *smallest of the African species and resident of the drier savannah regions.*

The Kruger – king of parks

South Africa's premier game reserve, sprawling over the heat-hazed Lowveld

plain, occupies an area the size of Wales and larger than the state of Israel, and

is haven to the world's most wondrous array of wild animals.

Early this century most of the Transvaal Lowveld was still a wild, savage and sun-blistered land with lonely islands of settlement linked by bone-jarring roads and tenuous railroad tracks.

Small groups of African people inhabited the flat Lowveld plains, but malaria, bilharzia, tsetse flies, predatory wild animals and sheer murderous heat kept the wider world at bay.

European settlement came late to this region, in spite of early reconnaissance ventures. In 1725 the Dutch East India Company, attracted by rumours of gold, sent an expedition from Baía de Lourenço Marques (modern Maputo) to explore the Transvaal interior, under the leadership of François de Kuiper. He was the first European to have entered the Lowveld and he got as far as Gomondwane,

near present-day Crocodile Bridge, before hostile local Africans sent him scurrying back.

In 1836 two separate Voortrekker parties set out to find a way which would lead from the interior to the east coast. Both expeditions were disastrous: Hans van Rensburg's group was slaughtered by Shangaan warriors, whereas Louis Trichardt's men were almost wiped out by malaria, although a few survivors managed to limp into Delagoa Bay.

When he saw the Trichardt group arrive, a remarkable Italian of Portuguese nationality, Joao Albasini, realized there was great potential for lucrative business between the hinterland and the coast. In the late 1830s he opened a trading post near the present-day Pretoriuskop rest-camp, and became the first European resident of the Lowveld.

Then, in 1870, gold was discovered in the uplands, and tens of thousands of fortune-seekers arrived in the region. As there were no towns, shops or farms, the speculators hunted for their food, and soon the depredation of animals in the area became wholesale. Adding to it were the transport riders, a hardy breed of men who lived off the land as they ferried supplies to and from Delagoa Bay.

Sustaining the heritage

Eventually, visiting Boer hunters, sensible men who shot only what they needed, observed the excessive killing and reported it to the Transvaal Republican authorities in Pretoria. In 1889, as the eastern gold rush fizzled out, President Paul Kruger urged his parliament to create a sanctuary to protect the remaining wildlife of the Lowveld, and eventually, in 1898, some 4 600 square kilometres between the Sabie and Crocodile rivers were proclaimed the Sabie Game Reserve.

That was the birth of the Kruger National Park, a project which fortunately the British endorsed when they took over the region. In 1902 a diminutive Scotsman named James Stevenson-Hamilton was appointed as the first warden of the reserve. During the next 40 years he did more than any other individual to nurture this splendid natural heritage.

In 1903 a second reserve was proclaimed, the Shingwedzi, which encompassed the land further north between the Letaba and the Limpopo rivers. In 1926 both reserves, and the farmland between them, were consolidated by the South African Parliament into the Kruger National Park. Later still, more land was added and the reserve reached its present size of about 21 000 square kilometres.

The park is not the world's largest of its kind, nor is it particularly scenic. Most of it is flat and rather dull, with only a few insignificant hills rising here and there, and the occasional giant rocky outcrop. It can also get exhaustingly hot. But it is recognized as the

TOP: CAMP-FIRE COMPANIONSHIP *on the Olifants wilderness trail, one of the park's seven foot-safaris.*
ABOVE: THE SHY WATERBUCK *thrives in the Kruger.*

world's leader in African fauna and flora research and in environmental management.

To the average person it offers the unique chance of observing an unequalled variety of wildlife creatures at close proximity. Up to 700 000 people flock here every year to escape the pressures of modern life and experience the wonders of the bush.

Facilities include 4 000 beds in 32 camps of various kinds and sizes, together with camping sites, restaurants, grocery shops, bakeries, laundries, an education centre, a library, and more than 7 000 kilometres of good roads.

The Kruger is, without doubt, a wilderness without peer, the monarch of game parks.

THE ENDURING LEGEND

He was born a mongrel runt in May, 1885, and nobody knew who his father was. His mother was Jess, a bull terrier bitch whose other five pups were quickly snatched up because, in those wild early days of the Lowveld, a good dog was a much sought-after companion.

Percy Fitzpatrick, a young transport rider plying his ox-wagon from Delagoa Bay to Lydenburg, Barberton and the other goldfields, took pity on the runt of the litter, and adopted him, naming him Jock.

For years Jock travelled with his master through the hot bush and the wild mountains.

They hunted together, and Jock proved to be an instinctive master of the game: he had astonishing courage and tenacity, and knew exactly when to move to down a wounded buck, keep a lion at bay or distract an enraged buffalo.

The strong, stocky, red-brown and brindle terrier saved Fitzpatrick's life on many occasions, and his legend grew even while he was still alive. Travellers stopped at the same places overnight and tales of Jock's prowess were told over campfires.

Long after Jock's death, and encouraged by Rudyard Kipling, Sir Percy (knighted for services to South Africa) wrote *Jock of the Bushveld* for his grandchildren. It instantly became a South African classic.

The routes Jock travelled and the scenes of many of his adventures have been retraced and today, all over the Lowveld – including the Kruger National Park – there are place names, plaques, statues (pictured) and signs that weave his story inextricably into the tapestry of the local history.

South of the Olifants

The Kruger Park's southern section, with its broad game-rich grasslands, was the first to be developed and its old-established camps, now supplemented by some splendid new venues, beckon the comfort-conscious safari enthusiast.

Being the oldest and most accessible part, the southern half of the Kruger National Park has more accommodation, roads, picnic places, viewpoints and, some even say, animals, than the northern half. It is served by seven main rest-camps, two bushveld camps, five private camps (for hire on a group basis), five wilderness trail camps and the park's only bush camp.

Outside these man-made pockets lies unadulterated wilderness. Each entrance to the Kruger Park is like a Wellsian time-travel machine: on the outside there is the crush and pollution of towns, farms, factories and traffic; take a step across the line and you are transported to Africa as it was a hundred, a thousand, ten thousand years ago.

The Kruger Park is crisscrossed by rivers and streams fringed with many kinds of trees, some of them very large. Leopards lie on the massive branches and store their prey in the forks. Foraging elephants stir the riverine undergrowth, and bushbuck appear magically, their spotted coats blending with the dappled shade, as colourful birds and butterflies flit about in the clear air.

Distinctive style

Away from the rivers the land changes from acacia woodland to scrub and grassy plains, home to sable antelope, rhino, reedbuck, waterbuck, duiker, steenbok, buffalo, impala, wildebeest and zebra. Here too are found their attendant predators, among them lions, cheetahs, wild dogs, hyaenas and jackals.

The seven main camps differ greatly from each other in character. The oldest is the highly popular Skukuza, on the Sabie River. Set amid trees and lawns, it is the focal point of the southern region, and is a veritable town: its thatched chalets cater for nearly 700 visitors a day and its amenities include a bank, a police station, a post office, a garage and two good restaurants, one of them housed in an old railway train.

Pretoriuskop, the Kruger's fourth largest camp, dates back to 1927, though many years before that transport wagons paused here on their way to and from Delagoa Bay to fetch machinery, food and liquor for the gold diggings. The old transport route, plied by Sir Percy Fitzpatrick and other intrepid men of the veld, is clearly signposted. Nearby, Jock of the Bushveld, one

Above: The Olifants Rest-Camp *is set atop cliffs high above the Olifants River and its game-rich valley.*
Right: A Young Chacma Baboon, *one of three species of monkey found in South Africa, surveys the bushveld terrain.*

Satara, well north of Skukuza, is a large circular camp in extensive bushy plains that teem with game, often seen in huge herds. Farther north still, Olifants camp, perched high on a ridge, has superb views across the Olifants River – where fish eagles cry – and the savannah beyond.

The two bushveld camps are special because, apart from having splendid game-viewing sites, they have no more than 15 chalets between them, and no public amenities to disturb the tranquillity of the veld.

Five simple but popular wilderness trail camps bring people even closer to nature. Rangers lead small parties along the trails each day, for easy walks during which they can study everything from elephants to ants.

The Kruger Park's one and only bush camp is used mainly for environmental courses: visitors sleep on the ground, do their own cooking and cleaning, and commune with the fauna, the flora and with each other.

TOP: WELL-FED ZEBRA *of the southern grasslands.*
ABOVE: SKUKUZA – *more of a village than a camp.*

of the southern region's five smallish private camps, is named after Fitzpatrick's famed dog.

To the south-east are the smaller, much-loved Lower Sabie and Crocodile Bridge camps, each sited beside a perennial river in thickly forested veld. Both have large shade trees and are known for their birdlife. In the mountainous south-west, Berg-en-Dal (Hill and Dale) is a camp of unusually modern design, where the buildings blend entirely with their bushveld surroundings. Wilderness trails in the neighbourhood lead walkers to a profusion of Bushman rock paintings.

THE BIG FIVE

In hunters' tradition the Big Five are the elephant, the rhino, the lion, the leopard and the buffalo. They are the most sought-after of all the wild animals and are all found in the Lowveld.

But why only these five? Why not also the hippo, which is as big as the rhino, or the cheetah, which is fleeter than the leopard? The reason is that the Big Five are the most dangerous; other mammals are seldom as dangerous unless they are cornered. The elephant, for instance, is immensely powerful and makes a terrifying opponent when challenged or wounded. The Kruger has around 7 000 of these giant pachyderms, many of them with unusually long tusks.

The rhino, and especially the black variety, is notoriously bad-tempered when aroused and is unstoppable when it charges. Demand for its horn in the Middle and Far East has led to its virtual extermination in much of Africa, but the Kruger's population is well protected and has shown steady growth since its reintroduction a few years ago. Lions are extremely strong and fast, and so are leopards, which in addition are also extremely stealthy.

Finally, the Cape buffalo, when wounded, cunningly ambushes its pursuer and wields its huge curved horns with awesome, single-minded power.

The Kruger: north to Pafuri

The wild northern segment of the Kruger Park beckons the serious game-viewer and the lover of unspoilt Africa. The birds, the animals and the enchanting forests of the Luvuvhu River region are especially magical.

For the purists there is little to match the natural treasures of the Kruger Park's northern half. Some of the landscape appears monotonous – from the Olifants River to the vicinity of the Zimbabwe border, mixed mopane scrub and forest stretch as far as the eye can see, an ocean of pale green in summer, rich glowing red in winter, and dead grey in times of drought. However, especially around the jungle-like reaches of the Luvuvhu River, gems of life and colour catch the eye. Flowers and creepers form spectacular displays along river banks teeming with birds, and rare roan antelope canter across open veld, while nyala and shy bushbuck step daintily through forests. Elephant appear out of nowhere – majestic old bulls, and herds of cows and calves. There are four main rest-camps in the northern Kruger, plus three bushveld camps, one private camp and two wilderness trail camps.

The southernmost venue is Letaba, a cool and pleasant oasis graced by bird-rich subtropical growth which overlooks a wide sandy bend in the Letaba River. Animals go to drink there, and two nearby dams also provide game and waterbird viewing sites.

North of Letaba are the two camps which many regular visitors vote their favourites: Shingwedzi and Punda Maria.

Shingwedzi lies beside a river of the same name, and is centred around a patio covered by an enormous thatched roof. The camp is a collection of long verandah-girded huts scattered beneath trees in flat bushveld countryside, and in the evenings the heady scent of woodsmoke from the cooking fires fills the air. Shingwedzi is popular because many kinds of animals stroll by casually. Baboons cavort in the big wild fig trees overhanging the river banks, waterbuck amble down to drink, and the occasional lion makes its regal appearance. Devotees claim they see more wildlife on the short access road which runs alongside the deep trench of the river than anywhere else in the park.

Downstream from the camp is the Kanniedood Dam, where one can observe hippos and waterbirds from log hides set high on stilts. The road leading to the dam is fringed with dense mopane bush from which elephant sometimes emerge with heart-stopping suddenness. Fortunately, these particular ones tend to be unusually mild-tempered.

The Punda Maria camp, spread across the flank of a bushy hill, derives half its name from the Swahili word for zebra – 'punda milia' – and the other half from the wife of the ranger who established the camp – Maria Coetser. Visitors enter via a short steep road which is flanked on one side by a row of

ABOVE: BUFFALO WEAVERS' NESTS *decorate the branches of a giant baobab tree, one of many around Pafuri.*
LEFT: THE LUMINOUS LITTLE LILAC-BREASTED ROLLER, *often seen perched in roadside trees.*

LEFT: BUFFALO SLAKE *their thirst. These animals look placid but are among the bushveld's most dangerous.* ABOVE: THE PLEASANTLY SHADY LETABA *rest-camp.* BELOW: A SPOTTED HYAENA *carries the bones of a carcass to the den to feed her young.*

white-washed thatched mud huts, with verandah roofs supported by trimmed ironwood branches. Built in the early 1930s, the huts retain the feel of pioneer days, although today they all have bathroom facilities.

The imperious sable favours this area, and can often be admired from a distance. The splendid view from the camp sweeps over hills and valleys blanketed by a dense growth of trees, shrubs, creepers, flowers and grasses. One of the nearby hills, Gumbandevu, is held sacred by the local tribespeople: legend has it that a rain-making princess wove her spells and made sacrifices there.

Punda Maria is the nearest camp to what many visitors believe to be the most entrancing part of the park – Pafuri. The road leading to it descends through mopane and fat baobab trees into the shallow valley of the Luvuvhu River. At the bridge, side roads lead you east and west into a world of awe-inspiring riverine forest, a fantasia of enormous jackalberry, nyala, leadwood, sausage, ana, ghostly fever and many other trees that spread a canopy of cool dappled green high over the still surface of the river.

Hundreds of different kinds of birds dwell in the dim green reaches, among them Cape parrots, luminous Narina trogons, Natal robins, hornbills, crested guineafowl, barbets, gorgeous bush shrikes, boubous and black-eyed Pel's fishing owls. Great crocodiles sprawl on the muddy river banks, while buffalo herds raise clouds of dust on their way to stand belly-deep in the shallows. Nyala, bushbuck, kudu and impala graze between the massive tree boles, leopards laze high up in the branches and elephants stride with stately tread through the forest.

The Luvuvhu River flows east into the Limpopo. At the fork the borders of South Africa, Mozambique and Zimbabwe meet. The spot is known as Crooks' Corner, because, early this century, poachers smugglers, and other shady characters established a base here, knowing that, if need be, they could quickly slip across a frontier to safety.

LEFT: THE COUNTRYSIDE *around Dullstroom village, on the western mountain slopes, is famed for its trout streams and its charming little country inns.*
ABOVE: BLYDEPOORT DAM, *in the grandest of canyons.*

The magical Escarpment – mountains of beauty

For sheer scenic beauty, few parts of Africa can compare with the Transvaal

Drakensberg, a wonderland of massive sculpted buttresses, precipitous ravines,

mist-wreathed valleys covered in a profusion of wild flowers, cool, deep green

forests and some of the most breathtaking vistas imaginable.

A wall of mountain topped by great, jagged battlements towering up to 1 200 metres above the humid Lowveld bush from Zimbabwe to Swaziland – such is the Great Escarpment, the northern segment of South Africa's Drakensberg, or 'Dragon Mountains'. Formed some 700 million years ago, the Drakensburg is the southernmost part of Africa's Great Rift Valley.

Near Zimbabwe, where the Escarpment meets the Soutpansberg Mountains, live the VhaVenda, a people who migrated from the north nearly three centuries ago. Theirs is a land of tropical crops and tribal legend, remote reserves and intriguing, little-known wonders hidden away in secret valleys. There is, for instance, the sacred Fundudzi lake whose fresh water is believed to reject foreign bodies and other impurities. Then there are the *zwidutwane*, malign half creatures who are thought to inhabit the rivers. Forests of giant hardwoods cannot be entered by anyone because tribal chiefs are buried in their deep green depths and ancient, sacrosanct ruins are scattered here and there.

South of Venda, as it approaches Tzaneen, the Escarpment erupts into a crescendo of valleys, forests, naked slopes, peaks and dark gorges into which streams tumble.

Spectacular roads twist down through Magoebaskloof, which boasts the Escarpment's largest patch of indigenous forest (the Woodbush), and Duiwelskloof past tea estates, chilly trout streams and deep-green natural woodland and emerge in the fecund tropical countryside around Tzaneen. Various hiking trails and some superb hostelries can be found in this area. In the nearby Modjadji nature reserve, the fabled Rain Queen presides over her forest of sacred giant cycads.

Nature's glory

From Tzaneen the Escarpment sweeps southeast in a solid massif, until a cleft gives space for the Abel Erasmus Pass. At the top the road forks, one leg following the edge of the 16-kilometre Blyde River Canyon: one can look down at the silver ribbon of the river more than 600 metres below, and across at the mountains rising monumentally beyond.

Nature endowed this region with an astonishing diversity of minerals: gold, emeralds, corundum, mica, mercury and such curiosities as chromite bands in anorthosite. In addition there are rich farmlands and breathtaking natural wonders, such as the deep dolomitic Echo Caves near Ohrigstad and the Sudwala Caves, not far from Nelspruit. Upstream on the Blyde River are the Bourke's Luck Potholes, where stones churned by water have carved a filigree of weirdly eroded rock.

Above the Escarpment rim one finds Lydenburg, an attractive farming and trout fishing centre founded by Voortrekkers in 1849, and Pilgrim's Rest, a fascinating village made up of corrugated iron shops and houses, looking still much as it did when it was built over a century ago, during the gold rush. Near Pilgrim's Rest is the famed physical feature known as God's Window, where the 1 500 metre-high Escarpment plunges in an almost sheer drop to the Lowveld below.

Farther south, the Escarpment loses its sharp edge, and spreads wide in a chain of enormous valleys ringed by peaks and cloaked in dense indigenous forest, plantations and mist. Sabie is one of the loveliest of these valleys, a great bowl embracing the river and a town of the same name. The town, at the bottom of the dizzying Long Tom Pass, was born because of gold and is now a placid timber centre.

Steep hills and fertile valleys

The Crocodile and Elands rivers cut through the Escarpment in the south, and run across long fertile valleys, until the mountains soar again to Kaapschehoop and form a high and narrow plateau. On the other side of the plateau, cliffs swoop down into the gigantic bowl of what is thought to be the largest volcanic crater on earth – the De Kaap Valley, studded with steep hills and ridges that add interest to the landscape and contain a great variety but no great wealth of minerals.

On the far side of the De Kaap Valley, more than 40 kilometres away, is the lovely, sleepy little town of Barberton nestling at the foot of the Makhonjwa Mountains. Beyond it

BELOW: THE MOUNT SHEBA HOTEL *and timeshare complex, centrepiece of an exquisite private forest reserve. The forest is in what is known as climax condition.*
BOTTOM: BOURKE'S LUCK POTHOLES – *an intriguing fantasia of rock shapes sculpted over the millennia by the erosive action of water.*

A FAIRYLAND OF FALLS

The Lowveld Escarpment is ribboned with streams and laced with waterfalls, the loveliest of them on perennial rivers near the mountain villages of Sabie and Graskop. Many are accessible only to hikers and, in some cases, only with the forester's permission.

One spectacular and easily reached cataract is at the point where the Elands River plunges from Waterval Boven into a gorge beside the main road, down to Waterval Onder.

At Sabie's northern edge, under the road bridge, are the pretty Sabie Falls; just to the west are the Lone Creek, Horseshoe and diaphanous Bridal Veil cascades. A little to the north, before the Pilgrim's Rest turn-off, the twin columns of the famed Mac-Mac Falls drop straight down into the magical pool far below. Nearby you'll find the Maria Shire Falls and, deep amid trees, the Forest Falls (pictured). Just outside

Graskop, on the brink of the Escarpment, lies the long, narrow Panorama Gorge with its several waterfalls; the exquisite Lisbon and the unfenced Berlin falls grace the area just north of Graskop. Beyond, between God's Window and Devil's Window, are the New Chum Falls, easily reached by one of the area's several hiking trails.

are a succession of deep, narrow valleys flanked by walls so steep they resemble the pages of some giant, loosely opened book. Gold and asbestos are mined in those valleys and old bottles, machinery and other relics of long-gone prospectors can still be found in the area, as well as remote Swazi villages that still have much of the old Africa about them, and a great number of wild animals.

Heavenly hikes – trails in the Lowveld

If the best way to see a country is on foot, then the Lowveld must surely be the

most visible part of South Africa – more than thirty splendid hiking trails criss-

cross the tumble of mountains and the torrid bushveld below.

The hiking trails of the Eastern Transvaal cover hundreds of kilometres, and are remarkably varied: many follow rivers, others climb hills, one leads through an old mining tunnel, another's base camp is a brace of old railway coaches, and so on.

One of the least-known yet most exciting of these trails is the 53-kilometre hike through the mountainous Makuya National Park in Venda, where an armed ranger escorts hikers because the paths are also used by elephants, leopards, buffalo and other wild animals. Also in Venda, and equally little known despite its breathtaking scenery, is the 53-kilometre Mabunda-Shango hike, which takes you to the magical, mystical and, to the VhaVenda, sacred locations of the Fundudzi lake and the Thathe Vondo Forest.

Among South Africa's oldest and most rewarding trails is the Fanie Botha trail, named after a former forestry minister. The 79-kilometre hike runs between the Ceylon State Forest and God's Window on the rim of the Great Escarpment. Its bunkhouses are sited so the route can be completed in one five-day or two three-day trips, but either way it is tough going: the trail follows a yo-yo path past the high peak of Mount Anderson above Sabie, the Mac-Mac Falls, Graskop, the Bridal Veil Falls, the Lone Creek Falls and other scenic jewels.

The Blydepoort Trail is another muscular marathon. It leads you from God's Window past Fann's Falls, New Chum Falls and the Bourke's Luck Potholes before dropping right down to the bottom of the awe-inspiring Blyde River Canyon. It then crosses the river

LEFT: A SEGMENT *of the lovely indigenous forests that mantle the reaches of the Blyde River.*
ABOVE: HIKERS TAKE *in the riverine splendour of the 23 000-hectare Blyde River Canyon Nature Reserve.*

THE SHY GARDENS

It is the second largest in South Africa and is second only to the Cape's Kirstenbosch in diversity and importance, yet for years few people had heard of, let alone visited, the National Botanical Garden at Nelspruit. It was ignored for the most practical of reasons: one could reach it only by following kilometres of badly marked dirt road winding past misleading turn-offs. All that has changed. Access is now easy, and there's a clearly signposted new entrance to this entrancing place, just outside Nelspruit, off the main road to White River.

The garden comprises 154 hectares spread along the east bank of the Crocodile River, of which 22 hectares have been groomed into beds, streams, walks and cultivated lawns. The remainder has been left intact as a completely natural habitat sustaining over 500 plant species indigenous to Nelspruit and its environs, plus many more from the rest of the

Lowveld. The grounds embrace several kilometres of cool, shady paths running between clumps of trees and flowerbeds (all clearly labelled) and alongside chuckling waterways. The most fascinating walk is along a wild trail which leads down to the river and opens onto a viewing area next to a tumult of rock, waterfall and cascade.

Among other pleasant features are spots in which to sit, rest and read; a nursery offers a superb range of indigenous plants for sale.

the Bushveld Trail along the Timbavati River near Hoedspruit, close to the edge of the Kruger Park, a five-day slog on which hikers, usually, are able to see plenty of big game.

The Gold Nugget Trail climbs up behind Barberton and continues more or less on the level for 37 to 44 km, depending on the precise route the hiker takes. Far up the dizzyingly steep valleys are large pieces of mining machinery that were carried up by the diggers more than a century ago. Also in the Barberton area is the Fortuna Mine Trail, a trip of only two kilometres, but demanding in a way because you negotiate 600 metres of it by torchlight through a dark tunnel.

Among many other choice hikes are the Magoebaskloof Trail, of either 36 kilometres or 50 kilometres, the latter route running through the Grootbosch, the largest indigenous forest in the Transvaal; the Kaapse Hoop Trail, which winds across 50 kilometres of mountain slopes, gorges and chilly grasslands (here the rare blue swallow breeds in dolomite sinkholes); and the Mapulaneng Trails near the Blydepoort Dam that cut through dense, dripping, riverine forest inhabited by such rare and striking birds as the Narina trogon and the Knysna lourie.

BELOW: NEGOTIATING THE RUGGED *floor of the Blyde River Canyon, the majestic sandstone gorge that ranks among Africa's great natural wonders.*

to the Blydepoort Dam and finishes at the pleasant, beautifully laid out Swadini resort.

In marked contrast are the many easy walks which can be enjoyed in the region, such as the 4-kilometre Forest Falls Hike in the Mac-Mac area and the 13,6-kilometre Loerie Walk near Sabie.

Others routes are known only to dedicated hikers, and wind their way through forestry areas that can only be entered with special permission. Some, like the two-day walk through the thick indigenous forest of the Wonderkloof Nature Reserve near the wondrous Sudwala Caves and their adjacent dinosaur park, are exceptionally beautiful.

South of Tzaneen, near the rugged Wolkberg Wilderness Area, the Lekgalameetse Trail winds through savannah and forest in high, dry valleys that sustain antelope, orchids and a myriad handsome trees. Much lower, and much hotter, is the Jock of

LEFT: THE QUIET LITTLE TOWN *of Barberton, once home to 20 000 diggers and enlivened by music halls, drinking dens and two busy stock exchanges.*
ABOVE: AN OLD-STYLE STORE *in historic Pilgrim's Rest.*

The golden thread

They came in their thousands to search for the glint of gold in granite outcrops,

to pan the crystal-clear streams of the high, rugged and beautiful mountains, to

wash the good earth and expose its nuggets – and in so doing they put the

Eastern Transvaal firmly on the map.

Gold – that most useless yet most beautiful and coveted of all metals – has been part of the story of southern Africa for at least two thousand years. The legend of King Solomon's Mines grew from the African kingdom ruled by monarchs titled Mwene Mutapa (Monomotapa), who built a great stone citadel and mined gold in what is now Zimbabwe and Botswana.

The precious metal was in common use in South Africa many centuries ago. The golden treasures of a vanished people – well-fashioned beads, bracelets and other ornaments –

were discovered on a low flat hill named Mapungubwe in the Northern Transvaal, and a similar but much smaller find was recently unearthed in the ruggedly beautiful northern Kruger National Park.

The modern quest for the golden lode began in earnest around the middle of the 19th century. In 1836 the first Voortrekkers to reach the far Northern Transvaal reported that the local Africans were mining iron, tin and gold and were wearing gold ornaments. In 1869 Edward Button, a Natalian, and his partners, found gold near Lydenburg and again, a

year later, near the Letaba River. Their discoveries triggered a frantic rush that saw thousands of fortune-seekers head for the Eastern Transvaal from all over the world, some braving the malaria-infested bush on the route from Delagoa Bay, others travelling the long roads from Durban and Cape Town.

They hunted for veins in outcrops of ore, panned for alluvial dust washed down by the streams, washed gold-bearing earth in sluice boxes to find nuggets and particles. Few could afford the equipment to extract the gold trapped in rock. On the Escarpment, tent and shack settlements mushroomed around Spitskop, Mac-Mac (named after the many Scots at the diggings), the Blyde River and the famed Pilgrim's Rest – the rich strike found by 'Wheelbarrow Alec' Patterson, so named because he carted all his possessions around in one. Today out of all these settlements only the sleepy village of Pilgrim's Rest remains, frozen in time, though a far cry from its spectacular beginnings in the early 1870s, when it was home to about a thousand diggers, traders, barkeepers, labourers, concubines and hangers-on and boasted a dozen pubs with names like 'Stent's Cathedral', 'The Spotted Dog' and 'Tom Craddock's Bar'.

The Pilgrim's Rest field yielded nuggets of astonishing size – the Reward piece weighed six kilograms, and three digger partners are said to have gathered another six kilograms of small nuggets in a single day. But then the alluvial gold ran out and syndicates and companies took over the area to start mining ore. By the early 1880s the population of Pilgrim's Rest had plunged to just over a hundred.

Meanwhile, a second gold rush, farther north, had produced another 'instant' town – Leydsdorp, set in the ferociously hot Lowveld near the Murchison range. In its heyday Leydsdorp was a lively little frontier-type settlement with a single row of wood-and-iron buildings flanking its dusty street, several pubs (one outside town, in the hollow trunk of a giant baobab tree, which you can still see), rough miners wearing pistols, a stage coach drawn by zebras, and Emerald Lil, who shrewdly bought the precious stones found in the diggings. Life was uproarious, and unhealthy – thanks to malaria the graveyard became better populated than the town itself. Here too the gold quickly ran out.

The glitter of Pilgrim's Rest was fast fading when gold was found on the high mountain plateau between the Elands River Valley and the gigantic De Kaap Valley. Because of its grotesque dolomite rocks and the chill mist swirling around them, the diggers named it Duiwel's Kantoor (Devil's Office). It later became known as Kaapschehoop but it, too, soon faded into obscurity. Fate stepped in again in the person of a tough, shrewd prospector named Auguste 'French Bob' Robert. On 3 June 1883 he was pottering

ABOVE: A GOLD-TAIL *glitters in the prospector's pan.*
BELOW: MAIN STREET, *Pilgrim's Rest - a 'living museum'.*

about a grassy slope down at the bottom of the De Kaap Valley when he chipped off a piece of yellow-speckled quartz, thereby exposing the Pioneer Reef, the richest strike yet made anywhere in the world – the vein measured less than one metre in width, but it was nearly two kilometres long.

Prospectors' luck

As the sensational news spread worldwide fortune-hunters streamed in, soon to form a sizeable part of the Transvaal Republic's 50 000-strong white community. Again, the surface and alluvial gold soon petered out and the Pioneer was taken over by companies with enough capital for deep mining, but by then other strikes were being made all over the De Kaap Valley. The evocative and sometimes eccentric names the prospectors gave them – Joe's Luck, Jam Tin Spruit, Forbes Reef, Eagle's Nest – survive to this day, though of course their treasures have long since disappeared.

The biggest strikes were around present-day Barberton, named after Graham Barber who, in 1884, found and worked the promising Barber's Reef. In May of the following year Edwin Bray discovered gold high in the nearby mountains, a stunning reef that was to become known as the Sheba. At the time the Sheba was ranked as the world's richest mine: it yielded a staggering 20 ounces of gold from each ton of ore, and gave its backers profits of millions in just a few years. The mine is still going strong today.

Barberton boomed: at one time it had two stock markets, a string of hotels and bars, shops, music halls, banks, a hospital, a club, a newspaper and all the other paraphernalia of new-found wealth – including 'Cockney Liz', who ran a saloon and sold herself each night to the highest bidder.

Other mines were started near Sheba and a new town, Eureka City, mushroomed on the uplands above the valley. This, too, had its amenities, among them a horse-racing track (set perilously close to a cliff). But almost nothing remains of Eureka. The De Kaap gold bubble collapsed in a heap of worthless share certificates. By 1888 most diggers had left, lured away by stories of new gold strikes at some forsaken place called the Witwatersrand, on the bleak Highveld plain to the west.

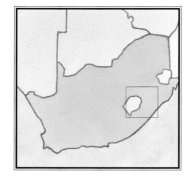

The craggy Drakensberg range, the most spectacular section of southern Africa's Great Escarpment, forms a natural divide between Natal and its neighbours on the high plateau to the west – Lesotho and the Orange Free State.

Mountains of the dragon

The gigantic rampart of mountains known as the Drakensberg is part – the highest and scenically most spectacular part – of the Great Escarpment that fringes South Africa's 3 000-kilometre coastal belt. The range is at its loftiest in the Kingdom of Lesotho, where it is known as the Maluti Mountains, but it is the Natal Berg that catches the eye and stirs the imagination: here, along the 95-kilometre eastern stretch, the cliff faces plunge – often precipitously, always dramatically – down to the foothills fully 2 000 metres below.

To the west and north of the Maluti bastion is the great plateau of the Orange Free State, a fertile countryside that rises to many-hued, picturesquely weathered hills, of which those in the Golden Gate Highlands National Park are perhaps the most strikingly colourful.

To the east, the Drakensberg's craggy slopes give way to the lovely rolling hills and misty valleys of the Natal and Zululand Midlands, a beautiful and peaceful looking land whose sweet grasses once sustained great herds of plains game.

The beauty and tranquillity, however, are deceptive: the region served as a monstrous battleground for much of the 19th century, and has suffered more than its share of violence in recent times – notably during the run-up to the 1994 elections.

But none of this has corrupted the essential character of what is known, aptly, as South Africa's 'garden province'.

OPPOSITE: THE RUGGED GRANDEUR *of the central Drakensberg, viewed from the Injasuti Valley.*

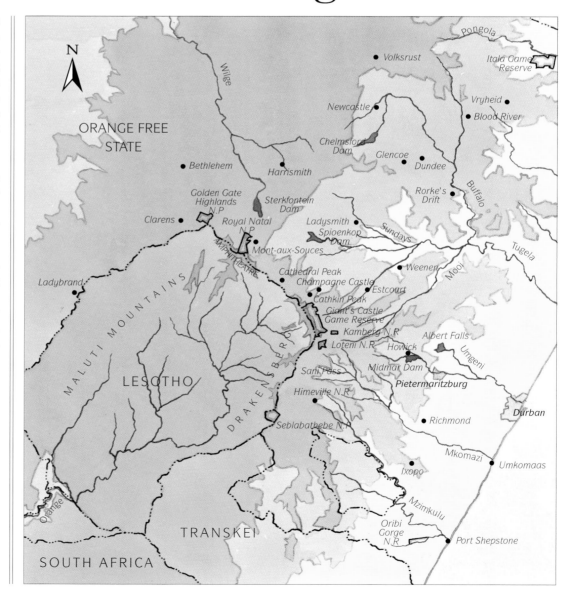

ABOVE: THOROUGHBREDS GRAZE *below the high Malutis.* LEFT: A PASTORAL SCENE *near Clarens in the Orange Free State's Golden Gate area, a name derived from its strikingly shaped and coloured sandstone formations.*

Under the Maluti Mountains

On the eastern side of the Orange Free State plateau, in the shadow of Lesotho's

Maluti Mountains, huge, strikingly sculpted and hued sandstone peaks and

buttresses rise to stand silent guard over the ancient plains.

The strange configurations of the eastern Free State's hills are as varied as the shades of their component sediment layers, dyed over the aeons by different iron oxides. Among the largest of the cliff-edged, flat-topped bastions is Thaba Nchu (the black mountain), the old stronghold of the Rolong tribe, a subgroup of the Tswana

people. Its ominous bulk lies between Bloemfontein and Lesotho. Dominating the coastal plain and closer to the Natal border is the Kerkenberg (Church Mountain), so named by the god-fearing Voortrekkers who camped in its shadow before venturing into the Drakensberg. Behind Harrismith, near the border with Natal and Lesotho, a table-like

buttress appropriately named Platberg (flat mountain) lies a few kilometres from the oddest of the configurations – the Tandjiesberg, whose contours are reminiscent of a set of giant molar teeth.

In early days these buttresses provided shelter for the Bushmen, and later they gave sanctuary to the dislodged tribes who, in the 1820s, were fleeing from the wrath of the conquering Zulus. Now, when the icy winds of winter blow down from the snow-capped mountains of Lesotho, their leeward side protects the Sotho and Tswana people and their livestock.

The place of vultures

The outcrops also provide eyries for many kinds of birds. Near Zastron, in the southeast, an imposing jagged cliff face is streaked white with the droppings of Cape vultures that nest among the heights. This Aasvoël-berg (vulture mountain) has an unusual geological feature – a gap, nine metres in diameter, known as the 'eye of Zastron'.

The eye, according to local lore, has interesting origins: a farmer was out hunting one day when he met the devil, who asked him for some tobacco. The farmer replied by showing him the business end of his gun, and while the creature was inhaling, he pulled the trigger. The shot knocked the devil's head against the mountain with such force that it cracked the rock face, and created the enormous hole we see today. The devil hurriedly withdrew, so the story goes, convinced that the tobacco grown in the area was too powerful for him.

A number of rivers flow between the rocky sentinels of the Free State. South Africa's largest, the mighty Orange, emerges from Lesotho near where the Maluti Mountains turn south. Stained with reddish silt, it follows a westwards route for 2 500 kilometres, meeting the Atlantic coast at the diamond beds on the border between Namibia and the Cape Province. Near Colesberg the river's course is interrupted by the H.F. Verwoerd Dam.

Flowing closer to the convergence of the borders between the Orange Free State, Lesotho and Natal, is the Vaal River, which separated the former Boer Republic from its northern neighbour, the Transvaal. Today the Vaal is the major source of water for the Witwatersrand industrial complex, though a multiphase complex, the Lesotho Highlands Scheme, is under construction on the upper reaches of the Orange to help meet Johannesburg's ever-increasing demand for water.

The ancient plains of the Orange Free State contain within their numerous sedimentary layers the evidence of many marvels of the

GOLDEN GATE HIGHLANDS NATIONAL PARK

The layered orange and yellow sandstone of a cliff-faced valley comes to glowing life in the setting sun. At moments like these the valley, carved by the Little Caledon River as it leaves Lesotho, can lay just claim to its name, Golden Gate.

This stark geological feature has been protected since 1963 inside a national park. The entrance to the park is near Clarens, named after the little town in Switzerland where Transvaal Republic President Paul Kruger died in exile in 1904.

The mountainous landscape of the 6 241-hectare park rises from 1 892 metres, at its lowest point, to 2 770 metres at its highest. In the natural highland vegetation of sour grasses and colourful herbs and shrubs, there is an abundance of indigenous wildlife, including black wildebeest, eland, the shy grey rhebok, the timid oribi, the red hartebeest, the blesbok, the mountain reedbuck and the zebra. There is also plenty for birdwatchers to study – from large raptors to blue cranes.

TOP: WINTERS ARE HARSH, *and life hard, in the uplands.* ABOVE: VILLAGE WOMEN, *on their way to fetch water, wend their way through fields of cosmos.*

evolving world. Extensive fossil beds have been uncovered, dating back to those immensely distant times when the plateau was part of an enormous flat lowland area.

At Damplaats, a farm near Ladybrand, fossilized remains of the oldest-known dinosaur, which lived about 200 million years ago, have recently been excavated. The Euskelosaurus, (Eu = first; skelo = skeleton; saurus = reptile) was a very large creature, but the bones of many smaller dinosaurs have also been found in the area. A number of dinosaur egg nests containing fossil embryos have also been uncovered in the Golden Gate Highlands National Park.

Peaks, parks and passes

Much of the Drakensberg is little changed since the days when Bushmen explored its deep gorges and hunted the abundant game that grazed on its lower slopes. Its majestic beauty provides an unforgettable experience which is enjoyed by thousands of visitors every year.

The Drakensberg mountain range stretches from Stormberg down in the Cape, right up to the border between northern Natal and the Transvaal. However, the section generally referred to as the Drakensberg starts in the north at the great natural amphitheatre of Mont-aux-Sources, where the Orange Free State, Natal and Lesotho meet, and from there runs south along the Lesotho border to Qacha's Nek. The main wall of this range of mountains comprises the 95 kilometres of weathered basalt cliffs stretching south-east from Mont-aux-Sources to Bushman's Nek.

Along the main wall the highest summits in the country follow one another in dizzy succession. Their dramatic beauty has inspired a plethora of evocative names: Windsor Castle, the Sentinel, the Monk's Cowl, the Outer Horn and the Inner Horn, the Bell and Champagne Castle and many more.

The Injasuti (meaning 'well-fed dog') Dome, behind the Injasuti Buttress on the northern border of Giant's Castle Reserve, stands at 3 410 metres and marks the highest point in the South African Drakensberg.

Giant's Castle itself, at 3 314 metres, is the fourth highest peak. Its massive bulk is so overwhelming, so menacing in its aspect that the Zulus named it iNtabayikonjwa, 'the mountain at which one must not point'.

Mont-aux-Sources, on the northern boundary of the mountain wall, marks the fifth highest point in the range, standing at 3 282 metres. Four rivers rise on this 'mountain of springs', including two of South Africa's largest – the mighty Orange, which runs west, and the eastward-flowing Tugela.

About midway along the wall, rising above a ridge of sheer rock faces which have defeated many an experienced mountaineer, the massive 3 004-metre Cathedral Peak dominates the landscape. Between Cathedral Peak and Injasuti, just below Cathkin Peak, the clear voices of the Drakensberg Boys' Choir (modelled on the Vienna Boys' Choir) can often be heard echoing down the valleys.

Thabana Ntlenyana ('the beautiful little mountain') can lay claim to being the highest point in Africa south of Tanzania's Kilimanjaro. It lies further west of the main wall, inside the Lesotho border. Ironically, it would take a stroll of only a few hours to climb it: although it is 3 482 metres above sea level, it appears to be an insignificant hill because it stands on a high plateau.

ABOVE: THE FOOTHILLS *are home to handsome blesbok.*

ABOVE: A HIKERS' HUT *in the Giant's Castle Reserve, originally created as a mountain sanctuary for eland.*

THE NOBLE LAMMERGEIER

Sometimes a lucky hiker will spot the rare bearded vulture, floating and soaring effortlessly between the spires of the Drakensberg massif on winds forced upwards by the mountain barrier. The bird has a rust-coloured underbody and black wings with a span of 1,5 metres, a diamond-shaped tail, a white head, a black bristly 'beard' and red-ringed eyes.

The vulture, commonly known as the lammergeier and prominent in African folklore, is also found in the mountains of Europe and Asia, and has been seen gliding at great heights over the Himalayas.

There are an estimated 200 pairs of this endangered species left in South Africa. Confining themselves to the Drakensberg area, the birds nest high up in the mountain crags, covering up to 40 kilometres in search of carrion and bones. They smash the bones they find by dropping them with impeccable accuracy from heights of up to 150 metres onto rocky platforms, and then use their tongues to extract the marrow on which they feed.

In order to encourage public interest in the species and its habits, an observation hide has been built in the Giant's Castle Reserve. It is open between May and September, the birds' non-breeding season. From this spot visitors have a superb view of the lammergeier, and of other vultures and birds of prey that live in the area. All are attracted to the hide by meat put out for them by Natal Parks Board officials.

The entire Drakensberg range is open to hikers and climbers, but the environment is well protected: the High Berg and the Little Berg are held in trust by the Natal Parks Board on behalf of the South African people.

Royal visit

In the north, beneath the Mont-aux-Sources amphitheatre, there is the Royal Natal National Park, where Queen Elizabeth II (then a princess) and her regal parents were hosted by Prime Minister General Jan Smuts during the royal visit of 1947. The park gained its 'Royal' prefix as a result of the visit.

The Giant's Castle Reserve stretches between the Injasuti and Loteni rivers, and with its rolling, grassy hills and high basalt cliffs is ideal for hiking. The reserve is also well equipped with caravan parks, camping grounds and holiday huts, catering for a wide variety of visitors. Both inside and outside the reserves there is an abundance of colourful flora. Tree ferns, orchids, ericas and gladioli grow among the towering, moist cliffs and crags, while proteas are scattered on the grassy pastures of the lower slopes.

The passes

The Drakensberg's passes are as spectacular as its peaks and parks. Some, like the breathtaking Organ Pipes Pass, are mere mule tracks; others are simply faint, perilously steep paths used only by intrepid hikers.

There are four national road passes which cut the Escarpment on the northern borders of Natal to reach the Transvaal and the Orange Free State. It is the route that leads up to the mountain kingdom of Lesotho, however, that provides the most memorable experience. The switchback corners of the Sani Pass take you 2 865 metres up to the highest pub in South Africa. On the way you follow the course of the Mkhomazana River, past caves which in many instances are graced by Bushman paintings.

BELOW: THE SWEET GRASSES *of the foothills sustain domestic stock and the antelope of the Drakensberg's reserves. Among the smaller and more inviting of these reserves are the Loteni, the Kamberg and the Vergelegen. All three are famed for trout-fishing.*

Barrier of spears

Three hundred million years ago, the foundations of the majestic Drakensberg range were laid down in a huge landlocked basin – part of the supercontinent of Gondwana that slowly, over countless aeons, broke apart to give birth to Africa, India, Australia, South America, Madagascar and Antarctica.

Dinosaurs evolved, lived and died in the basin from which the Drakensberg eventually emerged. Their fossils were to be discovered millions of years later.

Over time, layers of silt and sand that were carried down from the surrounding hills accumulated in the basin. Then, about 200 million years ago, weather patterns changed, and hot, dry westerly winds began to blow across the land mass, depositing dust and sand. Scientists have been able to pinpoint the several periods in the geological history of the region by identifying fossils found in the various strata: those of the Upper Beaufort Group, for instance, date back to 225 million years; the Molteno Formation to 200 million years; and the Elliot Formation to 190 million years. The light-coloured wind-deposited Clarens sandstone was the last of the strata to be laid down.

Then, 90 million years ago, giant convection currents in the molten interior of the earth began to break up the Gondwana continental strata. Fiery chasms hundreds of kilometres long opened up and molten lava poured from these giant fissures for several million years, finally cooling into a slab of basalt, as thick as 1,5 kilometres in some places, and which originally extended far beyond the present outcrop area, all the way from the Limpopo River in the north to a line running between Port Elizabeth and Kimberley in the south.

The dragon's back

As the continents tore apart, this multi-coloured geological sandwich tilted upwards on the south-eastern side of the African continent. The warm Mozambique current began to flow south from the tropics between the separating land masses, bringing moist air that combined with onshore winds to begin the long process of carving out the great buttresses and deep ravines of the Drakensberg.

Technically speaking the Drakensberg, unlike the Himalayas and the Alps, is not a

ABOVE: THE ROYAL NATAL NATIONAL PARK, *set beneath the imposing Mont-aux-Sources massif and its ampitheatre.*

ABOVE LEFT: THE 4000-HECTARE *Loteni Nature Reserve's rest-camp. Horse-riding is a favoured pastime here.*
ABOVE: STILL WATERS *reflect pinnacles of the Cathedral Peak area, renowned for its waterfalls.*

THE PAINTINGS OF THE PERSECUTED

Enthusiasts of rock art can expect a treat in the Drakensberg: the area boasts the richest collection of rock paintings in the world.

The paintings record the history, beliefs and traditions of the San – the little people of southern Africa, called Bushmen by the white settlers. Their ancient artists decorated caves and rocky overhangs using red, yellow and black oxides and white calcium and magnesium. No carbon was used in the pigments, so it has been almost impossible to date the paintings.

Some found in Namibia are thought to be 25 000 years old, while those in the Drakensberg are believed to be from a much later period.

Many of the scenes depicted are mystical, and are thought to reflect the workings and trances of medicine men. Most paintings though are of hunters and tracked animals; often the prey are attributed human features, while the people have animal qualities. The paintings are all that remain of the Bushmen in the Drakensberg: by the middle of the

19th century the last known artist in the area had been killed. The Bushmen knew no life beyond that of the hunter-gatherer; they took what they found as if by right. As a result they were persecuted by both the white man and the Zulu.

Diseases from Europe also decimated their numbers, and those who were left migrated to the remote deserts of the west. In a cave at Giant's Castle Reserve, a lifelike exhibit of a Bushman family going about its daily tasks has been recreated for the benefit of visitors. The cave also contains Bushmen paintings.

true mountain range, because it has not been thrust up in a powerful collision of land masses. The Drakensberg range is the eroded edge of an escarpment; at the summit, a plateau stretches out, sloping westwards towards the Atlantic Ocean. At a rate of less than one centimetre a year, over millions of years, rivers swollen by torrential rains have slowly eaten back the edge of the Escarpment by almost 200 kilometres.

Millennia of weather extremes have carved and reshaped the cliffs into steep spires, majestic peaks, narrow clefts and deep gullies. In the haze of a hot summer's day they appear blue and distant. As winter approaches and the air clears, they stand out, snow-capped and stark, sharply silhouetted against the bright sky.

The Voortrekkers who first saw the mountains named them the Drache Berg, because their jagged edges and isolated pinnacles, stretching for hundreds of kilometres, gave the impression of the ridged back of a storybook dragon. The Zulu, on the other hand, call them Quathlamba – 'the barrier of uppointed spears'. Both names convey the impression of an impenetrable rampart protecting some secret, magical world.

ABOVE LEFT: ONE OF THE SOUTHERN DRAKENSBERG'S *many resorts. Most serious hikers, though, use the trail-huts and caves of the remoter slopes.*
ABOVE: CLIMBERS NEGOTIATE *the last section of The Ampitheatre ascent by chain-ladder.*

Hiking in the Drakensberg

The Drakensberg is a hiker's dream. The scenery is awe-inspiring; the views are breathtaking; there are short rambles and there are long, exhausting treks. The landscape changes constantly: hilly grasslands; secret, trickling streams; forested glades; craggy mountain slopes.

Stretching from Mont-aux-Sources to the southern Natal border, the Drakensberg mountain range offers hundreds of kilometres of interlinked hiking trails. Most of them lie within the 200 000 square-kilometre Natal Drakensberg Park. In the north, this park is separated from the majestic Royal Natal National Park by the heavily populated Zulu tribal area, the Upper Tugela Location, which is crisscrossed by a number of dramatic but very demanding walking trails.

Hiking in the Drakensberg is extremely popular; the paths are well maintained and a permit system regulates the number of hikers so as to minimize trampling and ensure the preservation of the environment. In spite of the strict controls, or perhaps because of them, visitors can still experience the exhilaration of freedom, the feeling of isolation and remoteness often sought by city-dwellers.

Valleys and views

Hikes vary from easy strolls to challenging climbs to the top of the Escarpment. The popular 60-kilometre traverse between Mont-aux-Sources and Cathedral Peak takes hikers along hills with deep valleys and high peaks, and offers superb views over the most dramatic and magnificent part of the Drakensberg. The hike takes several days, and passports are essential, as the route meanders in and out of Lesotho.

Sudden weather changes, at any season, make hiking in the Drakensberg potentially dangerous. In winter there are frequent icy spells, and raging blizzards often cover the summits. In summer heavy thunderstorms sweep in from the coast, causing flash floods in the ravines. Swirling mists at any time of year can quickly disguise familiar landmarks. These weather vagaries make climbing the higher reaches of the mountains notoriously challenging; exploring the range is not for the faint-hearted, ill-prepared or inexperienced. Mountain rescue registers are kept at a number of set-off points as a wise safeguard: they have saved the lives of many a missing hiker.

The beauty of the Drakensberg is also accessible to the casual day-tripper. The lower reaches of the range are crisscrossed by safe walks and relatively easy climbs. Champagne Castle, with its proximity to Durban and Pietermaritzburg, is the most popular climb in the range. The soaring bulk of Cathkin Peak provides an uplifting backdrop to the many paths that explore the valley below, and there are many hotels, resorts and guest houses in the area that cater to all tastes.

Well-worn path

The seven-kilometre day-walk up the Tugela Gorge is probably the most frequented path in the Drakensberg. It starts at the gorge car park, below the Tendele hutted camp, and ends below the impressive Tugela Falls at The Amphitheatre. From various points along the trail, there are many spectacular views of the fledgling Tugela River as it falls in three breathtaking leaps from the top of the Escarpment. At one point the path crosses the river, which has sliced its way through basalt rocks, leaving high-sided cliffs that shelter pockets of lush, dense vegetation. There is a sturdy

TIGHT LINES

A flicking, brightly coloured fly is suddenly snatched from the gently flowing waters of the cold Drakensberg mountain stream – the trout on the end of the tight line has taken the hook.

Many a novice fisherman has been ensnared by the sport after having experienced the thrill of holding a fighting trout at the end of a whipping line and flexing rod.

Brown and rainbow trout are the most sought-after freshwater fishing available to the angler in the Drakensberg. Imported to South Africa from Britain, trout were first successfully introduced to the mountain streams below the Drakensberg in 1890. Keeping the streams well stocked is today the exclusive prerogative of the hatchery at Kamberg. The rivers under the Natal Parks Board's administration can be fished with permits, sold at the various resorts. The Underberg-Himeville Trout Fishing Club allows out-of-town anglers to purchase one-day tickets to fish on any of the impressive 22 dams and the 140 kilometres of the six rivers under its control.

LEFT: EXPLORING THE FOOTHILLS *on horseback. Among the more prominent of the riding stables are those of the Rugged Glen Reserve, next to the Royal Natal National Park. Most visitors, however, cover this area on foot along one or other of the numerous established trails.*

chain-ladder fixed to the rock face for those who want to venture higher. This, though, is three kilometres from The Amphitheatre wall and there are no direct paths.

Giant's Castle, the prime attraction of the Natal Drakensberg Park, offers a wide choice of exhilarating climbs and walks. Visitors can also admire Bushman paintings in a cave where a reconstructed scene shows a Bushman family going about its daily life.

There are numerous maps and books describing the multitude of marked trails in the Drakensberg.

Moreover each Natal Parks Board resort offers a comprehensive brochure which lists the established walks in its vicinity, giving such details as the time required to complete them, and the levels of difficulty of the various trails. Unaccompanied hiking is not recommended under any circumstances.

The Midlands

'There is a lovely road that runs from Ixopo into the hills. These hills are grass-covered and rolling, and they are lovely beyond any singing of it.' Such are the opening lines of Alan Paton's classic novel, Cry the Beloved Country, and they encapsulate the very essence of KwaZulu-Natal's Midlands region.

The hills of KwaZulu-Natal's Midlands region seem to unfold endlessly from below the foothills of the Drakensberg in the west to the coastal plain in the east. The spacious plain, stretching 220 kilometres from the Tugela River to the Mzimkulu River Valley in the far south is verdant and beautiful. At the lower altitudes, near the coast, the grassy slopes are green all year round, but closer to the mountains, in the cold of winter, they take on a reddish-golden hue.

Wrapped in the folds of the hills are numerous villages and towns, with names that reflect the origins of their various inhabitants. There are places called after the English aristocracy and the English countryside, recalling Natal's colonial history. Others point to the Zulu presence; Ixopo, for example, is an onomatopoeic name derived from the squelching sound made by cattle plodding through mud. Some names go back to the time of early Voortrekker settlements; Mooi River, meaning lovely river, not only shows the trekker origin of the town, but also touchingly reveals a pioneer's sentiments about the beauty of the area.

Old traditions

Most of the towns and villages in the Midlands serve farming communities, and were established by settlers who came from Britain in the mid-19th century. In many of these districts the highlight of the year is the annual agricultural show, where farmers show off their livestock and produce, and meet old friends, before taking part in the Royal Agricultural Show in Pietermaritzburg.

The influence of the British is still very noticeable in the Midlands. The settlers brought many of their traditions with them,

LEFT: MICROLIGHTING *is an increasingly popular sport; these aircraft are pictured near the town of Howick.*

ABOVE: PLOUGHMEN PLOD *their weary way over the undulating fields. The wealthier properties are mechanized, but most farmers in the former Zulu 'homeland' use the traditional methods.*
BELOW LEFT: THE HOWICK FALLS, *which plunge 95 metres into the Umgeni River, are one of the loveliest of the area's several cascades. Among its notable neighbours are the Shelter and the Karkloof falls.*

from cheddar cheese, made from the rich, yellow milk of Jersey cows, to daring polo matches. They also introduced the public school system or, as it is known in South Africa, the private school system to the area. Several of the country's most prestigious private schools are located in this part of Natal. Among them are Michaelhouse, Hilton College and Kearsney College for boys and St Anne's, St John's and Epworth for girls.

Majestic waterfalls

On an often misty ridge that cuts across the Midlands from north to south, there are great timber plantations of imported wattle and pine trees. Only patches of original indigenous forest remain, containing protected trees such as the large and lovely yellowwood.

Off the central ridge tumble numerous majestic waterfalls. The most famous are the magnificent but treacherous Howick Falls, near Pietermaritzburg, where the Umgeni River drops 95 metres. In a nearby forest, the even more spectacular Karkloof Falls begin with a series of cascades, before the Karkloof River plunges 105 metres into a wild gorge.

The scenic Midlands are dotted with nature reserves, guest houses, country inns, and art and craft studios, appealing to those who value the quiet life. Once these lush downlands were a hunter's paradise filled with wildlife, but today the antelope, along with zebra and other species, have been driven back to isolated reserves in the foothills of the Drakensberg, or to the great game reserves beyond the Tugela River in the north.

Many more hills

Once seen, the Valley of a Thousand Hills can never be forgotten. The huge valley, running down from a point near Pietermaritzburg to the coast close to the city of Durban, was carved out by the Umgeni River. Once the home of cannibals, it is now densely populat-

ed, especially in the parts close to the coast. Higher up, near Cato Ridge, along the old road between Durban and Pietermaritzburg, the area can still be seen in its original beauty, spreading out in a patchwork panorama of hills, valleys, and green undulations graced by a kaleidoscopic variety of flowering plants and aloes.

A number of country hostelries enable the visitor to stop overnight and enjoy the scenery, while regular performances of tribal dancing at a reconstructed traditional Zulu village give a fascinating insight into the way of life in centuries past.

BHACA REFUGE

The series of terrifying military onslaughts through which Shaka forged the Zulu nation drove many who were not prepared to live under his martial discipline deep into the mountains or the dark forests of the river valleys. When Britain annexed the province and brought in settlers, many of the refugees came out of hiding to seek shelter within the new colonial order. Near Richmond, in the Natal Midlands, the remnants of tribes shattered on Shaka's anvil, the amaBhaca (the people who hide), fused together and developed their own identity. They became renowned for their traditional costumes and elaborate beadwork. Beautifully dressed Bhaca women, each of whom displays a distinctive knob of ochred and beaded hair on her forehead to assert her status, can often be seen in town.

The hills of blood

The beauty of northern Natal and Zululand belies the area's bloody past, when

spears beat on rawhide shields and rifle-fire thundered across the hills in the

perennial struggle for power, prestige and land.

Some of the most scenic sites in Natal and Zululand have been named after the various battles and skirmishes which took place there, in haunting memory of the blood that was shed.

First there was Shaka who, in forging his Zulu empire from the polyglot of tribal fiefdoms, caused the blood of unknown thousands to be shed on the green hills of Natal. Then, from the early 1820s, vicious intertribal wars, known as the *Mfecane* (the crushing), raged across the eastern and northern part of southern Africa for over a decade.

More blood was spilled soon after the Voortrekkers peered in wonder between the peaks of the Drakensberg at the fertile and well-watered land below. In 1838, within days of the trekkers descending into Natal, the first clashes between the white newcomers and the Zulu occurred. At Bloukrans and Weenen (the place of tears) trekker families were slaughtered by marauding Zulu impis while their leaders, who had gone to the Zulu king Dingane to negotiate for land, were being clubbed to death. On 16 December 1838, at Blood River near Vryheid, the disciplined and well-armed trekkers exacted their revenge on the new Zulu nation.

Then it was the turn of the British, who had set up a trading settlement at Port Natal (now Durban) in 1824. It did not take long before the trekkers and the British were at

ABOVE: THE CLOUSTON GARDEN OF REMEMBRANCE *near Colenso, scene of one of the Anglo-Boer War's opening battles and a notable Boer victory.*

each other's throats. The first clash came in 1842 near Durban, with the British putting a quick end to an attempt by the Afrikaner settlers to establish a Boer Republic, based in Pietermaritzburg. But this was a minor skirmish compared to what was to come.

In the late 1870s, the British issued the Zulu king Cetshwayo with an ultimatum. It was rejected, and the British invaded Zululand in three columns in early January 1879. Cetshwayo immediately moved to confront the columns, and found one encamped beneath the mountain of Isandlwana on the northern bank of the broad Tugela River on 23 January.

Almost 1 200 British and colonial soldiers were annihilated in the ensuing battle, despite their superior weaponry of cartridge rifles, by the weight of over 20 000 Zulu warriors, lightly armed with hardened leather shields and short stabbing spears. On the same day another British column, after marching north across the Tugela River near the coast, met and defeated a Zulu army in a savage engagement at Khambula on the banks of the Nyezane River. At nearby Rorke's Drift the British recovered some pride when a tiny garrison held out against a 4 000-strong impi. Within weeks, the decisive British victory was gained at Ulundi – later the KwaZulu capital.

Beating the British

Meanwhile the Boer-Briton problem continued. After the South African Republic (the Transvaal) was annexed by Britain in April 1877, nationalists began to work for its freedom anew. On 16 December 1880, the republicans took up arms to eject the under-strength British forces. After a number of British defeats the final battle came on 21 February 1881, on the inaptly named Hill of Doves – Majuba – on the northern Natal border, where British reinforcements attempted, with catastrophic results, to break through into the Transvaal.

The South African Republic was independent once again – but not for long. Gold had

been discovered and the covetous eye of the Empire was once again straying across the border. A series of incidents led to a declaration of war on 11 October 1899. Within days, Commandant-General Piet Joubert had crossed into Natal with 16 500 men. Newcastle was occupied. At Talana Hill, near Dundee, the British forces were given a drubbing. A number of battles followed, and the British were forced to pull back to the small town of Ladysmith, where four-fifths of their forces in Natal would be locked up for 120 days.

At Colenso, on the banks of the Tugela, the British reinforcements were ignominiously defeated in one of their first tastes of a new type of conflict – it was the harbinger of

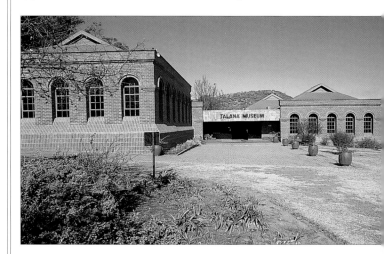

ABOVE: DUNDEE'S TALANA MUSEUM, *named after the first serious engagement of the Anglo-Boer War.*
LEFT: GRAVESTONES *near the battlefield of Elandslaagte. The Boer commander was among those who died.*

trench warfare, which would claim the lives of millions in World War One. At Spioenkop (Spy's Hill), further upstream, they suffered another defeat and again at Vaalkrans between the two, before finally breaking through. It was during this period that a young Winston Churchill was captured near Estcourt.

The various battlefields are scattered all over the spectacular landscape of rural Zululand and northern Natal. Rudimentary but effective stone forts, built by the British during the wars with both the Zulus and the Boers, are dotted about the countryside. There are several museums telling the stories of the battles and containing many of the relics of these historic events.

Wandering down Pietermaritzburg's lanes

Pietermaritzburg still shows signs of its Boer origins, but its quaint lanes and

pedestrian malls also display a strong British colonial influence that dates from

Britain's annexation of Natal in 1843.

Pietermaritzburg can be justly proud of its reputation as 'Heritage City'. At its centre the southern hemisphere's largest all-brick building, the red-faced City Hall, was erected on the site of the early Voortrekker government's meeting house (Volksraadsaal). With its 47-metre high clock tower and stained-glass windows, the hall was for long the seat of the regional administration. Its red brick architecture is echoed in many other structures, both old and new which contribute to Pietermaritzburg's distinctive character, as do the lilac-flowering jacarandas that line its streets.

The numerous brick-paved lanes of the town were originally designed for easy access between offices and were initially privately owned. They now serve as safe and convenient public links between the main streets. Lined with Victorian-styled buildings, the lanes were named after prominent business personalities or various trades. Change and Timber Lanes mark the locations of the three stock exchanges that operated in Pietermaritzburg at various times. Theatre Lane is the site of the first playhouse, long since disappeared. Shepstone Lane was named after the first Natal Secretary for Native Affairs, Theophilus Shepstone, who played a key role in 19th-century Anglo-Zulu relationships. Club Lane has the Victoria Club, which still stubbornly flies the Union Jack as its flag. There is a lane called Grays Inn, named after its London counterpart, where the legal fraternity established their first offices near the impressive brick complex of the Natal division of the Supreme Court.

Victorian cast-iron lamp posts and shopfronts decorated with hitching nails and metal filigree adorn Pietermaritzburg's lanes.

Yet the strong British presence cannot negate the fact that it was the Voortrekkers who, in 1838, founded this town on the

BELOW LEFT: PIETERMARITZBURG'S BOTANIC GARDENS *have a splendid avenue of planes, and a great wealth of indigenous and exotic plantlife.*
BELOW: A STERN QUEEN VICTORIA *presides over KwaZulu-Natal's provincial assembly buildings.*

ABOVE: THE ENCHANTINGLY FILIGREED *Victorian pavilion in Alexandra Park, one of Pietermaritzburg's many green areas noted for springtime displays of azaleas.*

Town Hill, one of the city's newer suburbs, is the site of Queen Elizabeth Park. This is where the Natal Parks Board, the guardian of the region's natural resources, has its headquarters. The 93-hectare park is a preserve for indigenous flora and fauna, and paths have been laid out for ramblers.

Events in Pietermaritzburg have been recorded by the town's journalists since 1846. The *Natal Witness* was the first newspaper in the province, and is now the oldest daily in the country. One of its biggest early stories concerned the serious schism in the colonial Church of England in 1869. The schism was caused by an attempt to replace the town's liberal bishop with a more orthodox one. Unity finally returned when the new Cathedral of the Holy Nativity was consecrated.

A phenomenon that continues to draw the attention of both the media and the public is the 'weeping' of the wooden cross dedicated to the South Africans who lost their lives in the First World War battle of Delville Wood, France, in July of 1916.

The cross, which stands in a memorial garden, exudes sap around the anniversary of the battle. Scientists maintain this is caused by humidity levels, but many believe it to have more spiritual origins.

banks of the Mzinduzi River. As they came down the hills to take possession of the bowl that was to become Pietermaritzburg, the fully locked wheels of their laden wagons left deep channels in the rock. These grooves are still visible today at World's View, the hill overlooking the city.

After the British took control of Pietermaritzburg, the town became a frontier centre. Mementoes of the British troops remain: behind the station there is the garrison itself – Fort Napier and St George's Garrison Church.

Parks fit for queens

Natal's long-time capital city boasts one of the loveliest and most ornate pavilions. Alexandra Park, named after Britain's Queen Alexandra, is almost entirely encompassed by a horseshoe bend in the meandering Mzinduzi River. The pavilion is built of red brick and trimmed with white-painted metal lacework. Beside it an old military bandstand, in the same style, is still used on Sunday afternoons in the summer. Eccentric students from the local University of Natal and other devoted royalists meet there every year to celebrate the Queen's Birthday with tea and thinly sliced cucumber sandwiches.

THE VOW

On 16 December 1838, at Blood River in northern Natal, the Voortrekkers wreaked terrible revenge on the Zulus for the murder of one of their leaders, Piet Retief, and a group of his followers.

The commander of the Voortrekker forces, Andries Pretorius, a few days before the battle, made a 'covenant' vowing that, if he was victorious, the day of triumph would be commemorated 'even to our latest posterity in order that it might be celebrated to the honour of God'.

As part of this oath an old Cape Dutch gabled church, the Church of the Vow, was built in Pietermaritzburg three years later. Today it serves as the Voortrekker Museum and contains a collection of pioneer relics as well as an ironwood chair, which had originally been carved for the Zulu king Dingane. It was on this king's orders that Retief and his followers were killed.

Next door to the museum, in the forecourt of the new Memorial Church, stand the statues of Piet Retief and Gert Maritz (pictured), the two leaders after whom the city is named.

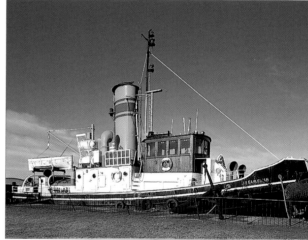

Valleys and gorges

Black, threatening clouds accumulate over the Indian Ocean. More often than not, as they try to reach the parched South African hinterland, they hit the barrier of the Drakensberg range and release their water over the rugged Escarpment to bring life-giving sustenance to the foothills and the plains to the east.

ABOVE LEFT: BIRD'S-EYE VIEW *of the Midmar resort near the town of Howick. Among the area's attractions are boating, bathing, fishing; a nature reserve, a Zulu homestead and a historical village.*
TOP: START OF THE WOMEN'S SECTION *of the 'Midmar Mile', a hugely popular annual swimming event.*
ABOVE: THE STEAM-TUG JG EAGLESHAM, *once Durban-based and now part of the Midmar historical village.*

Natal has no less than 20 major watercourses and innumerable streams. The coastline is punctuated by 73 river estuaries. The province is in fact the best-watered region in South Africa, and seldom suffers from the droughts that ravage many other parts of the country.

The Drakensberg presents perhaps its most spectacular faces on a late-summer afternoon after an electric storm. As the sunlight pierces through the breaking clouds, temporary waterfalls are brightly illuminated as they plunge over basalt cliffs on their journey back to the sea. The waterfalls and streams steadily converge into rivers that, over the aeons, have carved the underlying sandstone into sheer-sided valleys and magnificent gorges.

One such cleft is the famed Oribi Gorge, on the Mzimkulwana River in south Natal. It is 24 kilometres long, 5 kilometres wide and 400 metres deep. At one point a rock shelf, known as the 'Hanging Rock', protrudes over the valley floor far below, and provides a magnificent but hair-raising vantage point.

The canyon is the most striking feature of the Oribi Gorge Nature Reserve, an 1 837-hectare expanse of rugged countryside that serves as sanctuary for some 40 mammal and 270 bird species, including an array of raptors.

Natal is bisected by the Umgeni ('the river of acacias') which, with its tributaries, is the main source of water for the two major urban areas of the province. The river reaches the Indian Ocean at Blue Lagoon in Durban, and its course is blocked by four major dams in the hills overlooking Pietermaritzburg.

One of these, Midmar, has been turned into a popular holiday resort, which offers a wide variety of recreational attractions. Here the Natal Parks Board has created a historical village which includes an early white settlement and a traditional Zulu kraal. Bathing can be enjoyed in a large swimming pool, or in the dam, the venue for the annual Midmar Mile, a swimming race that attracts hundreds of entrants. In the adjacent nature reserve visitors can view varied and abundant wildlife, including zebra and white rhino.

The startling one

The Tugela or, more correctly, the Thukela River (the Zulu word for 'the startling one') marks the traditional boundary between Natal and Zululand. It is Natal's mightiest river and it proved its awesome power in 1984 when, running in full flood near the coast, it lifted a 450-metre, single-span concrete bridge and cast it aside like a piece of driftwood.

The river, one of the largest in South Africa, is dammed in its upper reaches, but runs unchecked for the rest of its course. It originates high up the Drakensberg at Mont-aux-Sources. Within the first few kilometres of its source it drops 2 000 metres in a series of spectacular, ribbon-like cascades, known

SPILLS AND THRILLS

Natal's rivers are the venues for two important canoe races – the Duzi, which attracts a record number of participants, and the Mkomaas, the country's longest distance race over two days.

In the Duzi canoeists take three days to cover 100 kilometres, starting from Pietermaritzburg and dropping about 800 metres to Durban at the coast, paddling and portaging along the Mzinduzi (or Duzi) River before it joins the Umgeni.

This is one of two great sporting events which link Pietermaritzburg and Durban. The other is the famous Comrades Marathon, which every year attracts thousands of runners and joggers to test themselves against the 90 kilometres of hills and valleys that divide the two cities.

The Mkomaas is a canoe race reserved for the very experienced or the very brave. It does not have a single dam to slow the daredevil competitors on their headlong two-day race. It starts near Richmond, and covers roughly 120 kilometres, plunging 1 300 metres over a seemingly endless and terrifying series of rapids and finishing near the Indian Ocean. The course is described by participants as 'downhill all the way', through wild and seemingly inaccessible gorges.

LEFT: THE ENCHANTING *upper reaches of the Mgeni River, Durban's main source of water. Among the attractions along the course of the river are the eye-catching Howick and Albert waterfalls.*

as the Tugela Falls. Rapids in the gorge below the falls provide what is reputed to be the best white-water rafting in the country. Further along, the Tugela meanders through the cattle and sheep farms of northern Natal before entering the wide open valleys of Zululand to discharge into the Indian Ocean.

At a point where the road running north from Greytown to Vryheid crosses the valley the majestic peak of Kranskop stands sentry. The Zulu living in its shadow have always held the cliff-faced sentinel in awed respect. Young girls carrying water from the river below ask the mountain for its protection. Legend has it that in such instances the rockface occasionally opens up, and the girls, attracted by tantalizing sounds of merriment, enter it, never to be seen again.

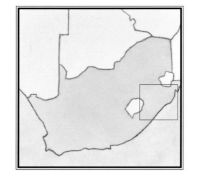

Broad acres of golden sand, superlative game reserves, a myriad marine resorts and the splendid city of Durban – these are among the more striking components of one of South Africa's prime tourist regions.

Subtropical KwaZulu-Natal

From Durban, the largest and busiest port in Africa, KwaZulu-Natal's Indian Ocean shoreline stretches north to the remoteness of the Mozambique border and south to the land of the Xhosa.

It is a coast stunning in its beauty and diversity, a 550-kilometre compound of blue sea, exquisite little coves, lagoons and estuaries, golden beaches, lushly evergreen hinterland, wetlands, forest, and superb game reserves that, together, make of the region one of the southern hemisphere's most entrancing tourist destinations.

This is also the country of the Zulu, harsh in its history, troubled in its present, but always vibrant and colourful.

Durban itself is the premier playground, numbering among its many assets a splendidly spacious natural harbour, broad thoroughfares, a handsome high-rise central area and the Golden Mile, a 6-kilometre stretch of seafront that holds everything dear to the heart of the holiday-maker.

The city and its surrounds are home to more than two million Zulus, to whites of largely English colonial extraction, and to a great many Indian people, some of them direct descendants of the indentured labourers brought in during and after the 1860s to work the great sugar plantations of the region. It is a unique cultural mix that confers a rich, dynamic quality and makes Durban special among South African centres.

OPPOSITE: LORDLY GIRAFFE, *tallest of the world's land animals, survey the lush terrain of the Hluhluwe-Umfolozi game reserve in northern KwaZulu-Natal.*

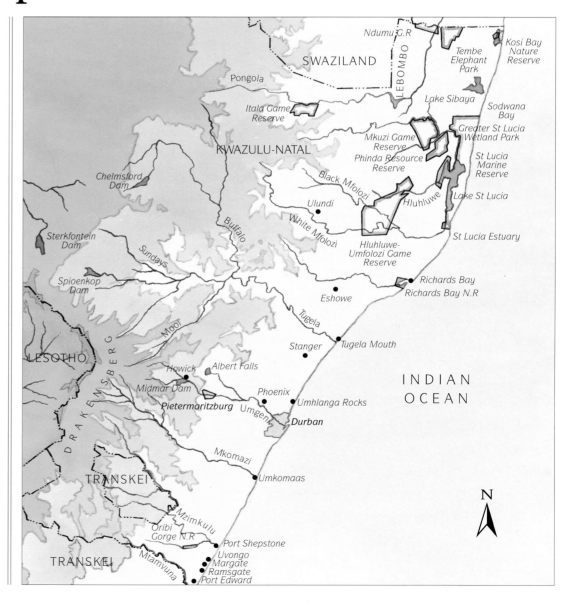

Where East meets West

On Christmas Day in 1497 Nguni tribespeople of the great swampy bay they

called Thekweni (the estuary) spotted a vessel with discoloured sails on the

horizon. This was a Portuguese craft, its captain seeking the holy grail of the

early navigators: the sea-route to the riches of the East.

Three and a half centuries after this first sighting European ships seeking shelter from storms, or intent on replenishing their food and water supplies, would stop at the Bay of Natal. Then, from the 1820s, the white people came to stay: the British arrived from the Cape to establish a trading post, and the Boer trekkers descended from over the mountains to do battle with the Zulu and then to put down roots. They founded Pietermaritzburg, in the misty hills 90 kilometres inland from today's great port city of Durban, as the capital of their short-lived Republic of Natalia.

Some of the early settlers led fascinating lives that passed into legend: among many others there was the intrepid Francis Farewell and his companion Henry Francis Fynn, close friends of the formidable Shaka Zulu; Capt. Allen Gardiner, who founded Durban and was eventually to die, in far-off Patagonia, of starvation, and later, the white adventurer John Dunn who married 19 African wives to establish a prolific dynasty.

In 1843, Britain, not content with mere trading posts, determined to expand its colonial empire and after a brief military stand-off, annexed Natal. Many of the trekkers loaded up their wagons once again and went back across the Drakensberg. The annexation prompted a steady influx of European settlers seeking a new life in the youngest and it seemed the most attractive of Britain's overseas possessions.

Large-scale private immigration schemes were launched around mid-century and, with a fast-growing Durban as the focal point, white settlement spread out across the colony. In due course the newcomers discovered that conditions were ideal for growing sugar cane, and thus the scene was set for yet another wave of immigrants.

Sugar plantations were labour-intensive. The Zulus who lived in Natal were more or

BELOW LEFT: SARI-CLAD SALESWOMEN *display sumptuous fabrics in one of Durban's many Indian-owned shops.*
BELOW: AROMATIC SPICES *tempt visitors to the Victoria Street market, an exotic downtown concentration of some 150 stalls, shops and inviting restaurants.*

ABOVE: ELABORATELY DECORATED *rickshaws and their Zulu 'drivers' are among Durban's major tourist attractions. Once plain looking, they took on a more ornamental look with increasing competition for custom.*
ABOVE RIGHT: A MUSLIM SHRINE *in the Umgeni area.*

less self-sufficient, and therefore did not need to work the long and hard hours required. The European settlers had to look abroad for their workforce, and they turned to British-controlled India, where landlessness, poverty and the pressures of a rigid caste system had combined to create a huge reservoir of inexpensive and readily available labour.

On 16 November 1860, the *Truro*, with 340 Indians from Madras and Calcutta, anchored in Durban. The men had been recruited with promises of eventual land ownership in the new colony. Thousands more were to follow, undertaking to work under arduous conditions for a monthly wage of 10 shillings (women were paid half the rate) plus food and free accommodation. Then, in 1870, another group of Indians, Muslims from Gujarat, arrived. They brought capital and trading talent with them, and were to establish a thriving commercial sector.

In their first hundred years in South Africa Indians faced a barrage of discriminatory and restrictive legislation. But they stayed, enriching all the many other groups with their skills, traditions and culture.

Durban, however, was and has remained, first and foremost, the home of the eastern Nguni people. Every day the city centre throbs with the bustle of thousands of Zulus who live in a great arc of townships nearby.

On the streets traditional healers and herbalists sell secret cures to the sound of African jazz blaring from music shops, while raucous street traders shout and call to customers in the daily battle to earn a living.

GANDHI – THE BIRTH OF SATYAGRAHA

In 1893 a small, unassuming, London-trained lawyer named Mohandas Gandhi arrived in South Africa to defend the rights of two Indian merchants. After the notorious incident of his ejection from a first-class train coach in Pietermaritzburg, he went on to fine-tune the political skills that would make him the liberator of India and an internationally revered leader.

In Natal and the Transvaal racist legislation had been enacted to keep Indians voteless and landless. Gandhi's response was to develop the political strategy of *Satyagraha* – passive resistance in its simplest definition. In the process he was persecuted, imprisoned and vilified.

In 1914 Gandhi returned to India, to take up the struggle against British imperialism in his homeland. There passive resistance flourished, and eventually was adopted as a non-violent option by people around the world in the fight for political rights.

Although the strategy would achieve only a small measure of success in South Africa, it was often used, in the years after Gandhi's return to India, to fight apartheid.

Gandhi achieved mystical status in India, where he came to be called the Mahatma (Great Soul). Sadly, it was his preference for compromise that ultimately caused his death. A Hindu fanatic assassinated him in 1948, a year after India achieved independence, believing Gandhi to have favoured the Muslims in the political settlement.

In Durban Gandhi established the settlement of Phoenix, which serves as a lasting reminder of his commitment to peace, to non-racism, and to a simple lifestyle.

The Bay of Natal – a refuge from stormy seas

In the balmy Bay of Natal, yachts glide past squat tug boats, Zulu stevedores

shout instructions to foreign sailors, fishing boats unload their catches, and

giant cranes shift thousands of tons of cargo with speed and efficiency.

Portuguese navigator Vasco da Gama first spotted the natural harbour, surrounded by swamps and mangrove forests, on Christmas Day in 1497. Soon after that, fragile sailing boats, making the dangerous journey between Europe and the spice markets of the East, began to use the Bay as a watering place and a refuge from the stormy seas of the southern Indian Ocean.

Those early sailors could easily recognize the port by the great bluff which protected the harbour from the south-easterly winds.

This landmark promontory is still covered with indigenous sand-dune forest, and is dominated by a white, red-roofed lighthouse.

Crossing the bar

Although it provided a welcome haven, the port was almost landlocked, blocked from the sea by a shallow sandbar that could only be crossed at high water. Early ships' captains had to time their manoeuvres to perfection in entering and leaving the harbour, and a sharp

eye can still spot pieces from the seventy-odd vessels wrecked by wild storms and driven ashore while waiting to cross the bar.

In 1895 the harbour mouth was dredged for the first time, making the port accessible to larger craft. During the Arab-Israeli wars, when the Suez Canal was closed, the only way for tankers to transport oil to Europe was via the Cape sea route. During this time up to 50 ships could be seen lying off Durban Bay, either queuing to enter the harbour or waiting for supplies to be flown out to them from the mainland by helicopter. Bystanders would gasp in amazement as gigantic supertankers squeezed through the entrance of the port for repairs and fuel. The opening is now maintained at a depth of almost 13 metres, allowing entry to ships of considerable size.

The harbour has changed dramatically since the time it was used as a refuge from rough seas. The swamps and mangroves are long gone and in their place are orderly, concrete-edged piers. Along the 12 kilometres of quayside, cargo ships offload heavy equipment used by the major mining and industrial complexes on the Witwatersrand; they load their holds again with sugar, subtropical fruits and other agricultural products, coal and manufactured goods. The sugar terminal, with its three giant curved silos, is a striking feature. Offshore, a floating terminal receives most of the oil used in South Africa.

Thanks to all this activity Durban has developed into South Africa's second largest metropolis. It started, less than two centuries ago, as a small trading post: in 1824 a tiny sloop named *Julia* crossed the sandbar into the estuary, carrying a Cape Town businessman, Henry Francis Fynn, and five other passengers. Together these men were to create the germ of a settlement that was to become Africa's largest and busiest harbour.

For a long time the harbour was the main focus of the city – it was a genial gathering place for the residents as well as a functional dockyard. The incoming ships brought news of friends and families abroad, and luxuries that could not be found in the colony.

ABOVE: WINDSURFERS PREPARE *to take to the waters. Durban is a mecca for aquatic sports enthusiasts.*

HISTORIC HEROES

Tales of brave deeds serve to inspire new generations, and become absorbed into folklore. Durban's colonial community produced two heroes whose stories bear retelling; each of them made an epic journey to save his fellow citizens.

In 1827, fifteen-year-old John Ross set off on a 40-day, 1 400-kilometre round-trip from Durban to Lourenço Marques (now Maputo), crossing wild and dangerous terrain on foot to obtain medicine for sick traders. Along the way the brave lad visited Zulu monarch Shaka, who was so impressed by his courage and devotion that he provided an armed escort for the rest of his journey.

Dick King also took to the road, but under far more dramatic and stealthy circumstances. In May 1842 the British unsuccessfully attempted to wrest control of Natalia, the newly established Boer trekker republic. In a minor battle at Congella, then on the outskirts of Durban, the trekker forces beat off the British, and went on to lay siege to the 250 British troops. Under cover of darkness one of the British settlers, Dick King, with his African servant Ndongeni, slipped across the Bay in a small boat, towing two horses swimming along behind. On reaching the southern shores the two set off on a perilous 1 000-kilometre, 10-day ride through difficult and hostile country, fording more than one hundred rivers and streams to reach the garrison town of Grahamstown.

In June a relief column arrived, and King was acclaimed the 'saviour of Natal'. Statues of both King (pictured) and Ross have been erected on Durban's Victoria Embankment, which runs along the landward side of the Bay.

Many Durbanites grew up with the sight of the bluish-mauve hulls of the Union Castle mail-ships gliding over the horizon, maintaining an umbilical cord between the old colony and Europe. But in the 1960s, as jet aircraft began to take off south of the harbour, the link between many ordinary citizens and the harbour was broken. The mail-ships called less and less frequently, and finally came no more.

The Golden Mile

In the early morning, when the shad are running, hundreds of fishermen line

the beaches and piers of Durban's famous Golden Mile. As the orange sun

comes up over the horizon, the fishermen make way for swimmers and surfers,

out to catch a few waves before going to work.

By breakfast-time Adonis-like lifesavers have taken up their stations, waiting for the locals and the vacationers who, in winter and summer alike, swarm to the beaches in their thousands.

In Durban the seasons make little difference. The shores of the Golden Mile lie in the subtropics, and are washed by the warm Mozambique current that flows down the east coast of Africa. This means that even in winter temperatures seldom fall below 15° C, while in the summer months they reach well into the thirties.

The Golden Mile begins on the seaward side of a spit of land known as the Point, which separates Durban harbour from the Indian Ocean. In the south, to the north of the harbour entrance, lies the first of the Golden Mile's sandy stretches – Addington Beach – which is overlooked by a hospital of the same name. Every year the hard-working staff of Addington Hospital treat, among other patients, hundreds of holiday-makers who have spent too much time in the sun, who have been stung by the long tail of a Portuguese man-o'-war (blue bottle), or who have ignored the orders of lifesavers to stay away from treacherous currents.

Addington Beach is followed by Pumphouse Beach, where tourists leave the waves to surfers and skiers, and are treated, in return, to a daily display of impressive skill and daring. South Beach, extremely popular because of its spaciousness, is next in line.

Here the famous golf-ball shaped Little Top open-air theatre entertains audiences with magic shows, music concerts, talent competitions and the like.

West Street – Durban's main commercial thoroughfare – forms the dividing line between the southern and northern beaches of the Golden Mile. It also marks the end of the spit of land which separates the harbour from the sea. The street begins at the aquarium and runs up to the Berea, the first of several ridges that march upwards towards the Drakensberg's foothills, and is the site of many of Durban's stately homes. African arts and crafts can be purchased at the bottom end of West Street, where Zulu women string intricate and

THE WONDERS OF SEA WORLD

A pair of dusky dolphins dance on their tails to cheers of delight, spraying spectators as they fall back into the water in the main pool of the Dolphinarium. The performance is repeated several times each day: they play football, do spectacular somersaults in the air, leap over ropes and give their trainers hair-raising rides around the pool.

The bottle-nosed dolphins are the main attraction of Durban's Sea World, a complex on the Golden Mile where you can find everything from delicate sea horses, only a few centimetres long, to great Zambezi and ragged-tooth sharks.

Seals and penguins, with their array of remarkable tricks and amusing antics, are also very popular with audiences both young and old.

In the aquarium, a circular tank with three viewing floors houses a wide and colourful variety of fish and turtles from the warm oceans of the world. The graceful fish can be viewed through large glass windows, and are at their most conspicuous when they are being fed by divers. The shark tank nearby offers a different kind of spec-

tacle. With unblinking eyes, its primaeval and fearsome inhabitants patrol their limited territory with measured precision, breaking into a sudden dash every now and then, as if to catch onlookers by surprise.

ABOVE: THE MILE – *a pleasure-seeker's paradise of pools, piers, pavilions and glittering emporiums.*
BELOW LEFT: THE END *of a long day's surf-riding.*

brightly coloured bead necklaces, anklets bangles and amulets, and sturdy grass baskets. Continuing along the shore past West Street one finds North Beach, where wildlife enthusiasts can enjoy a visit to Fitzsimmons Snake Park. The park houses a fascinating collection of snakes and crocodiles, and also has a research laboratory, where anti-snakebite serums are produced.

Beyond the Mile

The upper end of North Beach is officially the end of the Golden Mile, but more sandy expanses stretch beyond it. Battery Beach lies opposite the white façade of the Natal headquarters of the national defence force, and Country Club Beach takes its name from the nearby Durban Country Club with its gracious buildings and magnificent golf course. Nearby is a complex of water slides which locals claim is the biggest and best of its kind in Africa. Beyond the ocean breakers, red buoys anchor rows of regularly serviced nylon-mesh nets, protecting bathers from the sharks. On land the horned, feathered and colourfully beaded headdresses of Zulu rickshaw drivers bob up and down as the men take tourists for rides along Marine Parade.

Between the beaches and the hotels of the Golden Mile is a welcome strip of lawn, interspersed with swimming and paddling pools, entertainment centres and restaurants.

Sunshine, Dolphin and Hibiscus coasts

A balmy subtropical climate, the warm blue waters of the Indian Ocean, a

shoreline graced by lala palms and hibiscus, casuarinas and bougainvillea,

and a score and more of fashionable seaside villages and hamlets – these are

some of the delights of KwaZulu-Natal's sun-drenched seaboard.

Great flocks of diving, darting seagulls and cormorants plunge, head first, into the sea to emerge a few moments later with bulging beaks. The ocean is a surging mass of black and silver bodies.

The Sardine Run has begun! These enormous shoals, often kilometres long, start far out at sea in the cold waters of the southern Cape to make their way up the east coast of the African continent. In June, when they reach Natal's southern shores, powerful eddies from the south-flowing Mozambique current, together with sharks and other predatory species, drive the fish towards the beaches and the waiting onlookers, hundreds of whom rush into the waves to snatch the swirling fish up in buckets and nets. Seabirds, big game fish and dolphins follow the run in a spectacular procession. The run continues for about a week, and is then gone as suddenly and mysteriously as it appeared.

This lively phenomenon is just one of a great number of drawcards that attract holiday-makers to one of the southern hemisphere's most splendid holiday areas. From Port Edward in the south to the Tugela Mouth in the north, the coastline is a diamond-studded belt of stylish little resorts blessed with pleasant weather, and with golden beaches lapped by the warm, intensely blue waters of the Indian Ocean.

The southern shores are divided into two segments, known as the Sunshine Coast (from Amanzimtoti, near Durban, down to Mtwalume) and the Hibiscus Coast (from Hibberdene to Port Edward), and are slightly

ABOVE: FASHIONABLE NORTH-COAST *holiday apartments.*
LEFT: ONE OF THE MANY *secluded little bays on the subtropically balmy seaboard south of Durban.*

SWEET-TASTING SUCCESS

Among the biggest of South Africa's agri-business giants, Tongaat-Hulett and CG Smith, are the direct descendants of the wealthy sugar barons who established the multibillion dollar industry on Natal's subtropical seaboard.

Most of the sugar pioneers were British settlers, but they came from a variety of Victorian social backgrounds and were often in bitter dispute with each other over a wide range of issues – from the use of indentured Indian labour to the role of railway lines – but they were alike in their resilience and gutsy determination to succeed.

Ironically, though, one of the few who never made his million was the actual founder of the industry. Edmund Morewood was to leave the region a frustrated and disillusioned man, eventually to die in far-off Brazil. His farm Compensation and the remains of his first mill – erected in 1846 near Esenbi – are now national monuments. Also of visitor interest is the lovely old colonial homestead built by Horace Hulett in 1903: it has been converted into a country house whose guests enjoy a taste of a turn-of-the-century sugar magnate's opulent lifestyle.

At that time a mere half-dozen or so barons controlled the plantations. Today, in a good year, around 45 000 growers harvest an impressive 20 million tonnes of sugar cane to retain South Africa's ranking among the world's 'big five' producers.

ABOVE: THE LIGHTHOUSE AT UMHLANGA ROCKS, *an upmarket resort area near Durban and headquarters of the renowned Natal Sharks Board. The Board lays on lectures and demonstrations for the public.*

cooler and rather more popular than the seaboard north of Durban. Margate, Ramsgate, Port Shepstone, Uvongo – these are among the more evocative names, exciting many a surfer, sporting fisherman, yachtsman and sun-worshipper. With lifesavers on duty all year round, bathing carries little risk and the beaches are well patronized. The Hibiscus Festival, held every July, fills the streets of Port Shepstone and Port Edward with parades and parties.

The southern maritime stretch has also been dubbed, by players and followers of the game, the 'Golf Coast' for its superb courses.

The shoreline that extends away to the north of Durban, from Umhlanga Rocks ('the place of the reeds') to the Tugela River Mouth, is called the Dolphin Coast, a marvellously inviting 90-kilometre stretch of secluded coves and rock pools that shelter oysters and crayfish and that beckon those who prefer the smaller, more intimate kind of resort. The dolphins for which it is named are often to be seen riding the waves – indeed, it is not unusual for surfers to find themselves sharing a crest with one of these endearingly playful marine mammals.

The place of sharks

Sometimes schools of dolphins can be spotted from the 2,7-kilometre paved promenade at Umhlanga, from which there is also a fine view of the resort's luxurious hotels and holiday homes. The place has been compared in its sophistication to the French Riviera. But the entire coast hasn't always been a glittering success. There was a time when the holiday-makers stopped coming: a growing number of near-fatal shark attacks in the fifties and early sixties almost destroyed the local tourist industry. Then the Anti-Shark Measures Board found a way of safeguarding bathing beaches – with nets positioned beyond the breaking waves – and in so doing established its reputation as the world authority on sharks. Visitors are able to tour the Board's headquarters, located on the hill overlooking Umhlanga.

The coasts to both the north and south of Durban are lined by field upon field of emerald sugar cane, the plantations flowing like an immense and undulating sea of green as far as the eye can see. Although the sugar world is still dominated by the big producers and millers, small growers are being encouraged and, increasingly, given a say in the running of the industry.

ABOVE LEFT: SHAKA'S ROCK *whose headland once served as the great Zulu king's viewpoint.*
ABOVE: ZULU YOUNGSTERS *in traditional finery.*

In the steps of Shaka

In 1816, when Shaka became chief of the Zulu clan, his followers numbered just 1 500. He created a new kind of fighting force, set out on the bloody road of conquest – and within five years he was master of the land.

On 22 September each year Zulus in the traditional warrior garb – plumes and feathered anklets, patterned oxhide shield and the short, lethal stabbing spear that once struck terror into the hearts of thousands – gather at a small white marble monument in the Natal north coast town of Stanger to commemorate the death of Shaka, the ruthless and brilliant creator of the Zulu empire. It is an impressive occasion.

Shaka was enthroned in 1816, and in the 12 short years of his reign the shock waves of his bloody conquests spread beyond the Drakensberg to help trigger what became known as the *Mfecane* (the crushing), the vast and terrible forced migration of African peoples across the southern subcontinent.

Shaka was born in 1787, the bastard son of the beautiful Nandi and Senzangakona, a prince of the then tiny Zulu group, whose lands lay above the confluence of the Black and White Mfolozi rivers. The pregnancy, however, had been condemned by Senzangakona's followers as the workings of an intestinal beetle called I-Shaka – the name the clan elders, in ironic mood, gave the child.

Rejected by both the parental clans, Shaka and his mother spent the early years of his life as virtual outcasts. But Shaka's intellect, courage, strength and prowess as a hunter set him apart from other boys. His special qualities were quickly recognized when he joined the army of Dingiswayo, king of the collective Nguni peoples – a recognition reinforced when Shaka succeeded to the Zulu chieftainship and began to develop the battle skills that would make his small (1 500-strong) clan master of the entire land.

His first move was to replace the traditional light and often ineffectual throwing spear with the heavy-shafted, long-bladed stabbing assegai. With these the Zulu regiments would charge into the ranks of the enemy, using their hardened rawhide shields both for protection and to lever away the enemy shields to expose their bodies to the assegai's deadly thrust. Shaka also refined the *Amabutho*, the

THE LIVING MUSEUM OF SHAKALAND

In the heart of Zululand, within the beautiful Nkwalini Valley near Shaka's first capital, a new Bulawayo was built – not to house the massed ranks of a warrior people but as a film set for the epic *Shaka Zulu* (it was also used for a television series about the 15-year-old John Ross, whom the Zulu king befriended).

The kraal, named Shakaland, is now a unique tourist venue, a living and working museum of Zulu culture, customs and lifestyles. It's all there, as it once was and to some degree still is: vibrant Zulu dancing and colourful traditional dress; the rigorous formality of stick-fighting; the forging of assegais, the weaving of grass mats and baskets and the making of the great red-clay, fire-blackened, beer drinking pots; the stringing of brightly coloured

beads into message patterns. The daily menu features traditional stews served with staples of putu and samp made from maize and beans, cooked in giant, three-legged iron pots bubbling over open fires and served on carved wooden platters and bowls. For the more adventurous there is *utshwala*, the traditional millet beer, drunk from a communal clay pot. Visitors are housed in traditional, 'beehive' grass huts (pictured) – though modern conveniences have been skilfully incorporated.

LEFT: POTTERY AND PRODUCE *on sale at the roadside.*
RIGHT: A ZULU GIRL *of marriageable age. The patterns of beads often convey subtle messages of love and loyalty.*

age-graded regimental system in which warriors lived with men of their own age, each regiment taking pride in its own markings and regalia; and he discarded the cumbersome leather sandals of the Zulu warrior: bare feet, hardened by formidable route marches, conferred greater speed and agility.

Finally, he perfected the famed Zulu battle tactics, basing them on a formation resembling the horns and body of a bull buffalo. The regiments in the field – collectively known as the *impi* – were divided into four groups, the most powerful (representing the 'chest') clashing head-on with the enemy force while the second and third groups (the

'horns') flanked, encircled and decimated it. The fourth regiment remained in reserve.

Shaka established his royal kraal at Bulawayo (the place of killing) in the hills above present-day Eshowe. After the death of his mother, which drove him to a grief-stricken frenzy of slaughter (thousands of his subjects died, pointlessly), he moved south to today's Stanger area. The great grass-hutted city was called KwaDukuza (the place of hiding) for its size and complexity – its 2 000 beehive-shaped huts formed a labyrinthine maze. The change was prompted in part by a need to be closer to the first of the white traders who had settled around Port Natal's (Durban's) great bay in 1824.

Ivory and trinkets

The newcomers, whom the Zulus referred to as 'swallows', had helped Shaka during some of his military campaigns and were now the source of sought-after beads and trinkets (which they traded for valuable ivory). The old coastal road that now cuts through the sugar cane plantations, across the Tugela River to Eshowe, follows the old trade route along which the impis trotted, and is known as Shaka's Way.

One morning in September 1828, when he was at the height of his power, Shaka was reclining on his rock throne at the entrance to the royal kraal, waiting for a regiment to return from Pondoland in the south, when he was set upon and murdered by his half-brothers, Dingane and Mhlangana. His body was thrown into a grain pit, above which Stanger's later residents erected the modest marble memorial honouring one of the greatest of Africa's 19th-century leaders.

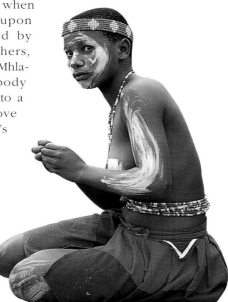

Zululand reserves: paradise regained

Earlier this century tens of thousands of Natal's wild animals were slaughtered

in a futile bid to destroy the disease-bearing tsetse fly. But the wildlife popu-

lations survived and staged a miraculous recovery to add immeasurable

richness to the region and its splendid game reserves.

The land that lies to the north of the Tugela River is subtropically lush, ecologically varied, beautiful, parts of it a splendid refuge for the wild animals of Africa, some of them severely threatened elsewhere.

A paradise indeed. But the story could have been very different: from the 1920s to the 1950s the authorities launched a deliberate extermination campaign in a sustained and tragically fruitless effort to stop the spread of *nagana*, the dreaded sleeping sickness that attacks both man and his cattle. Tens of thousands of animals were slaughtered, the roar of the lion was quieted, the trumpeting of elephant heard no more, a myriad wildebeest, zebra and antelope lay dead in the bleaching African sun. And the disease, carried by the tsetse fly, was eventually defeated not by the mass killing of wildlife but with insecticides.

However, while one group of people were seeking to destroy the animals and extend the boundaries of agricultural land, others were working hard to sustain game sanctuaries whose names would become shining beacons in the world of conservation.

The Hluhluwe and Umfolozi reserves, in fact, had been established much earlier and had suffered grievously from the hunter's rifle. But they survived, and over the years other areas, both publicly and privately owned, were added to the list. The two reserves previously separated by a narrow corridor, have been joined to create a 96 000-hectare area that boasts more than 80 mammal and 400 bird species. The wildlife complement includes elephant, lion, white and black rhino, buffalo, cheetah, leopard, wildebeest, giraffe and a variety of antelope.

Vines and vistas

Hluhluwe, which takes its name from the river that winds along like the twisted 'umhluhluwe' vine the Zulus pick from the forests along the river banks (and used to muzzle weaning calves), lies in moist, hilly country. It is the more scenic of the two areas, with magnificent views of forested river valleys.

Umfolozi is on the lower ground, in the V-shaped wedge above the confluence of the White and Black Mfolozi rivers, cradle of the Zulu nation. (Umfolozi, incidentally, is the Zulu word describing the special qualities required of a lead animal in a span of oxen.) Here the vegetation is drier and starker, and flat-topped thorn trees dot the grasslands in

BELOW: ZEBRA ARE COMMON *residents of Natal's parks.*
BELOW LEFT: THE MALACHITE KINGFISHER, *found among the reeds fringing streams and lagoons in Zululand.*

THE RARE RHINO: RESCUE AND RELOCATION

The Hluhluwe-Umfolozi Game Reserve is among the last of the safe havens for that most persecuted of animals, the massive, prehistoric rhino. The combined area sustains around 30 per cent of Africa's remaining rhino – the largest concentration in the world.

The Hluhluwe-Umfolozi areas are home to both the square-lipped white rhino (a grazer), and to its smaller, more aggressive black cousin, which is a browser. The two species are endangered, and have been so since the turn of the century, at which time the myopic, easy-to-hunt rhino had been wiped out in most parts of southern Africa. The southern white rhino had suffered especially severely: by the 1920s it was thought that only 25 individuals remained. But the numbers were steadily built up in the Umfolozi reserve, and in the 1950s the Natal Parks Board launched a programme to ensure the permanent survival of the species. Led by Ian Player, an internationally acclaimed conservationist, a team of Natal Parks Board rangers and scientists successfully pioneered drug-darting techniques to capture and translocate

white rhino to their former habitats and to game parks in many parts of the world.

The same methods are now being used to rescue the black rhino, whose continental population has been reduced from 65 000 in the early 1970s to a pitiful 3 500 or less today, of which 650 find sanctuary in Hluhluwe-Umfolozi.

To protect the animals from poachers (who hunt the rhino for its horn, in demand in the Middle and Far East for its reputed medicinal properties), the area is intensively patrolled by skilled, highly mobile anti-poaching squads.

of which can be seen on enchanting launch trips along the tree-lined Mzinene River. Phinda's lodge accommodation is superb.

The 30 000-hectare Itala, youngest of Natal's major game reserves, lies well inland, sprawling between the hills and valleys that sweep down to the Pongola River. The original animals of the area – among them elephant, rhino and lion – have been reintroduced, and some 80 different mammal species now roam the forested slopes and hilly bushveld. The Natal Parks Board has broken new ground with its magnificently designed Ntshwondwe rest-camp, set high on the escarpment with spectacular views across a great natural ampitheatre.

profusion. The Natal Parks Board has set aside 24 000 hectares of the reserve as one of a number of wilderness areas accessible only on foot; hiking parties are accompanied by trained game guards.

Mkuzi

The 35 000-hectare haven, now part of the Greater St Lucia Wetland Park, lies between the Mkuze and Umsunduzi rivers at the southern edge of the Mozambique plain. The reserve has had a checkered history: in 1931 there were near-successful moves to have its game destroyed, and the area de-proclaimed, in an attempt to eliminate the tsetse fly.

Mkuzi is much favoured as a winter game-viewing destination: this is the dry season and several lovely pans, of which the 5-kilometre Nsumu is the largest, attract a host

of animals and about 300 species of birds. Well-placed observation hides provide excellent viewing points for keen birdwatchers.

Phinda and Itala

The Phinda Resource Reserve is bounded by Mkuzi and the St Lucia wetland complex. It is owned and run by the Conservation Corporation, and was among the first to apply the 'sustainable resources' concept in the region. It is an imaginative approach, one which acknowledges the interdependence of various interest groups and the need to use Phinda's 15 000 hectares for the benefit of all the farmers, the owners of game lodges, the tourists, the local Zulu inhabitants, and the wildlife. The reserve embraces seven distinct ecosystems that, between them, support a splendid variety of animals and birds, many

TOP: INSIDE THE COMMUNAL AREA *at Mhlangeni, one of the Itala reserve's bushcamps.*
ABOVE: THE RESTAURANT *at Itala's Ntshwondwe rest-camp.*

Wetlands wilderness

KwaZulu-Natal's northern shoreline fringes the Greater St Lucia Wetland Park,

a remark-able, and fragile, melange of lake, estuary and lily-covered pan, game

reserve, forest, grassland, high coastal dune and marine sanctuary.

The Greater St Lucia Wetland Park, third biggest conservation area in South Africa after the Kruger and Kalahari Gemsbok national parks, extends over some 250 000 hectares of flattish bird-rich coastal plain. It could be described as one of the most varied – and most beautiful – protected areas of its kind in the world.

The giant, shallow, saline Lake St Lucia is the focal point, but the park also encompasses a massive spread of wetlands, estuaries, coastal forest, dune forest, mangrove swamps, African savannah and, in the adjoining marine reserve, coral reefs. This is a kaleidoscope of habitats that sustains a remarkable diversity of animal, bird, fish and plant life. Lake St Lucia is an extended estuarine system. This 60-kilometre estuary covers almost 37 000 hectares of mostly muddy expanses of water, and runs parallel to the Indian Ocean. Lake St Lucia is fed by five rivers: the Mkuze, Mzinene, Hluhluwe, Nyalazi and the small Mpate. The offshore coral reef provides evidence that the lake was part of the sea until about 20 000 years ago. During that period sea levels were very much lower than at present, and beach rock formed. This is the base on which the coral reefs have now grown. But over eons global sea levels changed and today the two are separated by a dune barrier running between the beach and the lake. The barrier, which rises 180 metres above the surrounding, flattish countryside, has served as the base for what are among the world's highest vegetated coastal sand dunes.

The depth of Lake St Lucia varies between one and two metres, the waters opening into the sea after following a twisted, thread-like channel to the south. Since the early nineties, when the Natal Parks Board (NPB) consolidated various parcels of land, the Greater St Lucia Wetland Park has extended from Mapelane in the south in a great sweep around the lake and its fringing game reserve to Sodwana Bay in the north. A corridor to the west links the park to the game-rich Mkuzi reserve, which is now considered to be part of the Greater St Lucia Wetland Park.

St Lucia is a dynamic and vital ecosystem which is in a state of continuous flux. In years of drought the rivers stop flowing, lowering the freshwater levels and so pulling salt water into the system from the Indian Ocean. The salinity is increased to above that of seawater, especially in the lake's northern reaches, through evaporation in the hot summer months.

The lake is subject to climatic cycles of drought and wet periods, during which the character and pattern of life within the system changes quite dramatically. At low salinity levels subsurface water plants abound, attracting a large variety of ducks; at mid-salinity levels the lake is home to estuarine fish and fish-eating birds (among them a breeding colony of about 6 000 pelicans); at high salinity levels up to 60 000 flamingoes strut the now nutrient-rich lake.

ABOVE: HALF-SUBMERGED HIPPOS, *one of them a lone egret's vantage point, bask in the Mkuzi Reserve's Nsumu pan. These giant semiaquatic mammals are even more numerous in and around Lake St Lucia and its estuary.*
RIGHT: THE GREY HERON, *commonly seen nesting in colonies near both salt and fresh water.*

DUNES IN DANGER

Save St Lucia! has become the rallying cry of South African conservationists in their fight to prevent a mining company from sending huge earth-gobbling machines onto the eastern shores of the lake to extract heavy metals. The company, Richards Bay Minerals (RBM), is primarily after the titanium that gives the sands a black tint which is often mistaken for pollution. The metal is used as a base for pigment in manufacturing paint.

The ancient dunes are covered with tall dune forest, scrub and a fire-maintained grassland, and RBM gave a firm undertaking that the mined dunes would be replanted with indigenous vegetation after the titanium was removed. The company also maintains that the enterprise will create jobs and earn millions in foreign exchange.

Conservationists argue that the project has a predicted life of only 17 years, that the damage to the wetlands system could be far more lasting, and that the tourist market, which could potentially generate many more jobs than mining, would suffer. Ultimately it is a matter of

exploiting the hidden riches now or having a long-term sustainable tourist industry.

The region is also one of the poorest in the country. Some of the local African people, displaced from the land in the 1950s, would like to see the mining go ahead. Others simply want the land returned to them for traditional agriculture.

In this emotive atmosphere, claims of fact are rejected by both sides. A full-scale environment impact study has been conducted and assessed, but the final decision has yet to be taken at a national level. A central issue in the argument is whether the dunes can be adequately rehabilitated after mining or whether there could be irreversible damage.

TOP: FLY-FISHING AT ST LUCIA, *one of the world's great wetlands and a paradise for the angler.*
ABOVE: WHITE PELICANS *flock at Lake St Lucia. Their feathers take on a pinkish tint in the breeding season.*

Development – notably irrigation projects and the planting of thirsty pine and gum trees in the catchment – has affected the cycle, but the Natal Parks Board keeps a careful eye on the natural balance and manages the estuarine system with sensitivity and skill.

There's much for the visitor to see and do within the St Lucia complex – hiking, estuarine and sea-water fishing, game spotting, birdwatching, diving and wilderness trailing. The main attractions, however, are fishing and scuba diving among the beautiful offshore coral reefs. Thousands of anglers, both local and foreign, beat an enthusiastic path to

the area each year. Hutted rest-camps and caravan-camping sites have been established.

The wetland park sustains an impressive 512 species of birdlife: great flocks of pink-tinted flamingo in the shallows of the lake, the stubby pelican with its elongated, fish-pouch beak, gangly marabou stork, goliath heron, saddlebilled stork and spoonbill all feed on the teeming shoals of fish (over 100 different species altogether) and other aquatic life. And then there are the migratory birds, among them a variety of terns and the boldly black-and-white avocet. Often, too, you can hear the plaintive cry of the white-breasted,

chestnut-winged fish eagle over the water, and see it swooping down dramatically to snatch a fish in its powerful talons.

Crocodiles, sharks and the wallowing hippos also share the lake. St Lucia was originally proclaimed a protected area to safeguard the hippo when, towards the end of the 19th century, hunters and poachers almost wiped them out. The crocodile remained vulnerable even after the reserve had been established. The vital role that each and every life form plays in the delicate natural balance is now better understood, and the wildlife has a more secure future.

The magic of Maputaland

A meeting of climatic zones and changes in the levels of the ancient seas have combined to create a region of stunning ecological diversity – one that may, one day, become Africa's finest national park.

The far northern extremity of Natal, the 9 000-square-kilometre region known as Maputaland that lies between the Indian Ocean and the splendid Lebombo Mountains in the west, is one of the most biologically diverse and loveliest parts of South Africa. This territory is a magnificent mix of evergreen woodland and savannah, dense forest, wetland, floodplain, river estuary and the world's highest forested dunes. Offshore are coral-encrusted reefs that entice scuba divers and marine biologists from afar.

Maputaland embraces a stunning variety of ecosystems, a product of both its position at the junction of the tropical and subtropical climatic zones, and of its origins: the land, not so long ago on the geological calendar, lay beneath the sea, which in due course receded to leave a sandy plain and a series of shallow depressions whose waters and their surrounds are now home to a wealth of animal, bird and plant life.

This is a fragile land, its many different components interdependent, their relationship finely balanced. And, like so many other parts of Africa, it is under stress – from a growing rural population, from wasteful utilization of land, uncoordinated planning, the burgeoning cattle herds, increasing afforestation, and insensitive tourist developments. Environmentalists would like to see the whole region proclaimed as a national park in which the needs of both man and nature are happily accommodated.

In the meantime, several of the pristine and more vulnerable areas have been set aside by the authorities for conservation.

A magnificent series of lakes and swamps extends north from the Greater St Lucia Wetland Park to the grandeur of the 18-kilometre-long Kosi Bay lake system, which opens into the sea just south of the Mozambique border. Between the two points lies South Africa's largest freshwater lake, the 18-kilometre-long Sibaya which, along with a number of other stretches of water – Kosi Bay, St Lucia and the pristine Lake Bangazi –

TOP: SODWANA'S VEGETATED DUNES – *highest in the world.*
ABOVE: A LOGGERHEAD TURTLE *scrambles up the beach.*
RIGHT: MARINE LIFE AT KOSI BAY *teems around the coral reefs, among the earth's southernmost.*

ABOVE: BOATING AT KOSI BAY, *a complex of four enchanting lakes in the far north.*

was once part of the sea. The lakes have been cut off from the ocean by the high, forested sand dunes built up on an underlying reef. An unusual feature of Lake Sibaya is the marine species that, over the millennia, have been forced to adapt to freshwater conditions. The beautiful reed-lined lake is home to hippo and crocodile and to the princely African fish eagle.

Inland a savannah woodland, characterized by its scrubby trees, spreads out in an impressive panorama. Interspersed on the plain are seasonal flood pans alive with waterfowl drawn by an abundance of fish and water insects.

Sanctuary for elephant

In the extreme north of Maputaland, the regional conservation authorities have set aside 29 000 hectares for the Tembe Elephant Park, a move designed to protect the remnants of the once great herds that, for thousands of years, wandered freely over the plain that stretches far into Mozambique. Their numbers have been grievously reduced, as a consequence of both human settlement and warfare, to about 80 individuals. But these few survivors are now protected by Tembe's electrified fences. Fortunately, the Mozambique government is now becoming increasingly aware of the tourism value of its country's natural heritage and is busy re-establishing the Maputo Elephant Park.

The park has other attractions, among them the giant sycamore fig trees, notable for their broad and spreading trunks, that dominate patches of forest. A wide range of animals forages between the dry-sand forest, shrubveld and areas of swamp and grassland.

Just to the west, close to the Lebombo Mountains, is the relatively small 10 000 hectare Ndumu Game Reserve, which boasts lovely riverine forest and a number of extensive pans. The sanctuary has a limited range of animals but its marshes and reedbeds, evergreen forest and fig- and fever-tree woodlands are haven to a flourishing array of birds – 420 different species in all, among them a great many waterfowl and some tropical varieties at the southernmost limit of their range. Some birdwatchers regard Ndumu as having the highest concentration of birdlife in one area on the subcontinent.

Most of the area is part of the Mozambique coastal plain and is subject to seasonal flooding, which replenishes the fish-rich flood pans and the wetlands of swamps and lakes. This process has been partly disrupted by the construction of a great concrete dam, at the point where the Pongola River breaks through the Lebombo Mountains in the west.

The sandy beaches that grace Maputaland's shoreline play host to the threatened loggerhead and the even rarer leatherback turtle, species that travel thousands of kilometres – some from as far as the Kenyan coastline – to find the precise stretch of sand on which they were hatched. There they nest, so perpetuating an ancient cycle of birth and life. Visitor access to the beaches is restricted as part of a successful move to protect the breeding colonies, which, by the 1960s, had been reduced to the point of regional extinction by human demand for their eggs and meat.

The cumbersome, gentle creatures come ashore at night to lay their eggs above the high-water line, then leave them to incubate in the warm sand. When the hatchlings emerge they are entirely on their own, and must run a gauntlet of ghost crabs before reaching the sea, where they face other, equally formidable predators. Less than one in 500 makes it to adulthood.

THE FISH KRAALS OF KOSI BAY

For centuries the local Tembe-Tonga fishermen have waded among an intricate system of fish kraals in the lower reaches of the Kosi Bay lake system, seeking and invariably making a good daily catch. The kraals, built with thick sticks embedded in the sandy bottom and interwoven with pliable tree branches or rope fashioned from plant fibre, are spread out in spirals across the lower part of the chain of four connected lakes. In the glint of a red-tinted sunrise, the structures and their surrounding waters take on the look of a futuristic work of art.

As the tides come and go the fish migrate from the sea into the lake system and its confining kraals. Some fishermen, wading waist-deep and armed with long, sharply pointed wooden spears, stalk their trapped prey, neatly impaling the silvery bodies in rapid and accurate stabbing movements.

The work is hard, and frustrating: the kraals must be constantly repaired as lumbering hippos barge their way through, moving from the daylight security of the lakes to their night-time feeding grounds on the reed-fringed banks.

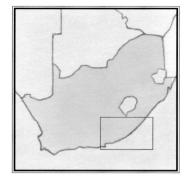

The Eastern Cape is a region full of contrasts, its different components unified only by history – a past fashioned by the perennial conflict between Xhosa resident and English colonial settler.

Xhosa country

The Eastern Cape stretches along the Indian Ocean coastline from beyond Cape St Francis in the west to the KwaZulu-Natal border, and inland to the semiarid plains of the Great Karoo and, to the northeast, the foothills of the Drakensberg. Until recently it encompassed three major political components: the former African 'homelands' of Transkei and Ciskei, and the once-colonial territory of the Eastern Cape, part of the wider Cape provincial division but in many ways divorced from the decision-makers in Cape Town, far away to the west.

The mountains of the Eastern Cape are rounder, greener, less jaggedly rugged than those of its western neighbour, and they lie farther inland, making room for a broader coastal plain. The many perennial and lovely rivers of the hinterland cut deep gorges as they snake their way to the sea. Farther north, between the coastal rampart and a second series of mountain ranges, is the plain of the Little Karoo, a gentler, better watered, far more productive land than its big brother, the Great Karoo, in the country's vast interior. The coastline, especially that toward the east, is world-famed for its wild beauty.

All this is traditional Xhosa country, much of it well settled long before the first European colonists made their landing at the Cape of Good Hope in 1652. The scene, in some areas, has changed little over the centuries: the rolling green hills are still dotted by simple thatched huts, and the people of the remoter parts have retained many of the ways of their forefathers. But the region is also the cradle of English-speaking South Africa, home to the first really big wave of foreign immigrants to wash over South Africa's shores. The settlers landed at Algoa Bay (now Port Elizabeth) in 1820, and the contribution they and their descendants made to the country's social and cultural fabric is preserved in the little city of Grahamstown, with its impressive 1820 Settlers Monument and its annual festival of arts.

The region received another substantial infusion of foreign culture in 1858, with the arrival of some 2 400 German immigrants at East London on the far eastern seaboard. The names of a number of Eastern Cape centres, among them Hamburg, Berlin and Stutterheim, reflect their German origins.

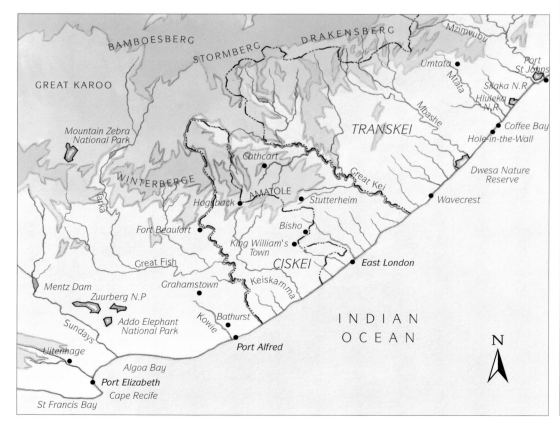

OPPOSITE: THE EASTERN CAPE *coastline, greener and softer than the southern seaboard and Western Cape, has many unspoilt beaches.*

Transkei's wild and wonderful coast

Transkei's ruggedly lovely shoreline, a compound of massively sculpted rocks

and long white beaches, is a hiker's and holiday-maker's paradise.

Transkei's seaboard runs from the Mtamvuna River on the Natal border to the Great Kei River to the south-east, a beautiful 280-kilometre stretch laced by lagoons, estuaries and sandy bays. Dramatic headlands, scoured by the sea into extraordinary sculptures, punctuate beaches lapped by warm water of a dazzling, tropical turquoise. All along its length the land merges with the sea in a series of ecosystems that are protected by the conservation authorities within the boundaries of eight lovely reserves.

But, for all its beauty and seeming tranquillity, this is the Wild Coast. From the earliest days of maritime travel, ships have been driven shoreward by the treacherously deceptive currents and contrary winds, to be smashed and swallowed by rocks and sea.

A modern explorer, though, can walk the coastline in just 25 days. The route is completed in easy stages, hikers overnighting in hospitable huts – a far cry from the anguish suffered by the sorry survivors of the shipwrecked *Grosvenor,* who walked the same path more than 200 years ago. The *Grosvenor,* reputedly laden with riches, foundered near the mouth of the Mzimvubu River, and its 135 survivors set out on the formidable 92-day trek to Algoa Bay (now Port Elizabeth). Only six men arrived to tell the tale of their 500-kilometre odyssey.

Scenic paradise

How different the journey is today! The trail traverses some of South Africa's most spectacular scenery, a compound of unspoilt golden beaches, mangrove swamps, broad estuaries, waterfalls and massive cliffs. The only man-made interruptions – apart from a few welcome hotels and casinos – are occasional, tiny coastal settlements, isolated trading stores and the circular, thatched mud huts of the Xhosa. Although western styles have

ABOVE: A SEA-SCULPTED ARCH *gouged from the detached and massive sandstone cliff at Hole-in-the-Wall. The Xhosa people call it 'the place of sound' because of the continuous roar that the waters make as they rush through the archway. Its flat top is large enough to accommodate several football fields.*

Mfihlelo Falls, where the stream gushes over the cliff directly into the Indian Ocean below. Port St Johns is an idyllic resort at the mouth of the Mzimvubu River and bordering the Silaka Nature Reserve. From here the five-day walk to Coffee Bay passes through the bird-rich Mngazi Valley and a superb mangrove swamp on the estuary of the Mngazana River.

Moving south, one comes to the dramatic dolerite intrusion of Brazen Head and the splendid evergreen forests and prolific water-fowl of Hluleka Reserve. Beyond Coffee Bay a black pebble beach lies alongside Hole-in-the-Wall, a massive, detached sandstone cliff through which the sea has eroded a perfect archway. There is a perpetual, thunderous roar as the water rushes through the opening, which has earned it the appropriate Xhosa name 'esiKhaleni' – the place of sound.

LEFT: ONE OF THE WILD COAST'S *many lovely estuaries.*
BELOW LEFT: *An age-old Xhosa indulgence.*

largely supplanted tribal dress and customs, these traditional brown and white structures have endured, their white sides confronting the sun to deflect the midday heat, their unpainted ones facing west to absorb the late afternoon warmth and conserve it for the night. Eminently practical, these homes dot the undulating pastoral landscape that eventually meets the straggling eastern bastions of the Drakensberg. Between Port Edward and Port St Johns, two dramatic sculptures have been gouged from the rocks by the perpetual pounding of the sea – Cathedral Rock and the Castle. The trail also includes Waterfall Bluff, where the route passes between the tumbling water and the cliff behind it, and

ABAKWETHA – PREPARING FOR LIFE

Many Transkei men work in the industrialized parts of South Africa, visiting their home villages for just a month each year to attend to domestic matters. The families who stay behind in the remoter areas rely on small, regular remittances to supplement a simple diet. Some families also earn an income from handicrafts they fashion with easy and enviable skill.

The Xhosa believe that preparation for life is a matter of example and of ritual: a man's success depends on how he lives and how he respects tribal lore, taboos and customs. Tradition is so highly regarded that boys return to the Transkei from distant Egoli (Johannesburg) to attend 'Khwetha' (circumcision school), the ritual transition to manhood and preparation for marriage that each boy must experience.

'Khwetha' involves a three-month period of strict seclusion, during which the young man lives in a beehive-shaped grass hut, in an all-male group, or in his own small hut near the home kraal. The initiates' identity is concealed behind masks and by white sandstone paint smeared from head to toe – both a symbol of purity and a defence against evil. Clothing is minimal, but ceremonial regalia (pictured) is elaborate, signifying the strength and virility of the initiates when they perform ritual dances at neighbouring kraals. On these occasions the boys wear masks, thick reed skirts, and high, pointed reed caps with horns. After the initiation period, the ritual burning of the hut used during the seclusion denotes the end of boyhood.

South of the Kei

Both sophistication and the simple life feature in this land of green-clad mountains and unending idyllic shores.

The Great Kei River, on its way to the warm Indian Ocean, has cut gorges so deep that they form a prominent boundary, a line that divides the land into 'beyond the Kei' and 'this side of the Kei'. In the course of a history too often marked by violent confrontation it also became a strategic and political division that separated the province of British Kaffraria – later called Ciskei – from the Transkeian Territories.

But there's more than history here to tempt the traveller. This is a region of surprising contrasts. Affluence rubs shoulders with soul-destroying poverty; casinos and luxurious marine resorts are the near neighbours of dwellings made of mud and reed. Yet the wider community has reason to bless the resorts: located on or near some of the most beautiful beaches, lagoons and mountains (notably the forest-clad Amatole range) in the country, they provide essential employment as well as attracting much-needed tourist revenue from beyond the borders.

Inland is the surprising little city of Bisho, administrative headquarters of the former republic of Ciskei – a city that rose from the veld in just a handful of years. Bisho provides an interesting contrast to neighbouring King William's Town, which dates from the 1830s and was once the capital of British Kaffraria and frontier headquarters of the British army. Bisho, indeed, was actually created from scratch as the capital of the 'homeland', because strokes of administrative pens placed the major centres of white settlement beyond Ciskei's borders.

But it is for the beauty of the coastline that the Ciskei and Border regions are best known. From the mouth of the Great Kei in the north, to the Great Fish River in the south, and beyond, to the Kowie River and Port Alfred, the seaboard is endowed with an entrancing collection of natural assets. Resorts such as that at the Mpekweni estuary have sensibly – and sensitively – capitalized on exquisite sites designed by nature. Separating these pockets of development is a string of beaches etched with estuaries, and dunes and coastal forests forming a barrier that still holds firm against too-civilized intrusions. Populated only by isolated fishermen or shell-seekers, they provide an undisturbed and beautiful habitat for the birds and wild creatures who left their transient prints on the sands long before man arrived.

The shoreline can be explored in a series of hiking safaris laid out along the paths followed by prehistoric coastal dwellers from the Kei Mouth to East London, or along another route past the Madagascar Reef, offshore of the Birha resort, from the Great Fish to the Chalumna River. The Strandloper Trail

ABOVE: THE GONUBIE ESTUARY *near East London. The Buffalo River, to the south, serves as the town's harbour.*
ABOVE RIGHT: *A fish eagle soars above the Birha, strewn by shells washed up from the Madagascar Reef.*

ABOVE: TIME-HONOURED TRADITION *survives in the rural Ciskei region. These women are grinding grain.* ABOVE RIGHT:THE FAR EASTERN CAPE *is renowned for its many rivers and scenically splendid shoreline.*

includes no fewer than 10 river mouths and two nature reserves along its 93-kilometre course. The route can be broken for overnight stops at numerous scenic points, or for digressive trips to the game lodges and historic settlements of the near interior.

Mammoth mussels

The 64-kilometre Shipwreck Route traverses coastal dunes and estuaries set against a densely forested backdrop, with some tough hiking in the final stretch between the Keiskamma estuary and the Chalumna River. This is legendary mussel, shell and bird country; the black mussels are meal-sized mammoths found in great clusters on the many rocky stretches along the coast, strewn with shells and with the worn debris of ancient wrecks washed up from the Madagascar Reef. Fish eagles are a familiar sight in the estuarine setting of the Birha resort, just one of the many bird-friendly habitats that sustain terns, gulls, cormorants, Cape teal, pochards, spurwinged geese and the many other birds of this extraordinarily beautiful coast.

THE COELACANTH – NOT ALL FOSSILS ARE STONE

The coelacanth had been extinct for more than 70 million years. At least, that was what scientists believed until a live specimen was trawled off the mouth of the Chalumna River near East London in 1938. It was discovered almost by accident. Inexplicably, the fish had wandered away from its haunts in the deep tropical waters off East Africa, and it was only by chance that Captain Goosen cast his net while homeward bound in the late afternoon of 22 December. Even then, the coelacanth had to be noticed and identified among two tons of sharks and other species when the nets were swung inboard.

The discovery of a fish that lived from 300 to 70 million years ago caused an immediate international scientific sensation and brought world renown to Prof JLB Smith of Rhodes University, Grahamstown, the man who identified it. The coelacanth became known as 'old fourlegs' from Smith's reference to its unusual arrangement of fins. Later specimens were found, as Smith predicted, in the vicinity of the Comoros. The first coelacanth caught in this area was flown back to South Africa by military aircraft, where it was put on view at the JLB Smith Institute of Ichthyology at Rhodes University in Grahamstown.

The original South African specimen, appropriately named *Latimeria chalumnae* in honour of Miss (later Dr) Courtenay-Latimer – to whom Captain Goosen first took his find, and who immediately recognized it as something exceptional – is housed at the East London Museum.

It's worth noting that the world's only dodo's egg is also an exhibit at this lively institution.

Hogsback and the Amatole

The lofty mountain peaks are often snow-capped in winter, wreathed in cool

mists in summer, and they rise above the slopes and foothills of a scenically

stunning region that the Xhosa herders called Amatole.

The gently rounded contours of the Amatole mountain range, of which the Hogsback is a prominent part, are known as 'the little cows' by the Xhosa people, who have long grazed their cattle on the lower slopes and along the banks of the serpentine Keiskamma River coiled at their feet. The slopes are densely forested with indigenous sneezewood, ironwood and yellowwood; in parts the tree canopy, up to 30 metres high, is so thick that no undergrowth can be sustained on the deeply shaded forest floor. The more open patches, however, are covered with shrub-like bush, grassland and fynbos (heath-type vegetation). Everywhere there are spectacular waterfalls, dappled trout streams and cold, clear pools, and the views from the unexpected windows in the forest are breathtaking.

Introduced species – gums and pines – form their own quiet forests or lend shade to roads and footpaths lined with brambles and the occasional, ancient tree bearing cherries, nuts or pears. Gardens display an abundance of plants from all parts of the world. The hedgerows are hung with berries, and there are banks of rhododendrons, while azaleas grow in profusion and enormous mushrooms sprout from the forest floor. There's a distinctly English countryside air about parts of Hogsback, and this, as much as the mountain and woodland splendour of its southern African setting, accounts for its wide appeal.

Among the peaks and valleys is a line of three arched ridges, the one known as 'First Hogsback' most closely resembling the back of a sturdy pig. The rock strata near the top even suggest the bristles along its spine, or so the local inhabitants tell you. Others make reference to a Major Hogge of the British Army, to a place called Hog's Back in England, and to the wild boar or hogs that once roamed these forests. Whatever its origin, though, the name is an old one, going back to at least 1848.

Redcoat Lane is a reminder that the British Army was indeed here, as part of the system of fortification of the Eastern Cape frontier in the long struggle for land between white farmers and black pastoralists. But war seems remote at Hogsback, and although grassy

ABOVE: CARPETS OF IVORY-HUED *arum lilies decorate the forest floor around Hogsback.*
LEFT: A PAIR OF WOOD OWLS, *common residents of the Amatola forests.*

CONSERVATION AND CASTLES

You find the ruins on hilltops or covering the river-fords, all that's left of forts where the soldiers of King George, of King William and of Queen Victoria kept uneasy watch during the colonial wars against the dispossessed Xhosa.

Fort Michel at Hogsback has crumbled away, but the gun-tower of Fort Armstrong, romantically decrepit, still stands overlooking a meander of the Kat River near Balfour. A circular drive from Hogsback, taking in Fort Beaufort, Grahamstown, Peddie and Alice is a journey through country rich in a history that rings with the clash of arms. Now a new war is being fought – to preserve the wildlife and its environment from both neglect and over-exploitation. Regional policy places emphasis on the community, on its role in and the benefits it derives from conservation.

The region's several sanctuaries are run in close co-operation with the local villagers; each has its drawcards, all offer comfortable country-lodge type accom-

modation. Tsolwana Game Reserve provides superb wildlife viewing, hiking and pony trekking as well as hunting opportunities. Mpofu, the home of the eland, is being restocked with a wide variety of game. Hippos live in the Double Drift Game Reserve, farther south in dense valley bushveld vegetation and expanses of spekboom (*Portulacaria afra*). Here, foot safaris, conducted by experienced guides, enable you to see kudu, black rhino, Cape buffalo (pictured) and leopard among other mammal species.

mounds may hide ancient fortifications and long forgotten graves, the very air seems alive with a sense of freshness and wonder.

Exploring Hogsback

Hogsback and its forests and falls should be explored on foot. The paths are well planned and have rest stops that are usually outstanding view sites, but some, especially to certain waterfalls, are strenuous. Wherever you go, and in whatever season, take warm clothing as insurance against a sudden change in the weather. This gently capricious climate is itself a part of Hogsback's charm and it would be a pity to have memories of the rising mist from Kettle Spout Falls marred by recollections of discomfort caused only by lack of foresight.

This is a quiet country, one that seems to offer the ultimate in solitude. But you are not alone: the shaded depths provide habitats for a whole community of small and busy an-

imals, and the immense silence is broken by an occasional small rustle or a discreet but unguarded grunt. Hidden close by you are Amatole toads and Hogsback frogs, giant golden moles and earthworms up to three metres long, wide-eyed bushbuck and the rare blue duiker. Every now and then you'll hear the babble of a Samango monkey calling from a hidden perch and the shrieks of Cape parrots and Knysna louries somewhere above you. But always the silence returns to wrap you in its comforting mantle.

There is spiritual comfort, too, in Oak Avenue. With cut logs for pews, it serves as the nave of a great outdoor cathedral, notably at Easter and at Christmas, when it is the venue for open-air services. Rather more formal is the small, round church of St Patrick's-on-the-hill. It lies next to Hogsback's 'through road' that runs past charming hotels, the post office, and side roads that invite exploration of this enchanted place. You'll come to Hogsback if you drive up the Tyume Valley

from Alice, or from Cathcart, through Happy Valley and up past Gaika's Kop, or even up the steep and narrow Michel's Pass, also known as New Katberg Pass, from Seymour. However you approach it, there is no really major road, which is also a part of the enduring charm of Hogsback.

BELOW: THE WOODLAND MAGIC *of the Hogsback.* BOTTOM: SNOWSCAPE *along the Hogsback-Cathcart road. The area is best explored on foot.*

Port Elizabeth – the friendly city

Several informal epithets have been attached to the seaport that hugs the shores

of Algoa Bay, among them 'The Windy City' and, because of its vehicle assembly

plants, 'The Detroit of South Africa'. It is best known, however, for the amiable

nature of its citizens, deemed the friendliest people in the country.

Port Elizabeth offers an extraordinary diversity of attractions as well as its legendary friendliness. It's an ideal leisure location from which to explore not only the endless beaches of the Sunshine Coast but also some fascinating natural and social history, the heavily laden orchards of the hinterland and the small towns and remote landscapes of the central and eastern Great Karoo. But start with the city itself.

LEFT: HOBIE CATS *of the highly active Port Elizabeth Yacht Club take to the warm waters of the Indian Ocean from the sands of Summerstrand.*
BELOW RIGHT: A POIGNANT *Victorian memorial.*

The Heritage Trail through the city centre shows off some of Port Elizabeth's intriguing 19th-century architecture. Queen Victoria, regally robed in Sicilian marble, overlooks Market Square, where the trail begins. The nearby Victorian Gothic library opened in 1902, its terracotta façade manufactured in England and shipped to South Africa in numbered pieces to be assembled on the site.

The Campanile, east of the square, commemorates the landing of the 1820 Settlers. This 51,8 metre high structure, with its carillon of 23 bells, was erected in 1923 just north of the beach on which the settlers landed. Progress, sadly, has ensured that the beach is no longer to be seen, not even if you climb the Campanile's 204 steps and look for it from the viewing platform.

Victorian heritage

Radiating out from The Hill, the city's oldest residential area, are the earliest streets, each with its handful of perfectly preserved Victorian homes. The most venerable, Victoria House at 31 Constitution Hill, was built in about 1825. In Donkin Street an entire row of terraced houses, stepping sedately down the hill, dates from 1870, and has been proclaimed a national monument, to be preserved and occupied by yet more generations. On the open space of the Donkin Reserve, near the old lighthouse, a small stone pyramid erected by a grieving husband commemorates Elizabeth Donkin, whose first name was given to the city at its birth, a city she never saw.

The trail includes a stop at the Railway Station, built in 1875 when railways in South Africa were still something of a novelty. The ornate and much-admired cast-iron pillars that support the roof were added 20 years later. Nearby is The White House (the old Harbour Board Building), one of the best examples of Art Nouveau architecture in the country (many other examples of this style are being uncovered and restored). The old Feather Market Hall – now an upgraded conference venue and concert hall – opened for

THE FOUNDER: SIR RUFANE DONKIN

Irish-born Rufane Donkin had reached the age of 43 and the rank of Major General before he lost his heart.

The lady, much younger than he, was Elizabeth Markham, daughter of an eminent churchman. They married in 1815, just before Donkin was due to leave for an important command in India. He had already survived soldiering in the West Indies, had been wounded in Belgium and had fought against Napoleon in Portugal, Sicily and Spain. But the lovely Elizabeth was to prove a less robust campaigner.

Their son was born in 1817 and then, just eight months later, Elizabeth died of fever in the northern Indian town of Meerut. In declining health and shattered by grief, the recently knighted Donkin was invalided home to Britain. At the Cape of Good Hope, however, he was persuaded by another bereaved soldier, Governor Lord Charles Somerset, to stay on for a while as acting governor while Somerset went on furlough to England himself.

It was Donkin who organized the settlement of the 4 000 British immigrants after their landing at Algoa Bay in 1820. On 6 June that year he named the embryonic city after his late wife. Still mourning, he planned another lasting memorial to her name, on an open sea-facing hill overlooking the town. The pyramidal sandstone cairn erected here is similar to one in the grounds of Castle Howard in Yorkshire, Elizabeth's home county.

The Elizabeth Donkin Memorial carries two plaques, one to the memory of 'One of the most perfect human beings, who has given her name to the town below', the other to 'The husband whose heart is still wrung by undiminished grief'. Despite a later, distinguished career that included being elected to the House of Commons three times, Sir Rufane Donkin ended his own life in 1841.

business in 1885 as a clearing-house for ostrich feathers, wool, hides, skins and fruit.

Among Port Elizabeth's best-loved buildings is the Opera House, the only surviving example of a Victorian theatre in South Africa. The Heritage Trail also includes a number of historic churches and St George's Park, where the country's first cricket test match (against England) was played in 1889.

Famous dolphins

For years Port Elizabeth rested rather modestly on its tourist laurels, woven in part around the famous dolphins Haig, Dimple, Daan and Dolly, the first of several bred-in-captivity infants raised at this world-renowned institution. Dimple, now over 30 years old, is still an amusing and energetic performer in the daily performances, and is the undisputed matriarch of the dolphin lake. The superb Oceanarium, Museum and Snake Park complex still, deservedly, attracts innumerable visitors. Gradually, however, the benefits of a kindly climate, beautiful beaches and the abundant enticements of the surrounding area have created a fuller awareness of the city's real potential.

BELOW: THE COASTS *to either side of Port Elizabeth are a mecca for holiday-makers. The city itself is set on the shores of Algoa Bay, scene of the first major landing of British immigrants.*

Adventures in Albany and Addo

Albany, Bathurst, Grahamstown – these are some of the very English names that colonial rulers and their dogs of war superimposed on a land ancient in the ways of Africa, a land wracked by a century of bloodshed.

Look at a large-scale map of the eastern Cape and you'll find fragments of England, places and their names redolent of the 'old country' scattered across the region's plains and hills. Here, in 1820, in the province called Albany, several thousand British immigrants were settled along a restless frontier and expected to survive as farmers. Most of them, in time, moved to towns where they could practise the skills they had used in England. But their names have endured, carried by proud people, carved on stones or adorning the homes they built. Here are Glenthorpe and Trentham Park, Broadfield and Oakdale, and they keep company with many others around the little city of Grahamstown.

Custodian of culture

Grahamstown was named for a soldier of long ago, when small armies, British and Xhosa, clashed violently over possession of this land. Hills and river crossings on the old frontier are still watched over by forts. They were small, functional places of barracks and squat gun-towers, some with taller towers on which were mounted semaphore arms for signalling to the next garrison in the line. There's one at the heart of Grahamstown itself: Fort Selwyn, on Gunfire Hill. Close by is a large piece of bronze statuary that pays homage to the British settlers and, an infinitely more practical memorial, the vast hall and conference centre of the imposing 1820 Settlers Monument.

This is the heart of the annual winter Festival of the Arts, when Grahamstown, the home of Rhodes University, celebrates its English heritage and, especially, the language (though the festival has taken on a much more catholic character in recent years, both honouring the African legacy and reflecting the contemporary scene in dance, theatre, music and painting).

The town sees itself as custodian or, at least, repository of that culture, and its museums reflect its traditions. An unusual museum is the Observatory, once the home of a jeweller and amateur scientist who helped to identify South Africa's first diamond. The chief attraction of his old home is his camera obscura, an instrument that still delights chil-

ABOVE: PORT ALFRED'S *fine golf course. The charming little town is set on a navigable river, and 19th-century settlers expended a lot of time, effort and money in developing its harbour, but the project was abandoned with the coming of the railway in 1881.*
RIGHT: COOLING OFF *at an Addo waterhole.*

The nature reserve at Bathurst is called Waters Meeting, a reference to the great horseshoe loop that the Kowie River makes on its way to the sea at Port Alfred where, for a while, there was a fair-sized harbour. Today, pleasure boats rock gently at an elegant marina, but no old-time schooners venture timidly up the winding channel. The days of maritime glory are reflected in the local museum, readily identified by the old ship's figurehead displayed outside.

To the west are other rivers – Kariega, Bushmans and Boknes – that wind to the sea through sheltered lagoons. The terrain is rich not only in its history but in floral variety, and is well served by reserves and resorts.

LEFT: FORT SELWYN, *built in 1836, originally served as a semaphore station linking Grahamstown to a chain of other fortified settlements.*

dren of all ages as it once delighted their young Victorian ancestors. The churches, in their way, are museums too, and there are many of them – about 40 all told – giving Grahamstown the well-deserved nickname of 'the city of saints'.

The old Cape Parliament met here, just once, in the 1860s, to mollify the Eastern Cape secessionists who believed that their province should have its own separate government. But Grahamstown never did become one of the world's capital cities, although it is certainly the centre around which the district of Albany revolves. This is the Zuurveld, the 'sour fields', a land for grazing and crop-raising and where, within a short drive of Grahamstown, are to be found other small towns and settlements with their own particular charm.

Village of peace

There's little Salem, for instance: a sprinkle of white cottages and a church of sternly unadorned design on a plain of scrubby bush and aloes. 'Salem', taken from the Biblical Psalms, means 'peace'. It seems appropriate here, but this place also knew stress and clamour during the long agony of frontier warfare. Farther afield is Bathurst, with its ancient angular pub and a church that sheltered women and children while their menfolk patrolled the grounds.

HUNTER'S HELL OR ELEPHANT'S PARADISE

It was a famous hunter who remarked of the Addo bush country that 'if ever there was a hunter's hell, here it was'. It is the sheer impenetrable denseness of the thorn

trees and the close-growing bush known as spekboom or elephants' food (*Portulacaria afra*) that allowed the pachyderms of Addo to survive – that, and their massive bulk that enables them to push on through areas where humans cannot go. The plant is well named: its nutritive value sustains more than 200 elephants within the Addo Elephant National Park – more than three times the usual carrying capacity for an area of close to 12 000 hectares.

The park lies in the valley of the Sundays River at the foot of the Zuurberg Mountains and is home also to eland, kudu, red hartebeest and several other varieties of antelope as well as to the endangered black rhino, the Cape buffalo and to 170 bird species, among them hawks, finches and moorhens. A pleasant rest-camp (pictured) has been established for overnight visitors

Once, elephants ranged as far south and west as Table Mountain, but within a century or so of European settlement at the Cape they were all but eradicated west of Algoa Bay. At Knysna, where the thick forests provide shelter, a few elephants still survive today, but they are rarely seen.

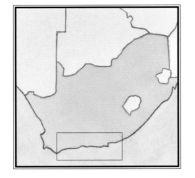

The Cape south coast's 'garden' stretches 230 kilometres from Mossel Bay in the west to Storms River in the east – a scenically stunning region that offers a multiplicity of enticements and which is superbly developed for tourism.

The Garden Route

A Frenchman named François le Vaillant travelled along the Cape's southern coastal belt, the aptly named Garden Route, late in the 18th century and, more than two hundred years later, his description of the countryside is still appropriate.

He wrote evocatively of a 'chain of mountains, covered with lofty forests' and of 'agreeable hills, variegated in an infinite number of shapes'. He wrote, too, of 'the most beautiful pastures' and of the flowers, 'their colours, their variety, and the pure and cool air which one breathes – all engage your attention and suspend your course. Nature

has made these enchanting regions like a fairyland'. To 'suspend your course' is a sound piece of advice for the traveller along this plateau between coast and mountain. There are many places at which to stay and, as Le Vaillant noted, there is much to see.

When he passed this way, of course, man's impact on the landscape had been negligible. A handful of farmers and woodcutters had left some slight scars, while small clearings marked the few villages of the indigenous peoples, such as the Outeniqua (the name means 'men laden with honey'), who were settled at a place the Dutch recorded as

Hooge Kraal (now Pacaltsdorp), close to the present and most attractive town of George.

Over time man has built other towns, and created roads, dams and bridges. Today jet aircraft trail feathery lines high above the range that Portuguese explorers called 'the Mountains of the Star'. But there are still great forests that clothe those mountains and quiet lakes that reflect their green slopes. The sea still washes the lovely, lonely beaches.

OPPOSITE: BIRD'S EYE VIEW *of the charming Wilderness Lakes region. This particular stretch, among the area's most attractive, is known as The Serpentine.*

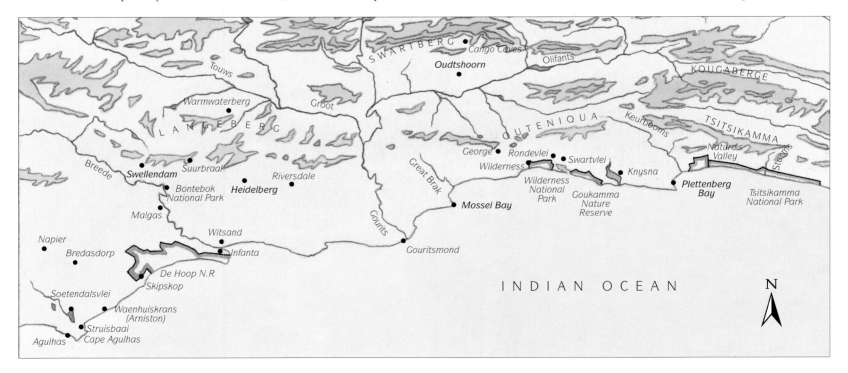

Plettenberg Bay

Affectionately known as 'Plett', this beautiful bayside resort lies beside lagoons and river mouths towards the western end of the Garden Route, in one of the most lushly afforested and scenically exquisite regions of the country.

Named variously Algoa Bay (Bay of Lagoons), Bahia Formosa (the Beautiful Bay) and the Bay of Content, the place was finally and officially christened by Cape Governor Baron Joachim van Plettenberg in 1778. But for the thousands of summer visitors lying supine on the beaches, it certainly appears to be the Bay of Content. Plettenberg Bay and its surrounds are spectacularly beautiful; the area is blessed with 320 days of virtually uninterrupted sunshine a year; its clear warm waters, safe swimming and fine white sands are incomparable. It is also here that you'll find the exquisite little pansy shell (*Echinodiscus bisperforatus*), symbol of Plettenberg Bay and a holiday souvenir that will outrank all others.

Flanking the fine resort hotel on Beacon Island, site of a former Norwegian whaling station, are two of the three major swimming beaches, Central and Robberg. The former is quite literally on the hotel's front doorstep and is favoured by families; the latter is a long curve of golden sand ending in a rocky punctuation at the Robberg (Seal Mountain) Peninsula, a 240-hectare nature reserve endowed with rich bird and intertidal life. The red sandstone peninsula throws a protective arm round the bay, and shields the beaches from the westerly winds.

The Robberg reserve embraces an important archaeological site. Nelson's Caves on the south side, once occupied by coastal Bushman people, can be reached along a pleasant, quite leisurely ramble along the ridge, with magnificent views and a super-charge of ozone along the way. The early inhabitants of the region followed clear seasonal patterns which have been traced in recent excavations: it appears that they spent their summer inland and the winter on a seaboard well stocked with shellfish and other marine foods. A fairly well-preserved child's skeleton, dating from about 700 BC, has

ABOVE: PLETTENBERG BAY'S *fashionable Beacon Island, flanked by magnificent beaches.*
TOP RIGHT: CANOEISTS *on the Keurbooms River. Rambling, fishing and bird-watching are other attractions.*

ALONG THE OTTER TRAIL

South Africa's first organized hiking trail is still one of the country's most popular. It follows the rockbound and scenically superb coast from Storms River Mouth (starting point shown here), headquarters of the Tsitsikamma National Park, to the lovely village and reserve of Nature's Valley.

Walkers take five days to cover the 41-kilometre route. Although each day's distance is short enough, the terrain can be tough and includes crossing – by swimming or wading – the mouth of the Bloukrans River. For most of the way one follows the shoreline, with occasional forays to the coastal plateau through forest and fynbos, and there is time enough to travel slowly and take in the spectacular scenery, the birdlife, the trees and the mounds of shells left by shore-dwellers of centuries ago, the baboons and, not too far out to sea, dolphins, whales and seals.

Africa: it lies back-to-back with an inlet of the great Bietou Lagoon, meeting place of the Bietou and Keurbooms rivers, the whole a paradise for the water-skier and yachtsman. Worth visiting are the Keurbooms River and Whiskey Creek nature reserves, where you'll find timber holiday chalets tucked away in idyllic shady glades and, occupying the only river-island, an unusual guest-lodge.

A holiday in Plettenberg Bay is largely but by no means exclusively for the wealthy. Some of the rich and famous do fly in by private aircraft; other devotees use the regular commercial services or drive down the Garden Route from Cape Town and Port Elizabeth with bicycles, surfboards and other holiday toys lashed to roofracks and carriers.

To accommodate the influx there's an airport, an 18-hole golf course and country club set in a nature reserve, speciality shops, boutiques, galleries, interior decorating services, banks, travel and tour firms – and as many restaurants to the block as there are olives in a salad. Nor are these naïve village establishments: most offer superb local linefish, caught fresh each day, and a range of cuisine that straddles the continents.

been found in one of three Robberg burial sites that have also yielded a wealth of shells, stone artefacts and ostrich eggshell beads.

Robberg Beach is overlooked by discreet duneside homes buried up to their eaves in lush vegetation and which, on closer inspection, are quite clearly the seaside retreats of the truly wealthy: multiple garages and landscaped gardens are among their more obvious features. Separating Plett's most prominent beaches is the lagoon at the mouth of the Piesang River, which snakes languidly into the wooded valley beyond. Here, too, there's evidence of luxury living: splendid townhouses overlook the lazy peat-coloured water, ruffled here and there by the occasional not-too-energetic canoeist.

Holiday-makers' allure

East of the sophisticated little hilltop town of Plettenberg Bay are Lookout Rocks, from where you can observe the giant southern right whales that come inshore to mate in the winter months. Beyond is Lookout Beach, reputedly the finest stretch of sand in South

ABOVE: SUN-WORSHIPPERS BASK *in the warmth at the Storms River estuary, eastern extremity of the Garden Route.*
OPPOSITE LEFT: THE DISTINCTIVE *Knysna lourie, charming resident of the indigenous forests.*

LEFT: THE LIMPID WATERS *of Knysna lagoon, centre-piece of a prime holiday area.*
BOTTOM: KNYSNA'S FOREST FLOORS *are mantled by a multiplicity of plant species.*

Knysna – the land of forests

A hundred years ago men dug for gold in the hills around Knysna, and

unearthed it. But the real treasure of the place is to be found in the beauty and

peace of its lagoon, its surrounding uplands and its ancient, brooding forests.

The tidal lagoon, fed by the Knysna River, covers some 17 square kilometres and is one of the largest South African estuaries. It's also an 'ecological battery' of diverse habitats for birds and fish, the country's largest oyster-farming centre and home to a rare species of sea horse, and to the little echinoid, or sea urchin, that is cast ashore in the delicate, petal-etched pansy shell. Its waters, now peat-brown, now blue, wind-whipped or placidly reflecting the embracing hills and cliffs, are an artist's delight and a holiday-maker's paradise.

Early mariners saw these waters differently: a treacherous sand bar lies between the imposing sandstone cliffs, known as The Heads, that flank the lagoon's entrance channel. Negotiating the bar is still a tricky procedure. Knysna no longer functions, officially, as a harbour, but it was once a haven for a small fleet of fishing boats and, for a few years, coasting steamers regularly braved the terrors of the bar. Today the lagoon is home to the local yacht squadron, houseboats for hire, a myriad small leisure craft and to a few pleasure cruisers that carry visitors across the waters to the western headland, where there is a private nature reserve. But the eastern bluff, sprinkled with expensive homes and easily reached by road, has the grand view of sea and lagoon, town and mountain.

The central part of Knysna is on the north shore – a small commercial and residential district with numerous pubs and restaurants and an immense range of accommodation for tourists. Two former islands in the lagoon have been connected to the mainland by causeways; the larger was once Steenbok Island, but now, as a dreamy lagoonside suburb, is called Leisure Island. On Thesen's Island, named after a Norwegian family that settled in the region in 1869, is a busy, bustling bar on the jetty that was once the heart of the forgotten fishing harbour.

Royal beginnings

Knysna residents may tell you, with modest pride, that their town was founded by the son of an English king, and an old gravestone does indeed proclaim a George Rex to be the 'proprietor and founder of Knysna', but makes no mention of his origins. In the early-19th century George Rex was proprietor on the largest scale, and owned almost all the land in the region. He sold an estate on the western shore to a son-in-law, who called it Belvidere; a retirement village, designed in an

early colonial style, has recently been developed there. But the interesting part of Belvidere remains the charming little stone church of the Holy Trinity, built in the mid-19th century, a faithful copy, in every respect, of an early Norman church.

Wood used in the building of the church was cut in the forests that still surround the town and extend for almost 200 kilometres along the Outeniqua and Tsitsikamma mountain slopes. Formerly even more extensive than they are today, these dense indigenous woodlands with their tangles of fern and other ground cover are almost impenetrable in parts. Their density provides security for the last few survivors of the once numerous Knysna elephants, the most southerly herd on the African continent. The region's trees, on which the early economy of Knysna depend-

ABOVE: LAKESIDE PANORAMA. The 17 square kilometre lagoon yields fine oysters, and 'pansy' shells.

THE OUTENIQUA CHOO-TJOE

A familiar call to many Knysna residents is that of the narrow gauge steam locomotive – SAR Class 24, locally known as the Outeniqua Choo-Tjoe – as it makes its daily approach to Knysna station across a railbed raised on piles above the lagoon. The run between the inland town of George and Knysna is on the last stretch of railway in South Africa routinely worked by steam traction. It is also one of the most enchantingly scenic stretches of track in the world, a gently moving view site that commands vistas of cliffs precipitously rising above the Indian Ocean, river crossings and beaches, lakes and forests and the final, triumphal sweep into Knysna.

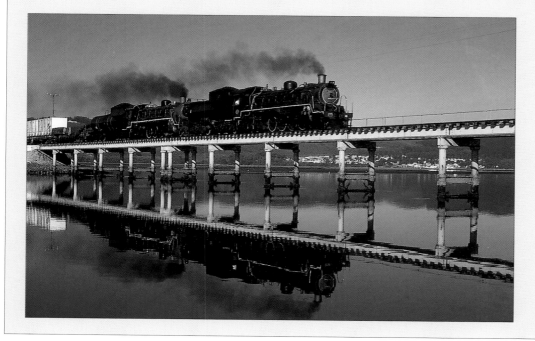

ed almost exclusively, include ironwood, white alder, stinkwood and yellowwood.

Each of the 'big trees' of the Knysna Forest – and several specimens are signposted – is a yellowwood, some of them perhaps over a thousand years old, with a girth close to 10 metres. But the magical tree is the stinkwood, its hard, beautifully grained timber making beautiful, enduring and sought-after furniture. The name, derived from the odour it emanates when freshly sawn, offended an early settler from a noble British family, who insisted on calling it 'stingwood'. But stinkwood it remains, and it is sold annually in limited quantities at auction in Knysna. Along with other rare indigenous trees it is protected by strict regulations.

Today there are huge tracts of plantations of introduced species such as pine and eucalyptus, but it is the indigenous high forest that fascinates the nature lover. Leopards and vervet monkeys, wild pigs and several species of small antelope are among the numerous creatures that live beneath the great forest canopy, rarely disturbed by human intrusion. Birdlife, too, is prolific, and this is the preferred habitat of the vividly coloured and crested Knysna lourie that, usually invisible among the dense foliage, sends its raucous, repetitive call echoing across the cathedral-like stillness of the forest.

The Wilderness

'Like pearls from a broken necklace', a chain of lakes lies scattered along the strip of densely wooded plateau between the mountains and the sea.

Travelling eastwards from Knysna, the first glimpse of the lakes, and of the Wilderness village and resort, comes as the road soars gracefully up from the cool depths of the Kaaimans River gorge and curves high above the sea at Dolphin Point. The view site here commands long lines of white beach and breakers that fade into misty distance and, inland from high dunes and a ribbon of road and rail, the village of Wilderness and its beautiful lagoon lying at the mouth of the Touw River.

This is a favourite place for holidays and honeymoons, a place to walk in the quiet of primaeval forests, or to drive along dusty roads from which wagoners' children once looked out over an incomparable expanse of woodland and water. Today's children find fascination enough along the shallow shores of the lagoon, while the deeper channels provide an ideal venue for watersports. Surfers favour nearby Victoria Bay, which also offers the best bathing in the area.

It was a real wilderness a century ago, when only a few farmers and fishermen knew the place, and access was by a difficult track from the inland way the locals call 'the old road' and signposts label 'the passes

BELOW: WOODLAND MAGIC: *A secluded corner of the enchanting Kingfisher trail.*
BOTTOM: THE DRAMATIC *Kaaiman's River gorge and estuary near the village of Wilderness.*

route'. Thomas Bain built it in the 1860s to accommodate lighter and more leisurely traffic between the towns of George and Knysna. It winds through forest and farmlands, and up and down gorges of rivers whose quiet, tawny waters, are crossed now, not by Bain's simple fords or drifts, but by little bridges of

Nature and the bounty that sustained the Outeniqua are today the subject of energetic conservation efforts that have resulted in the creation of the Wilderness National Park, incorporating five rivers, four lakes, two major estuaries and 28 kilometres of coastline. Largest and deepest of the lakes, and the largest natural saltwater lake in South Africa, is Swartvlei – the 'black lake'.

On a cloudy winter's day its vast surface may indeed seem forbidding, but in sunlight it sparkles and reflects the surrounding hills with their orderly plantations of pine and eucalyptus. Lines cast by anglers glisten like silver webs along the shoreline, as speedboats carve their wake along the sparkling surface, and bright sailboards dart back and forth across the silvery expanse. The major part of Swartvlei, together with Island Lake and Wilderness lagoon, have been set aside for recreational use.

ABOVE: THE REED-FRINGED *Groenvlei, one of the larger lakes in a chain stretching between Wilderness and Knysna. It is renowned for its birdlife.*

stone or cast iron. The road that links it with Wilderness is called White's Road, after an enterprising investor who opened the first boarding house of the area early this century. Regularly maintained, it offers the most comprehensive view of the lakes.

There are five major lakes to the east of Wilderness, all saltwater and linked to the sea with the exception of the most easterly one. This is freshwater Groenvlei or Lake Pleasant and, like the other lakes, including Wilderness lagoon, it owes its creation to some complicated geomorphological sequences. This shaping of the landscape over many thousands of years saw the sea advance and retreat, and there were times when the lakes area was marshland, the home of hippos. Then the sea beat against the cliffs that, today, lie inland from the lakes in an arc that extends from Wilderness to Swartvlei. More recently, and for many centuries before the arrival of the first European explorers, this was home to the Hottentot hunters and gatherers who must have delighted in the beauty of the place, and in its abundance of food and water. Envious clansmen who lived in less idyllic surroundings called them Outeniqua - 'men laden with honey'.

A WEALTH OF WATERBIRDS

Wildlife conservation within the Wilderness National Park is focused on Rondevlei and Langvlei. This is an intermediate zone where the semiaquatic vegetation of reeds and sedges mingles with the ubiquitous coastal fynbos or heath. The resultant mix of plantlife, together with abundant water, provides a sheltering habitat for what is probably the greatest variety of waterfowl in South Africa. Some 95 species (including the purple heron, pictured) have been recorded in the entire country, and 75 of them are to be seen in this relatively small area.

There are bird hides at both Langvlei and Rondevlei, and a boardwalk of one kilometre along the Touw River at Wilderness provides splendid opportunities for birdwatching. Another haven for birdlife is Groenvlei which, although it lies just beyond the eastern limit of the park area, is within the contiguous Goukamma Nature Reserve. Groenvlei – the green lake – is a popular venue for freshwater anglers, who are drawn to the waters by the introduced population of black bass.

While anglers drift lazily on Groenvlei's waters, other visitors take to canoes and dinghies to explore the further delights of the area, each of which contributes another perspective to the Wilderness experience. This is a restful and tranquil corner of the country, its tranquillity complemented by the small black and brass locomotive that trails its shrill wail and brief plume of smoke across the landscape.

Ostrich capital

Oudtshoorn began, as so many South African towns did, as a cluster of houses

in which farmers spent a few days when they rode in from their lands for the

quarterly 'nagmaal' or communion service of the Dutch Reformed Church.

Oudtshoorn began life, modestly enough, in 1853 and, across the mountain, the people of George looked down their noses at this upstart settlement and dubbed it Velskoendorp, after the rawhide shoes of the simple countryfolk. Perhaps they laughed when their magistrate's wife gave it its official and rather aristocratic name of Oudtshoorn, after one of her distant and distinguished ancestors, but the new town was eventually to have its day.

This dawned when, in the salons of Europe, ostrich feathers became accessories of high fashion from the 1860s. It was a slow boom in the beginning but, once it took off, it lasted more than 50 years, and Oudtshoorn became one of the busiest and most prosperous towns of the old Cape Colony.

The climate of the semiarid Little Karoo, of which Oudtshoorn is the unofficial capital, is suited to the ostrich as well as to the growing of lucerne and the making of hay, with which the big birds were fed. Given this combination, farming – and Oudtshoorn – prospered. Laid out along the banks of the Grobbelaars River, the town grew into a palette of golden sandstone buildings set against a backdrop of the Swartberg Mountains. 'Feather barons' built 'feather palaces' – lavish, ornate, romantic monuments to the staggering wealth of the early 1900s. The Art Nouveau 'town house' in High Street is one such example, carefully preserved with original wallpaper and carpets, and so are the many surviving buildings still liberally adorned with the cast-iron trimmings so loved by the late Victorians.

Less cluttered lines are seen in the later, vast Edwardian mansion of Pinehurst and in Welgeluk, the homestead on Safari Ostrich Show Farm. Both were designed by the Dutch-born architect Johannes Vixseboxse, who was also responsible for the relatively sober South African Museum building in Cape Town. Vixseboxse was just one among the many professionals, artisans, adventurers and entrepreneurs who flocked to Oudtshoorn during its boom era. In the CP Nel Museum, again designed by Vixseboxse,

ABOVE: PART OF THE CANGO CAVES COMPLEX. *Cango One, the first of four sequences to be discovered, is a remarkable labyrinth of 28 chambers linked by 2,4 kilometres of passages. Part of the interior is floodlit.*

ABOVE: RIDING THE BIG BIRDS *on a farm near Oudtshoorn. Feather auctions are still held in town.*

THE FLIGHTLESS BIRD OF THE KAROO

The largest of living avifauna, the ostrich, belongs to a family of flightless birds which has distant relatives in Australia and South America.

The wings, although useless for flight, help maintain balance, provide shade for eggs and newly hatched chicks, and also assist with body cooling. The ostrich's curious appearance and arrogant strutting may seem comical, but there is enough strength in each powerful leg and two-toed foot to disembowel a man with a single, downward-raking kick.

Not that the ostrich is a notably aggressive creature, except when it is guarding its nest of massive eggs or its brood of chicks (pictured). The eggs, which take 42 days to incubate, may weigh up to 1,25 kilograms, and are equivalent to 24 hen's eggs. They have immensely strong shells that, when upended, will not crack under the weight of an average adult man.

The wings of males have the finest feathers, and plucking takes place throughout the year, with the exception of the two coldest months. Ostrich skin is tanned to

produce much sought-after leather items. Ostriches thrive on lucerne and hay and, like other birds, they also ingest grit in the form of stones to assist in crushing their food. They are also likely to snatch and swallow any shiny object within reach.

cian, whose modestly attractive home in the town, Arbeidsgenot, is now also a museum.

In winter the peaks are covered in snow, but Oudtshoorn still basks in sunshine. A traditionally healthy place for invalids, the warm dry air and well-irrigated soils make the region ideal for products as diverse as tobacco, onions, walnuts, grains, honey and grapes. Wine is an attraction that visitors are discovering with approval in the Little Karoo and nearby Langkloof – the flatlands between two east-west inclining chains of mountains.

The mountains themselves are remarkable. Within the Swartberg to the north of Oudtshoorn is the world's most extensive system of limestone caverns, known as the Cango Caves. They were discovered in prehistoric times by people who never ventured beyond the sunlit chamber at the entrance. The great darkness and silence of the inner halls and passageways remained unexplored until 1780, when a local farmer made the first foray beyond the light.

Massive, ancient stalactites and stalagmites extend from the caverns' roofs and floors, as well as other, more recent formations: the intricately curled helictites for example, only a few centuries old, or the great sheets of dripstone that defy any assessment of age.

BELOW: ONE OF THE FEW *'feather palaces' to have survived from the boom years of the ostrich industry.*

among varied relics of days gone by, is acknowledgement of the contribution made by the Jewish community.

Carl Otto Hager of Stellenbosch was another architect who contributed to the charm that still mantles Oudtshoorn. He designed the central Dutch Reformed Church erected in the 1870s, during the early years of prosperity. The stone-built St Jude's Anglican church dates from the same period, but its structure reveals that its congregation was less numerous, and also less prosperous. A London creation is the 91-metre long suspension footbridge, erected in 1913, which used to be the only link between the east and west banks of the Grobbelaars River.

Cosmopolitan though its origins may be, town and setting are indisputably of the Cape. South Africans who live here speak Afrikaans, a language championed by the late CJ Langenhoven, journalist, poet and politi-

Mossel Bay to George

The two major centres of the Garden Route's western approaches, each with its own attractions and distinctive personality, are full of fascinating stories from the past, and hold a wealth of interest for the modern traveller.

The highway between the Garden Route towns of George and Mossel Bay is one of those rare roads that, rather than simply connecting two points by the shortest route, seems to display its surrounding countryside to the greatest advantage.

There are towns along the way, and places with ancient seafaring connections. At Mossel Bay, Europeans stepped on South African soil for the first time when, on 3 February 1488, Portuguese explorer Bartolomeu Dias landed to fill his water casks. Vasco da Gama later named the bay *Aguada de São Bras* – the watering place of St Blaize. Human settlement in this area, however, dates back to much earlier times: stone implements and middens of shells (including the mussels that gave the place its name) which have been found here tell of beach parties which took place long before recorded history began.

The town of Mossel Bay officially only dates back to 1848, although its 'post office', the country's first, is almost 500 years old. Mossel Bay is South Africa's fifth-largest harbour, and is also the base for the exploitation of offshore oil and gas fields. Luckily these have not spoiled the town's seaside holiday atmosphere, and safe bathing is still widely enjoyed from the white, sandy beaches.

Slightly removed from the sea and nestling beneath Cradocksberg and George Peak (both higher than Table Mountain) is another interesting little town – George, named after King George lll of England, and originally established in 1811. The town claims city status because of its charming Anglican cathedral of St Mark, one of the smallest cathedrals in the southern hemisphere.

Growth and change

Motor vehicles registered in George carry the letters CAW, which wags interpret as 'Cold And Wet', a description residents hotly deny. Rainfall, however, is generous in this area, and forestry and agricultural activities are vital economic contributors to the town's prosperity. Once described by an eminent Victorian novelist as 'the prettiest village in the world', George has grown considerably over the years, and has become the commercial centre of the Garden Route.

It is ideally situated for explorations of the Garden Route, and for ventures over the

ABOVE: GEORGE'S HANDSOME *Dutch Reformed Church, earliest of the town's places of worship.*

ABOVE: MAGNIFICENT SEASCAPES *unfold from this Mossel Bay view site. The town, once a quiet fishing village and holiday resort, has grown quickly since the recent discovery of oil in the offshore waters.*

Outeniqua, Tsitsikamma. There are other roads that follow the contours of the mountains east and west, venturing no farther than sheltered glens and valleys where farms and villages now blend into the lush landscape.

Roadmakers saw the mountain ranges as an obstacle and a challenge, but to others they represented home and shelter. The early Portuguese navigators, boldly pioneering a sea route from Europe to the Indies, gave them the lovely name of *Serra da Estrella* – 'the Mountains of the star'.

Navigation by trial and error

But to the early Portuguese even the stars in these far southern latitudes were strange and compasses were unreliable. So these seafarers found their way by the perilous method of hugging the coast, except where offshore gales forced them farther out to sea. Dias, for instance, rounded the Cape of Good Hope without ever being aware of its existence. Far out in the southern ocean, he steered his small ships to the north, to reach again the precarious proximity of Africa's seaboard.

ABOVE: THE STATUE OF BARTOLOMEU DIAS *at Mossel Bay. The great Portuguese navigator made his landfall in 1488; a later seafarer, João da Nova, built a small chapel here in 1501 - the first European-type structure to be erected on South African soil.*

Outeniqua mountains into the Little Karoo, land of the ostrich. The easiest way across the mountains is via the Outeniqua Pass, built in part by Italian prisoners of war during the 1940s. From this tarred highway one can admire Cradock Kloof Pass, built in 1813 and now considered fit only for baboons, and Montagu Pass, a gentle, narrow route which is still in daily use and looks much as it did on the day it was opened in 1847.

Other attractions of George are scenic drives, walking trails and its proximity to nature reserves and to the beaches of Herold's Bay, Victoria Bay and Wilderness.

Among the drives are several routes to the interior, some of which begin at Mossel Bay, from where the Robinson Pass rises effortlessly to the inland plateau of the Langkloof and Little Karoo. The mountains they cross carry old names evocative of the early Hottentot inhabitants of the area – Attaqua,

THE POST OFFICE TREE

The first Portuguese sailors took water from a little stream and were stoned by a small group of Hottentots who regarded the precious fresh water as their own. The Portuguese, wary and as nervous as the Hottentots, responded with crossbow fire, and the first meeting on South African soil between people of two different worlds ended in bloodshed.

Later vists, though, were usually fairly amicable and led to mutually profitable barter. In 1500, the Portuguese commander Pedro d'Ataide penned a message for others of his storm-scattered fleet. Curiously, he placed his letter in an old shoe which he hung in the branches of a white milkwood tree. This 'post office tree' still stands, close to the stream of the Hottentot and to a superb museum complex that houses, among its many exhibits (including an arts and crafts centre) a

reconstructed Portuguese caravel that, 500 years after Dias' epic voyage, was sailed from Lisbon to Mossel Bay.

ABOVE: COLOURFUL *holiday homes at Still Bay.*
LEFT: THE 12-MILLION CANDLEPOWER *lighthouse at Cape Agulhas has been warning ships since 1849.*
BELOW: THE DE HOOP NATURE RESERVE, *among the Cape's most important, is home to the once-rare bontebok.*

To the end of Africa

The same Africa of Egypt, Morocco and the shores of the Mediterranean in

between has its southernmost end at Cape Agulhas. This desolate, rocky

promontory lies 5000 kilometres south of the equator, on a shoreline of wide

beaches and sweeping bays interspersed with rugged cliffs.

Inland are rolling fields of wheat, barley and oats, and some of the finest stock-raising country in South Africa. This is the Strandveld, where the dunes and the coastal plains merge gradually with the ridges and undulating hills that lead up to the southern Cape's impressively rugged mountain chain.

The region's natural vegetation includes the small-leaved and hardy fynbos as well as gnarled and ancient specimens of the low-growing white milkwood. The local villages

are steeped in history and cloaked in the mystique of a harsh sea and those hardy mariners who have sailed it since Portuguese navigators, late in the 15th century, named the place Agulhas ('needles').

They suspected that the needles of their compasses here pointed true north, with no magnetic deviation, but other sources claim the name was given for needle-like rocks that showed above the sea. A lighthouse was built in 1849 and the beam from this stately tower

still warns ships off the treacherous cape and its rocky seabed. The lighthouse at Agulhas is one of 14 such beacons on the southern Cape coast between the hamlet of Paternoster in the west and Arniston in the east. Enthusiasts can follow a documented lighthouse and shipwreck route all the way round this tip of Africa, an excursion that could occupy an absorbing two or three days.

A few kilometres along the coast is Struisbaai, a popular resort where a picturesque, thatched-roof church and a few restored fishermen's cottages have gained national monument status. Beyond Struisbaai, where ostrich once roamed freely, is Arniston, named after a ship wrecked there in 1815.

The village is officially known as Waenhuiskrans ('wagon house cliff') because of a nearby cave big enough to house a wagon and team of oxen. Beyond Arniston – the unofficial name refuses to die – at Nacht Wacht farm on the road to

Bredasdorp, are the remains of a fence built in 1837. This was a private and noteworthy attempt at nature conservation, to protect the small local bontebok population after its cousin, the graceful bluebuck (*Hippotragus leucophaeus*), had been shot to extinction. Survival of the bontebok, it is hoped, has been assured by the creation of the Bontebok National Park near Swellendam.

A major attraction of the area is the De Hoop Nature Reserve, incorporating 46 kilometres of shoreline east of Bredasdorp. One of 12 marine and adjacent onshore conservation sites in South Africa, De Hoop is distinguished by the inclusion of an additional marine section to conserve a part of the Agulhas Bank, the richest fishing grounds in the southern hemisphere. The reserve also protects one of the largest remaining areas of coastal fynbos in the south-western Cape and is renowned for its diverse birdlife, including the endangered Cape vulture, nurtured within its seven distinct ecosystems. Moreover, it is an important site on the Whale Route, where great numbers of southern right whales

BELOW: FISHING BOATS *at Still Bay. The nearby and navigable Kafferkuils River is famed for its eels.*

gather offshore for several months of the year. Sightings are most common between May and November at Koppie Alleen.

On opposite banks at the mouth of the Breede River (or Breë) lie the bleakly beautiful settlements of Infanta and Witsand. The latter is still known, alternatively, as Port Beaufort, although its glory as a harbour was short-lived: the real port was almost 30 kilometres upstream at Malgas, where South Africa's only surviving pont still carries vehicles and stock across the river.

Inland lies Bredasdorp, home of South Africa's merino sheep industry. Visitors can tour local sheep farms on the Wool Route from April to October. A lucrative export business has evolved around the everlastings (*Helichrysum* and *Helipterum* spp.) that grow here, providing employment for the people of the little missionary village at Elim, the oldest settlement in the district.

One of the outstanding features of Bredasdorp's Heuningberg (honey mountain) reserve is the flowering of the spectacular, flame-red Bredasdorp lily in April and May. Known as 'the garden of Bredasdorp', the Heuningberg also has a beautiful hiking trail of about seven kilometres through a country-

side of fynbos and wild flowers. Among the many unusual special-interest sites in the country is the Bat Cave in nearby Napier. The 'cave' is a 30 metre-long tunnel of rock housing a prolific colony of bats and several baboon families. It is located in a narrow gorge through which flows a tree-shaded mountain stream and, although the land here is privately owned, visitors are welcome.

The Strandveld area was beautifully observed by South African essayist Audrey Blignault, who particularly loved Bredasdorp and its environs. A permanent exhibition in her honour is housed at the publicity offices in the centre of the town.

TEMPESTS AND TRAGEDY

The Shipwreck Museum in the south coast town of Bredasdorp tells part of the story of some 124 ships that have foundered within 80 kilometres of Agulhas during the past 300 years. Here are figureheads and furniture, cannons and crockery. A wealth of relics has been retrieved from the depths or from lonely beaches to be displayed in memory – and in honour – of seafarers and travellers who met disaster along Africa's farthest shores.

Beneath the great sunlit plains of the semiarid interior lies a wealth of precious minerals and fossils; above, the startling extremes of its climate have produced some of the most extraordinary floral and faunal adaptations in the world of nature.

Boundless spaces

The landscape alters dramatically beyond the rim of the southern mountain rampart, giving way to a vast, dry, brilliantly sunlit upland plateau that makes up the greater part of the South African inter- ior. Its semidesert vegetation, flat landscapes, harsh climate, oddly adapted plants and scattered towns might hold little attraction for most travellers, but there are those who are captivated by the clarity of the air, the stillness and the freedom of its boundless spaces.

More than half of the country's interior plateau is occupied by the immense basin of the Karoo with its characteristic vegetation capable of surviving droughts and extreme temperatures; the remainder is made up of three other major ecosystems – grassland, Kalahari, and the coastal sandveld of the west. The first two meet at the diamond capital, Kimberley. A man-made green belt lies along the southern bank of the mighty Orange River where hundreds of hectares of grapes, cotton and exotic plantations of date palms and other crops are cultivated.

Belying their barren appearance, the plains of the interior plateau are able to support life, and flocks of merino sheep – the wealth of the Karoo – thrive on the scrubby vegetation in the south, while a great diversity of game – most notably the springbok and gemsbok – occupies the dunelands of the Kalahari in the extreme northern corner of South Africa abutting the borders of Namibia and Botswana, home to the Bushman people.

To survive the extremes of heat, cold and drought, the flora and fauna have produced some extraordinary adaptations. And in springtime the bleak landscapes of Namaqualand in the west, even those of its forbidding Richtersveld region, are gloriously transformed by endless carpets of wild flowers. The far-flung towns of the interior largely serve the needs of the surrounding farming communities. Many are architectural and historic gems. Several, such as the museum town of Graaff-Reinet, are contained in conservation areas to safeguard the buildings and other artefacts of earlier lifestyles.

OPPOSITE: IN SPRINGTIME, *Namaqualand's normally bleak countryside is mantled by wild flowers.*

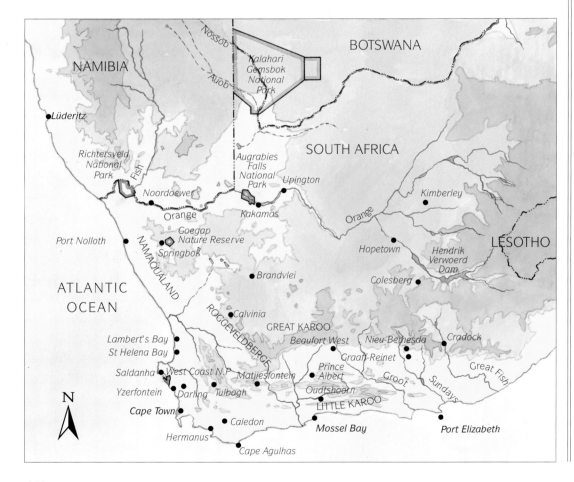

Forgotten treasure

Thousands of windmills punctuate the vast Karoo plains, indicating that most

precious of resources – life-giving water. But under the sun-seared surfaces lies

other bounty, rich fossil remains that, taken together, provide an almost

unbroken record of 50 million years of evolution.

South Africa's central plateau covers almost 400 000 square kilometres, well over half the total area of the Northern Cape Province and almost one-third of the whole of South Africa. This is the Karoo – the Bushman's 'dry and dusty plain', with such blurred boundaries that a precise geographical definition is almost impossible.

The Karoo is a seemingly endless area dominated by distinctively drought-resistant Karoo 'veld' – a vegetation compromised over aeons into manifold adaptations to survive the bone-dry years, extremes of heat and cold and intense sunshine. For the most part surprisingly nourishing, the Karoo veld sustains flocks of sheep, imparting a tenderness and herby flavour that has made Karoo mutton a delicacy.

Mountain rampart

Roughly divided into the Little and Great Karoo – of which the famous plains of Camdeboo occupy the far eastern interior – the plateau is deprived of coastal rains by a high boundary of continuous mountain ranges – the so-called Cape fold mountains – along its southern and south-western rim.

Two hundred years ago, great herds of migrating springbok thundered across its empty plains in search of fresh grazing, crossing the trek-paths of early explorers. Thunberg, Le Vaillant, Lichtenstein and Burchell left priceless records of the plant and animal life of the Karoo. Modern palaeontologists, geologists and botanists follow in their footsteps, drawn by the wealth of information frozen in the fossil-bearing rock strata. An almost unbroken record of the 50 million years of the Mesozoic era is contained in the horizontally bedded shales and sandstones of the Karoo hills. Here and there, the landscape is broken by dolerite dykes and sills, relics of volcanic action.

The tiny towns of the Karoo lie hundreds of kilometres apart, undisturbed, peaceful oases in a desert of dust, serving the needs and demands of the sheep- and stud-farming communities of the surrounding district. All are dominated by the spires of one or more churches, and the dominee's (minister's) house is in a prominent position. Many Karoo towns date from loan farms granted in the mid-1700s to free burghers who left the Cape and established farms, prospered, and attracted other settlers to the remote interior.

A number of small towns have survived the centuries; villages with wide streets and honest architecture. These serene settlements have been rediscovered and are being enjoyed for their pristine state of preservation. Many have been declared areas of historic interest and are thus protected.

Below the hard-baked surface lies the Karoo's most precious asset – water. And it is this buried treasure, rather than the ancient heritage of fossils and minerals, which preoccupies its people: access to and preservation of precious water resources. Windmills march across the vast and empty landscapes, drawing moisture from beneath the ground and pumping it to remote farms and grazing outposts, providing the only interruptions in otherwise unbroken horizons.

ABOVE: WINDMILLS DRAW PRECIOUS *water from the Karoo's abundant underground supplies. These, together with the region's sweet grasses, sustain a large proportion of South Africa's 28 million head of sheep.*

FEMINIST OF THE VELD

Olive Schreiner is considered South Africa's 'founder writer' – a child of the veld, whose feminist philosophies and free-thinking attitudes were formed far from the influences of the so-called civilized world. She gained international standing despite her status as a woman and one who was denied the education her equally brilliant brothers received.

Olive was strong-willed and independent, her life shaped by the hardships of her parents. She was born on 24 March 1855 at Wittenbergen Mission in the north-eastern Cape and named Olive Emilie Albertina, the ninth of her missionary father's 12 children. Only six of her siblings survived.

Poverty broke up the family when Olive was 12, forcing her into an itinerant lifestyle as governess, companion and sometimes nurse on remote Karoo farms and settlements. Her miserable existence as a governess in Colesberg shaped elements of her celebrated book *The Story of an African Farm*.

At 26 Olive went to England, where her manuscript was published in 1883. For six years she travelled, made a network of influential friends – and lived with philosopher-

psychologist Havelock Ellis. Asthma drove her back to the Karoo, to Matjiesfontein (pictured). From there she journeyed occasionally to Cape Town, spending time at Groote Schuur with Cecil John Rhodes; ultimately her friendship turned to revulsion for his 'contemptuous imperialism'.

In Cradock she met a young farmer, Samuel Cronwright. They married in 1894, he taking the name Cronwright-Schreiner and, for the sake of Olive's health, giving up his farm Krantz Plaats. Their daughter, born in 1895, lived only 18 hours.

Olive died in Newlands, Cape Town, on 10 December 1920. Cronwright reburied her the following year at Buffelskop on Krantz Plaats, and with her, the coffin containing their baby – which, in a sustained and eccentric paroxysm of grief, Olive had carried on her wanderings for 25 years.

ling, preserving and stockpiling of valuable foodstuffs for the leaner months, or for entry at the competitive annual agricultural show. And then there may be unexpected guests: with farms and villages many kilometres apart, a visit to the neighbours is nothing less than a major journey and guests – whether there are two or 20 – must be fed.

To the casual observer the Karoo may be nothing more than a barren plateau with a harsh climate. But it inspired Jacob Pierneef to paint, and Olive Schreiner and Sir Lourens van der Post to write, to mention just three among the many who have been charmed and then helplessly seduced.

BELOW: MATJIESFONTEIN'S ELEGANT *Late-Victorian Coffee House and antique petrol pumps.*
BOTTOM: GARDEN OF THE OWL HOUSE, *Nieu-Bethesda.*

In the towns, open water furrows line the streets, taking *leiwater* into backyards and gardens. Using a complicated system of 'water turns' residents can divert the water onto their own land for a specified period. Water rights are highly prized and fiercely guarded, and even a few minutes of *leiwater* once or twice a week will add a large sum to the price of a property.

The system allows even the smallest village garden to produce a generous harvest of extraordinarily sweet, sun-ripened fruit – apricots, peaches, nectarines, cherries, oranges and lemons – and a profusion of roses.

Life is regulated by the rhythms of the climate; at the height of summer when maximum temperatures head for the forties, housework is finished by 6 am. Curtains, shutters and windows are closed to preserve the interior cool, not to be opened until 6 pm with the rise of an evening breeze.

Although the Karoo is renowned for its dry, bright and usually sunny winter days, there is also bitter wintertime cold with frosts and snow which puts stock and crops at risk.

Throughout the year there is sowing and reaping; lambing and shearing, hunting and biltong-making. There is the bottling, pick-

LEFT: THE SPECTACULAR VALLEY *of Desolation near the historic Karoo town of Graaff-Reinet.*
BELOW: THE LUSH BASIN *of the Little Karoo.*

them, Meiringspoort, and the second, Seweweekspoort, lie along river gorges and were vulnerable to flood; at times they were closed for months on end. The third, and most recent – the Swartberg Pass – is a scenic marvel and a model of engineering.

Swartberg Pass

In 1879, the job of designing a new, reliable route over the Swartberg fell to the renowned engineer Thomas Bain. The Swartberg Pass between Oudtshoorn and Prince Albert is a 30-kilometre engineering miracle of sheer drops and twisting hairpin bends climbing to 1 615 metres above sea level.

It cost the lives of dozens of the 240 convicts employed during the seven years of construction. Part of the road is still untarred and definitely barred to large vehicles and caravans. Travel over the Swartberg Pass is inadvisable in wet weather, or for anyone with a less-than-reliable vehicle and a bad head for heights. But the views are panoramic and can be savoured from several vantage sites and picnic spots along the way.

Meiringspoort

Bordered by Klaarstroom at the north entrance and De Rust at the south, Meiringspoort was the first link between the Little and Great Karoo. As it weaves between cliff faces with almost vertical contortions in their Table Mountain sandstone strata, it criss-crosses the

Links in a mighty chain

Cutting a way through the towering southern mountains was a formidable

challenge. Three Swartberg passes were built, with Bain's tour-de-force perhaps the

most spectacular – a breathtaking switchback of hairpin bends and scary drops.

The Little and Great Karoo are separated from the coastal strip and from each other by a series of more-or-less parallel mountain ranges penetrated by some of the most spectacular *poorts* – narrow gaps – and passes in the country.

Nearest the coast, and forming the southern boundary of the Little Karoo, are the Langeberg and Outeniqua mountains. Further inland, spread out across the plains from west to east and beyond a ridge of lesser ranges are the majestic Klein Swartberg and

Groot Swartberg ranges, towering barriers between the Little Karoo and the vast, dry central plateau of the Great Karoo.

Crossing the Swartberg presented the greatest challenge of all but, in the last 150 years, its great cliffs and gorges have been probed with oxen, wagons, convict labour and the determination of men who saw the need to open pathways for trade between the coast and the interior. The result is three principal routes, all with unforgettable scenery and all built between 1858 and 1888. The first of

LEFT: FARM TRANSPORT *on the plains below the Swartberg: a fertile region despite appearances.* BELOW LEFT: THE DRY BED *of the Groot River.* BOTTOM: ALOES ARE PROMINENT *among the region's hardy and highly adapted succulents.*

names at the river crossings tell the story of long-ago journeys by oxwagon carrying wool and livestock to the coast, wood and potatoes back to the Karoo. Herrie's Drift was named after CJ Langenhoven's imaginary elephant, whose name was carved on a roadside stone by his creator in 1929; Waterfall Drift takes its name from the 60-metre cascade which drops into a pool of clear mountain water below. Access is by means of shallow steps cut into the rockface for the Prince of Wales' visit to the waterfall in 1925.

Seweweekspoort

West of the Swartberg Pass and opposite the tiny mission settlements of Amalienstein and Zoar, is the entrance to Seweweekspoort, 20 or so kilometres of old wagon road linking Ladismith and Calitzdorp with Laingsburg on the great north-south highway between Johannesburg and Cape Town. The road follows a narrow course along the Seweweekspoort River between vertical cliff faces of folded bands of sandstone topped with a wedge of blue sky. Here, too, convict labour was used for building the road, which opened to the travelling public in June 1862.

North and south of Calitzdorp are two equally memorable mountain passes – the Huis River Pass and the Rooiberg Pass, with bizarre colouring and rock formations reminiscent of Bryce Canyon and other parts of Utah in the northwest United States.

path of the Groot River 25 times. The mountain unfolds in a continually surprising series of vistas, each more dramatic than the last. Throughout the poort there are tranquil riverside picnic sites thrown into deep shade by the cliff walls above, and it is here that Karoo families come in numbers to picnic and find some relief from the blazing heat beyond.

The poort supports a rich pocket of vegetation that is anomalous in the Karoo, though common enough in the acidic soils of the southern Cape coastal regions. Many of the

Kimberley – home of diamonds

The discovery of diamonds marked the start of an economic revolution in South

Africa – and sparked the world's most frenzied diamond rush. More than

50 000 diggers converged on the dusty settlement of tents and tin shacks and,

while many foundered, a few struck fabulous wealth.

The late 1800s saw boom times for three South African towns which found themselves endowed with natural, very marketable, treasures. Oudtshoorn was blessed with ostriches and their fashionable – and valuable – feathers, Johannesburg with gold and Kimberley with diamonds.

The small, shining pebble discovered in 1866 at Hopetown, 125 kilometres south of Kimberley, precipitated the most frenzied diamond rush in world history – and led to the digging of the greatest man-made crater on earth – the Big Hole – now no more than a fascinating tourist attraction.

The pebble was identified as a 21.25 carat diamond and named 'Eureka'; the 83.50 carat 'Star of South Africa' followed, as did further finds in 1869 and 1870 at the farms Bultfontein and Dutoitspan. Encouraging deposits of alluvial diamonds were found on the banks of the Orange and Vaal rivers.

The discovery of diamonds in 1866 and gold in 1886 led to rapid industrialization, the development of road and rail links, employment and in many cases undreamed-of prosperity for the white people of the Boer republics and British colonies that were to become a unified South Africa.

In 1871 two significant deposits were uncovered on the farm Vooruitzicht, owned by two brothers whose name was to be written in South African history – De Beer. This was just the first chapter in the history of fabulous wealth gleaned from the depths of the earth at Kimberley. The founding of the De Beers Mine was followed by that of the Kimberley Mine on a nearby koppie.

Within two years the rudimentary settlement was swarming with more than 50 000 diamond diggers, and Kimberley became a town of shanties and tents. Relentless flies, inadequate water and lack of sanitation spread disease among the diggers, many of whom died in their attempts to get rich overnight. Gambling dens sprang up in the tent towns and fortunes made by day were often lost the same night. Everybody who was anybody came to Kimberley to stake their claim, including Cecil John Rhodes, and

ABOVE: THE HEADGEAR *of a working mine.*
RIGHT: THE BIG HOLE, *long worked out.*

Dr Leander Starr Jameson – leader of the infamous Jameson Raid which, in the 1890s, snowballed into a bitter war between the Boers and the British. Others, like the flamboyant Barney Barnato, became legends in their own lifetime, overnight mining millionaires who had both the wisdom and good fortune to be in the right place at the right time and the good sense not to gamble.

Today, Kimberley's older diggings are all but worked out, though the Dutoitspan, Bultfontein, and Wesselton mines still produce over half a million carats a year. And the Big Hole, partially filled with water of an extraordinary shade of green, is simply an ever-fascinating tourist attraction. More than 22,6 million tons of 'blue ground', or kimberlite, which yielded 14 504 566 carats, were excavated from the Big Hole from the start of the diggings until it finally closed in 1914.

Kimberley remains the head office for De Beers, whose former chairman, Mr Harry

ABOVE: PART OF KIMBERLEY'S MINE MUSEUM, *a complex comprising the Big Hole, an evocative re-creation of the early town, a hall of diamond displays and a splendid exhibition of early transport.*

STUNNING STONES

Two of South Africa's greatest diamonds are embedded in the British Crown Jewels: a pair of fabulous gems cut from the biggest diamond in the world (the 3 106-carat Cullinan), discovered at the Premier mine near Pretoria in 1905. Although the fabled diamond yields from Kimberley's Big Hole have been worked out, large diamond deposits still occur in the pipes of the Transvaal and Bushmanland, in alluvial beds along the Orange and Vaal rivers and in marine beds off the West Coast from Lamberts Bay to Lüderitz. One of the newest and richest mines is Venetia in the Northern Transvaal, which became operational in 1992.

The Kimberley area is still exceptionally rich in mineral deposits and, lured by the potential of the alluvial pickings along the banks of the Vaal, hopeful prospectors trek to Barkly West, 40 kilometres northwest of Kimberley, to try their luck seasonally. Here they vie for the limited number of permits issued each year from June to September.

On Saturdays the town buzzes with diggers and dealers, haggling over prices for the week's finds. Gemstone buffs can watch prospectors at work on the river bank or visit the Canteen Kopje archaeological site – an open-air museum and nature reserve – where diamond diggers have unearthed more stone age artefacts than diamonds. Their finds are on show in the Mining Commissioner's Museum.

Many precious and semiprecious stones are simply varieties of common minerals: agate, chalcedony, jasper, opal and citrine are quartz varieties, while ruby and sapphire are corundum.

Emeralds, aquamarine, morganite and heliodor belong to the beryl family, and amazonite and moonstone to feldspar. South African jade is a variety of garnet. Although no opals, sapphires or rubies are found in South Africa, there are good quality emeralds at Barberton in the Transvaal.

Oppenheimer, and his father, Sir Ernest Oppenheimer before him, benevolently influenced the social, political and cultural development of South Africa through their management of the vast wealth of the company. And history lives on in the grand old homes of the mining magnates, and museums filled with evocative relics of its prospecting days.

The Big Hole and Kimberley Mine Museum form a living, open-air replica of a section of the town in its diamond heyday so realistically reproduced that you almost expect a jovial Barney Barnato to pop through the doors of his Boxing Academy. The museum incorporates a transport hall and art gallery as well as a permanent display of uncut diamonds, jewellery, Kimberley's first diamond find, and the '616' – the world's largest uncut diamond. Visitors can see a Kimberley diamond mansion at Dunluce, Belgravia – a fine example of domestic Victorian architecture.

Kimberley also has an important military history, much of it preserved in the beautiful McGregor Museum where Cecil John Rhodes lived during the siege of the town in 1900. Thirty kilometres away on the Modder River Road is Magersfontein, site of one of the bloodiest battles of the Boer War. Here the British forces lost 2 400 men on 11 December 1899. The remains of the trenches into which the defending Boers were packed, stand as stark reminders of the day.

Fall of the mighty

Its fertile banks and floodplains make a striking impression in the barren

Northern Cape, but the Orange River is at its most magnificent as it thunders

through the Augrabies Gorge, and plunges over its falls in a series of cascades.

To visit the spectacular Augrabies Falls, it is usual to join the great Orange River at Upington and follow its course for 120 kilometres through the riverside settlements of Keimoes and Kakamas to the Augrabies Falls National Park.

Upington revolves around the rich harvests of fruit cultivated on the banks of the river made arable by one of the world's most sophisticated irrigation schemes, and fertile by rich river silt. Thousands of hectares of sultana and sweet hanepoot grapes are cultivated along the southern river bank and two giant cooperatives process and distribute wine and dried fruit. Two other major products are cotton and dates – grown in sprawling plantations that lend a distinctly Eastern air to the region. The river island at Upington, Die Eiland, has a kilometre-long date palm avenue which is one of the most unusual national monuments in the country.

In contrast to the fertile lower banks of the river, Upington's northern landscapes change to red Kalahari dunes, which start eight kilometres outside the town on the road to Keimoes, 40 kilometres downriver. En route is Kanoneiland where grapes, lucerne, cotton and deciduous fruit grow abundantly under advanced irrigation methods.

The little town of Keimoes has a Victorian waterwheel which is still in use, and can be seen in Main Road, where there is also a tiny historic mission church. The graves of German soldiers killed in battle in the First World War are a national monument, located at the foot of a small hill four kilometres west of the town. Here too is a small nature reserve, Tierberg, which contains prodigious

numbers of springbok as well as winter-flowering aloes. From the lookout, there is a panoramic view across the irrigated, densely cultivated lands of the Orange River Valley.

The town of Kakamas, 80 kilometres from Upington, is located in one of the most fertile

RIGHT: THE ROSYFACED LOVEBIRD, *endemic to the woodlands and semidesert of the north-west.*
BELOW: THE AUGRABIES FALLS *in quieter mood.*

areas of the lower Orange River Valley. It was named Kakamas (poor pasture) by the Hottentots, before the wealth of irrigated water transformed the arid desert into an oasis. Kakamas is the site of a massive hydro-electric power station, but the town's most historic relationship with the river and its waters can be seen in the old canals, water-wheels and network of irrigation tunnels built by immigrant Cornish miners. Still farther west lies the scenically dramatic Augrabies

SOUND OF SILENCE

No less dramatic than the colours, textures and forms of the Northern Cape landscape is the immense stillness which envelops these great wilderness spaces. It is a healing silence, and one which cannot be heard above the invasive drone of an engine. This is where mechanical transport should be abandoned in favour of more traditional locomotion – on foot, on horseback or afloat on the majestic Orange River.

These are adventures made easy by organizations offering canoeing, rafting and 'paddle and saddle' combinations along the river reaches. Days are spent paddling downriver at a leisurely pace and nights under a canopy of stars. The practical business of camping is taken care of by professional guides.

The journey may start at Noordoewer (north bank), just across the Namibian border. Getting there involves a substantial journey by car, 800 kilometres from Cape Town or 1 200 kilometres from Johannesburg, or by charter flight organized by the river-rafting companies. Another option is to paddle from Goodhouse to the historic mission station at Pella.

After breakfast each day one paddles at a stately pace for about 25 kilometres – a five hour stretch – in canoes and inflatable rafts carrying two to six people. There are frequent stops for swims, photography, exploring the old fluorspar and copper mines and examining the extraordinary rocks and plants along the way.

Although summertime temperatures reach 40 °C or more in this desert wilderness, there is always a drift of cooler air on the river and paddling is painless.

The final stretch, along the Richtersveld's northern and eastern boundaries is particularly scenic with views of a stark lunar landscape and strangely adapted plant species. Ending at the confluence of the Fish and Orange rivers, about 250 kilometres from the mouth of the latter, the six-day trip covers 120 river kilometres. Return transport to Noordoewer is provided by local farmers.

series of turbulent rapids takes the river down a further 35 metres from the highest falls.

The park's indigenous flora includes the quiver tree or kokerboom, *Aloe dichotoma*, whose soft branches were used by Bushmen to make quivers for arrows. Drought-resistant aloes are among the most conspicuous plants throughout the park, but camelthorn, white karee, wild olive and tamarisk, and Karoo-boerboon trees are also found.

Baboons and vervet monkeys are abundant throughout the park, as are small antelope such as klipspringer. Small mammals abound, with the endearing meerkats or suricates one of the most common species. Their curious upright stance and bright-eyed curiosity delight visitors. On the north side of the river, which is not yet accessible to tourists – large game – including eland, springbok, kudu and black rhino – has been introduced.

One of the most pleasant ways of exploring the Augrabies Falls National Park is to do the three-day Klipspringer hiking trail through the major sights and landmarks of the southern area of the reserve. Although named after the nimble klipspringer, which leaps from rock to rock and scales virtually sheer cliff faces at high speed, the trail does not demand anything too arduous from hikers.

Falls National Park, which spans the Orange River and covers 80 000 hectares of semi-desert wilderness. The park has a rich variety of drought-resistant flora and over 40 species of mammals. But it is the spectacular Augrabies Falls that draws visitors here time and again, to the 'place of great noise' as the Nama people called it.

The Orange River seems to gather speed as it approaches the narrow channels along the gorge, accelerated by smooth slipways of granite. It is released in turbulent torrents of white water, plummeting into the ravine below, roaring like thunder as it goes.

The granite gorge is among the most spectacular of its kind on earth; its walls of black and grey have been polished by the passage of the water to a deep gleam. Visitors' look-out points are clearly and safely defined. South African author Lawrence Green wrote about the falls, describing 'mile after mile of gigantic rock faces, washed and polished by the floods of centuries, naked, slippery, steep and deadly'. Legend has it that a treasure of diamonds, washed out of the earth along the river's path, lies on the floor of the 130-metre deep pool directly beneath the falls.

Throughout the 18-kilometre length of the deep ravine, below the falls, striking rock formations show how, over many millennia, incalculable masses of rushing water have eroded the granite faces. A giant needle-shaped sculpture stands several metres high, like a primaeval monument, on one side; a

ABOVE: WEIRD-LOOKING KOKERBOME *are a common feature of the semiarid north-western region. Bushmen used the tree for making quivers.*

The great thirstland

Only the hardy survive this hostile, arid environment, which is one reason

why the Kalahari Gemsbok National Park, with its notable variety of plants

and animals, intrigues the tourist and is a focus of scientific scrutiny.

bok, followed by wildebeest, red hartebeest and the more mobile eland. The black-maned Kalahari lion is king of the park's large predator population, which counts leopard and cheetah as well as black-backed jackal, bat-eared fox, the brown and spotted hyaena, and tiny suricate, African wild cats, caracal and mongoose among its numbers.

The Kalahari's duneland formation is seen at its most striking from the air, with vast reaches of lateral, wave-like ripples in an ocean of red sand reaching from the equator south to the Orange River, and from Angola to Zimbabwe – more than 1,5 million square kilometres. This mantle is the world's largest

ABOVE: THE KALAHARI *Gemsbok Park's Twee Rivieren rest-camp offers fully equipped cottages.*
RIGHT: SPRINGBOK THREESOME *drink in unison.*

For roughly 40 000 years Bushmen were the sole human inhabitants of the Kalahari. With their bush-wise survival systems, they shared the sandy plains and isolated water pans with the animals and plants of this great wilderness, living in natural harmony. It took only 15 years for white settlers to decimate the animal population.

The first came in 1914, appointed as caretakers of a line of boreholes along the Auob River bed, sunk in anticipation of an assault on German South West Africa during the First World War. At the same time, a handful of agricultural land grants were issued. While these settlers battled to make a living, they hunted springbok and other antelope to supplement their meagre incomes and food stores, and game numbers dwindled alarmingly. The Kalahari Gemsbok National Park was born in 1931, as a strip of protected land between the Auob and Nossob rivers.

Additional land purchases and a management partnership with the adjacent Botswana National Park have today increased its effective size to 36 000 square kilometres – bigger by far than the Kruger National Park. It is one of the world's largest conservation areas. With no dividing fences, the animals are able to migrate freely between the two territories. Most numerous are the gemsbok and spring-

continuous stretch of sand. The only punctuation is provided by bleached river beds with their windmills, watering holes and camel-thorn trees, and here and there the scattered patches of the thousand salt pans which gave the Kalahari its name – derived from Kgalagadi (salt pans) in the Bushmen language.

There is no perennial water in the Kalahari Gemsbok Park – the Auob flows perhaps once every five years, the Nossob once every fifty. The rain comes sporadically, usually as a dramatic thunderstorm preceded by a blackening sky and ominous winds. The air is left fresh and welcome water lies in the river beds. More often, the skies are clear and this absence of cloud cover causes temperatures to rocket to 40 °C in summer and drop to a freezing -10 °C on winter nights. Even in midsummer, nights are cool, with a rise in humidity that allows plants to absorb moisture.

The dunes, river beds and plains of the Kalahari support shrub savannah vegetation interspersed with scattered trees, providing the animals with a surprisingly reliable and nutritious diet. One of the most common Kalahari trees is the witgat or shepherd's tree *Boscia albitrunca*. Often referred to as the 'tree of life', its leaves, flowers and fruit provide year-round fodder.

The camelthorn trees, *Acacia erioloba*, thrive in the two river beds, where they may grow to a height of 15 metres, rising above their dune-bound brothers, which exhibit stunted shrub-like growth. Camelthorns are slow growing, and they spend years developing complex root systems that probe deep beneath the surface sand to locate water before risking growth above the ground.

Desert plants

Where there are no dunes, as along the banks of the Auob and lower reaches of the Nossob, the sloping calcrete plains support only shrubby driedoring, *Rhigozum trichotomum*, and the silky white Bushman grass, *Stipagrostis uniplumis*. The dunes, however, host numerous grasses as well as blackthorn, *Acacia mellifera*, candle-pod acacia, *Acacia hebeclada* and brandybush, *Grewia flava*, which old-timers ferment to produce a powerful alcoholic brew called 'mampoer'. After rain, a short-lived blaze of colour lights the river beds and dunes as plants hurry to reproduce, flowering and going to seed in an incredibly accelerated cycle.

The most life-giving Kalahari plants are the tsamma melon and gemsbok cucumber, which have a 90 to 95 per cent water content and provide both food and moisture to insects, worms, birds, rodents, ground squirrels, porcupines and antelope. Jackals and other carnivores eat them too. For the Bushmen, they are often the only source of water for many months.

For plants and animals in the Kalahari, survival depends on extraordinary water-retention adaptations evolved over centuries of exposure to heat and moisture deprivation.

Even the process of excretion has evolved to minimize loss of water. Carnivores may drink the blood of their prey – but for herbivores such as antelope the problem is more complex. Gemsbok and other antelope have adapted by feeding mainly at night when moisture from plants is at its greatest.

BELOW: TWO OF THE FAMED *Kalahari black-maned lions quench their thirst at a waterhole.*
BOTTOM: TERRITORIAL MALE *gemsbok fight for dominance. These strikingly marked antelope are superbly adapted to semidesert conditions: they can go for long periods without water, obtaining moisture from succulents and other dryland plants.*

The glory of springtime

For most of the year the plains lie parched and panting. But beneath the sun-

burnt soil countless seeds of flowers and plants lie dormant until the rain brings

life – and then an explosion of colour as millions of flowers carpet the land.

The far-western Namaqualand region is characterized by immense stretches of semiarid, thinly vegetated plain punctuated by domed granite outcrops that gleam with strains of copper. The land stretches from the Orange River south to Doringbaai and includes about 1 000 kilometres of coastline, backed by a narrow strip of red and white sand known as the Sandveld, often mantled by a disturbing, dense mist.

In a region of searing summer temperatures and erratic annual rainfall, this mist is life-sustaining for an enormous variety of plants, many of which have had to produce some outrageous adaptations to survive. These are the members of the palaeotropical plant kingdom, and they make a massive contribution to the floral heritage of South Africa.

For the greater part of the year the plains lie panting. Nomadic Nama herdsmen retreat to their domed reed shelters, and even the

wild irises and lilies, the dazzle of mesembryanthemums, and the bizarre forms and flowers of succulents create an extravaganza of colour on the landscape, aggressively and without apology for the gaudy mix of pink, red, purple, orange and magenta.

The Namaqualand flowers create a spectacle that is at its best from mid-August to late September, and even October if the rains are late. The spring-flower season starts early in the south and moves northwards as the weather gets warmer. Tour operators post lookouts along the flower route to ensure that their travellers get the best sightings.

ABOVE: FARM BUILDINGS *near Nieuwoudtville.*
LEFT: A CORNER *of Namaqualand's Biedouw Valley.*
BELOW: GEOMETRIC TORTOISES: *unique to the drylands.*

hardy goats seek the thin shade of stalwart aloes. But beneath the sunburnt soil, the seeds of a million plants and flowers lie dormant – until the first drop of rain. Then, almost instantaneously, they push through the earth and the dehydrated wilderness is awash, flooded with lakes of colour.

The bold brilliance of the daisies, the pastel fields of pale

A sudden change in the weather can close the flowers for the day (they open only to the sun), and at any time an insidious, hot berg wind will bring the show to an abrupt end.

Many Cape country towns – Clanwilliam, Calvinia, Darling, Nieuwoudtville, Tulbagh, Caledon – have superb shows of spring flowers, but the drive from Cape Town 550 kilometres up the West Coast to Springbok and beyond takes in the finest flower country and some fascinating towns to boot. Along the first, coastal portion of the drive, there are widespread displays of typical Sandveld flowers, ephemeral varieties that show their bright faces for only a few short weeks each spring. They include daisies, nemesias, gladioli, ixias and moraeas. Among the ixias is a bloom, *Ixia viridiflora*, of a curious green that defies description – one of the few green flowers in the world – along with some species of the damp-loving genus *Disa*.

Living curios

Springbok, town of pioneers and prospectors, is the capital of Namaqualand and a convenient base for exploration either towards the coast, or the interior. Fifteen kilometres south-east of the town lies the 6 500-hectare Goegap Nature Reserve where 481 known plant species flourish. Typical succulents here

include the strange stone plants, or *Lithops*, with their bizarre adaptations. With uncertainty ruling their lives – annual rainfall can vary from 80 to 280 mm – these plants have evolved to withstand the most arduous conditions in the quest for survival. Some have immensely long roots that seek moisture deep in the earth. Others have superficial, broadly spreading root systems to absorb the moisture provided by dew. Many of the plants have lethal thorns or tough spiked stems; other protective mechanisms include fleshy branches that conserve moisture, and nonentities for leaves, the better to withstand dehydration from the air and blistering sun.

From Springbok, 145 kilometres more or less, along the course of an old railway line

LUNAR LANDSCAPES

The Richtersveld occupies the north-ernmost reaches of Namaqualand. At its very tip in a ragged protuberance outlined by the Orange River and neighbouring on Namibia is the Richtersveld National Contractual Park. Here 160 000 hectares of mountain and sandveld scrub have been set aside as a protected area after years of negotiation with the local Nama pastoralists. These stock-farmers have occupied the area for generations, and they will continue to do so, but they have now 'contracted' with the authorities to help maintain the land, its flora and its fauna as both an ecotourism destination and a national asset. In return they share in the park's resources, and benefit from the money and employment that tourism generates.

This is vast, stark and silent countryside with extraordinary lunar landscapes and unnerving plant adaptations such as the 'halfmens', *Pachypodium namaquanum*. A first encounter with a group of these 'plant beings' can be rather disconcerting: they bear an uncanny resemblance to a family group of extraterrestrials. They usually face north, towards the sun.

The Richtersveld is rich with flora and is reputed to have one of the highest concentrations of endemic succulent species in the world. With spikes, thorns, fleshy trunks and other survival tactics evolved over aeons, they thrive in their desert domain.

The kokerboom, *Aloe dichotoma*, is conspicuous on slopes and hilltops. Its pliable branches were once used by Bushmen to make arrow quivers, and it is also referred to as the 'quiver tree'.

Visitors are advised to be well prepared with water, first-aid equipment, vehicle spares and clothing to cope with this dramatic and challenging environment.

that carried copper to the coast, is Port Nolloth. This is the capital of the Diamond Coast, centre of the South African alluvial diamond industry where diamond dredging boats are a permanent presence offshore. Port Nolloth is a delightful desert port with clean beaches, safe swimming and excellent line- and lobster-fishing.

The northern boundary of Namaqualand is the great Orange River, eight kilometres wide in parts, extensively used for irrigation, with industrious settlements on its islands and along its green, cultivated banks.

RIGHT: THE FLOWER-GARLANDED *and fertile Olifants River Valley, southern boundary of Namaqualand and a region of wheat, fruit, wine and rooibos tea.*

Harbours and hamlets

A feast for the eyes is no empty cliché – the West Coast's springtime wild-flower

bonanza really does feed the senses. But there is also more robust fare: the rock

lobsters caught in the waters are said to be the best in the country.

What was for long the single province of 'The Cape' – now divided into three – is truly a Cape of contrasts, and nowhere is this more dramatically evident than in the differences between the east and the west coast areas.

The east, lapped by the benevolent waters of the warm Indian Ocean, is soft, green and pretty. The west, scoured and scrubbed for aeons by the chill Atlantic and its dour winds, is a hard place of herders and fishermen, shipwrecks and divers – and of the best lobster in the country. It has a remote and haunting beauty which, once seen, can never be forgotten. The term east and west coast is loosely used; the true West Coast starts immediately west of Agulhas, the southernmost tip of Africa, where the Atlantic and Indian oceans meet. Colloquially, however, the West Coast is the seaboard running northwards from Cape Point, and the wealth and variety of its birdlife, its wild flowers and excellent shellfish and other seafood bring seasonal visitors from north and south by the coachload during the spring and early summer months. In response, accommodation has been created in some unexpected and delightful locations, from fishermen's cottages to luxurious lodges – and natural assets have been given a new profile.

Taking pride of place in a region boasting extensive sanctuaries for marine and terrestrial flora and fauna is the West Coast National Park. Just 124 km from Cape Town, the park has at its core the lovely Langebaan lagoon, separated from the sea by a narrow isthmus with an old whaling station at the tip of the peninsula. The park is acknowledged by ornithologists as a truly significant wetland area and is one of the world's more important bird sanctuaries. The shallow lagoon comprises about one-third of the total area of the park, and has both an exceptionally rich food web and unusual clarity. These attributes are due in part to a tidal, salt-water system and the hard-working colonies of white clams at the lagoon's mouth which clear the water in the process of filter feeding.

At least 550 species of invertebrates provide a rich diet for the sandpipers, turnstones, sanderlings and other migrant waders.

BELOW: HARD-WORKING FISHING BOATS *rest up at Stompneus Bay on the western side of St Helena Bay.*

HARVESTING THE ATLANTIC

The dense beds of kelp in the cold Atlantic Ocean are the habitat of the West Coast rock lobster, *Jasus lalandii,* also known as spiny lobster, crayfish, and in Afrikaans, *kreef.* This valuable – and vulnerable – crustacean is the basis of a R100-million industry concentrated on the southern African coastline from Cape Town all the way to Lüderitz in Namibia.

Around the many small harbours of the area live communities of fisherfolk whose livelihood is threatened by the alarming decrease in the numbers of fish, and particularly rock lobster, in South Africa's coastal waters. Although strictly regulated, the rock lobster industry has seen a dangerous decline: from 10 000 tons a year in the early 1960s to 2 200 tons in recent years. Among the major causes of this shrinkage is a decline in black mussels as a food source for lobsters, and rampant poaching. According to some estimates, the numbers poached are almost as high as the legal fishing quotas.

To help conservation it is forbidden to take out lobsters between July and October when most females are in the reproductive cycle. They are fully protected in several areas along the coast; recreational fishing is limited, and a minimum size is stipulated each year at the same time as the annual quota is announced.

Overfishing of undersized breeding females, and sexually immature males and females, is a massive threat. Lobsters have an extremely long period of maturation. It takes 10 to 12 years for a male lobster to reach a carapace length of 75 millimetres, when it can be harvested, and while a mature female can lay up to 150 000 eggs a year, the survival rate is extremely low as the larvae are a sought-after food source for many other forms of marine life.

ABOVE: SALTED FISH *are hung to dry out.*
BELOW LEFT: THE COAST *hosts a myriad gannets.*

Locals smother the fish with a baste made with apricot jam before grilling, which produces an excellent colour and flavour. One of the many delightful restaurants is the Muisboskerm near Lambert's Bay. This unusual eatery is set in a beachside *boma* where guests feast on shellfish prepared and served out of doors.

The superb Sandveld potatoes grown in the area combine particularly well with snoek, tomato and onion to make the robust *smoor-snoek* – a popular South African dish which may well have originated in the fishing communities of the West Coast.

South Africa's seafood has long been taken for granted: for generations of fishermen harvesting the sea has been the traditional way of earning a living. The fruit of the ocean also provided an unlimited supply of food. But seafood has now become a precious resource, one that requires careful management to maintain the precarious balance between promotion and preservation. While the rock lobster harvest has dipped dangerously in the last few years, the demand for these delicious marine creatures continues to grow and a recently established West Coast seafood route attracts hundreds of visitors in season.

The route starts at the small fishing harbour of Yzerfontein near Cape Town, and will keep hedonists happy for 300 kilometres, all the way to northern Doringbaai.

Summer also brings tens of thousands of Arctic visitors including curlew sandpipers that breed in Greenland and Siberia. Several islands in the lagoon support various other resident species of seabirds – black-backed gulls, cormorants, jackass penguins and a large population of African black

oyster-catchers. At the entrance to the bay, Malgas Island teems with great numbers of cormorants and Cape gannets. The park offers excellent accommodation and facilities as well as nature education courses, hiking trails and boating excursions.

Along the West Coast, the meals on offer tend to the simple and hearty with the emphasis on seafood. Regional cuisine predominates and menus invariably include *lewer-in-netvet* (liver wrapped in caulfat); *heerbone* (white beans); and *veldkool* (wild cabbage), which is exclusive to the area. Snoek, a game fish caught on lines, is a dietary staple. A curious sight during the season is washing lines hung not with laundry but with fish. The snoek, bought daily from the boats, is salted and hung for a few hours to draw off excess water, then washed, patted dry and barbecued.

The Cape Peninsula could be described as no more than a rocky limb of land protruding into a wild ocean and begging for abuse from the elements; more often, this legendary Peninsula is described with great passion.

Fairest Cape and winelands

In describing the Cape Peninsula as the 'Fairest Cape in the Whole Circumference of the Earth' Sir Francis Drake may have been a little exuberant, especially for an Englishman. However, over the centuries, few visitors have not been captivated by its spectacular shores and dramatic mountains; by the richness and variety of its unique flora, and by the largesse of the food, wine and good hospitality offered by its inhabitants.

Presiding over the Peninsula is the mother city of Cape Town. Backed by the famous Table, which is frequently covered with a generous white cloth of cloud, the city welcomes all visitors. It also stands guard to the entrance of the capacious larder of the Boland (the 'highlands'), where a cornucopia of wheat, grapes and other fruit is grown in abundance and is matched only by the plentiful bounty that is offered by the Atlantic and Indian oceans.

For much of the year life proceeds at a sedate pace in Cape Town, but come summer, the city bursts into a frenzy of activity as tourists arrive, lured by the spectacular beaches and the proximity to the winelands.

The Cape, sometimes viewed as a colonial relic by the rest of the country, has a historic and cultural heritage made up of an intricate patchwork of influences. Most notable are those of the British, the Dutch and the Malay people, whose architecture, art, cuisine, customs and traditions have been carefully preserved over time.

The rest of Africa – the 'real Africa' to some – seems remote when viewed from the verdant vineyards and oak-lined avenues of the small world at the southern tip of the continent. Although one can hear a distant African drumbeat, the Western Cape, quite simply, dances to a different tune.

OPPOSITE: GILDED BY DAY and bejewelled by night, Clifton's beaches are strung along the western Peninsula shoreline close to Cape Town.

Table Bay, gateway to Africa

Portuguese navigator Antonio da Saldanha trudged to the summit of the flat-topped mountain that rose from the bay where he had anchored, and named it 'Table of the Cape'. The year was 1503.

Da Saldanha was the Cape Peninsula's first European visitor, but many were to follow. Portuguese and Dutch sailing ships called at Table Bay in the ensuing centuries, eventually giving way to great steamers and mailships. These, from the 1860s onwards, brought fortune-hunters to the diamond diggings and goldfields of the north; they also transported the leisured classes to the then new and exotic holiday destination of Cape Town. The once tiny 'Tavern of the Seas', so named for its early tradition of hospitality to seafarers, grew into a vibrant international city which today is home to more than 2,6 million people. Table Bay's status as 'Gateway to Africa', however, had become mainly symbolic by the late 1970s, as air travel largely replaced the unhurried option offered by ships. Now, 20 years later, luxury cruise liners have begun to call again: *Achille Lauro*, *QE2*, *Sea Princess*, and *Europa* to name but a few.

Heading into the wind

Table Bay has two distinct harbour areas: the Victoria and Alfred Waterfront, a new leisure and entertainment development clustered around the old Victoria and Alfred basins, and the commercial port, which comprises the Duncan and Ben Schoeman docks. More than 2,25 million tons of containerized import and export cargo pass through the latter each year, making Cape Town a major international container seaport.

South-east of the commercial harbour lies the breezy Royal Cape Yacht Club, which encompasses two basins and provides mooring for more than 600 yachts. This is the scene of many national and international yachting events: the three-yearly Cape to Rio Yacht Race in January; Rothman's Week Regatta each December; the Lipton Cup, South Africa's prestigious one-design keel-boat race, in August; and the BOC Round-the-World Single-Hander, which usually includes a call at the Cape on the first leg.

Preserving the past

In the past 50 years, Cape Town's harbour and Foreshore areas have been enlarged by massive land reclamation – held to be among the most extensive of its kind in the world – which has added 303 hectares of increasingly valuable real estate to the central business district. Strand Street, once so appropriately named, is today the start of a major south-bound freeway; buried beneath it lies the old Imhoff Battery, which stood before one of the Castle of Good Hope's bastions.

The Castle is a massive pentagonal fortress, and the oldest occupied building in South Africa. Its walls were once lapped by the sea, but it is now landlocked between the city

LEFT: A LUXURY LINER *at rest in Table Bay harbour, entrance to the Tavern of the Seas.*

ROBBEN ISLAND

BELOW: ONE OF THE HARBOUR'S *sturdy working craft.*
BOTTOM: A PAIR OF JACKASS PENGUINS. *Colonies of this endangered species find safe havens near Table Bay.*

The sorry history of South Africa's Alcatraz, spanning 350 years of human degradation and suffering, is ironically overshadowed by the recent liberation and subsequent rise to international prominence of just one of its inmates – Nelson Mandela. From June 5, 1963 until his transfer to Pollsmoor Prison on the mainland on April 7, 1982, Mandela was confined to the 5,2 square-kilometre island, just 9,3 kilometres north of the Cape Town suburb of Green Point.

When the first Dutch navigators entered Table Bay, they found the island covered with birds and seals, and named it Robben (seal) Island. Its geographical position suggested its use as a maximum security dumping ground for prisoners, and it was used as such by both Dutch and British authorities from the very early days.

In the 19th century Colonial Secretary John Montagu enlisted the prisoners held there as cheap labour for building roads and mountain passes in the Cape. He increased their numbers by confining to the island inmates of leper colonies and any person who was considered useless to Cape society, so that by 1846, inhabitants included '50 lepers, 50 lunatics, 150 chronic sick and paupers'.

Today, the island still houses 700 prisoners, as well as 500 prisons department staff and their families, but it is no longer a maximum security prison, and the official secrecy that for so long surrounded it has finally been lifted. Proposals to redevelop it have ranged from the purely outrageous to the commercial and practical. Tourists can now book a ferry passage and a half-hour bus tour. The tour includes a trip to a lighthouse, built on Minto Hill in 1864, a visit to the Herbert Baker Church of the Good Shepherd and a stop at a kramat, or Muslim shrine, which commemorates Malaysian and Indonesian prisoners banished to the island by the Dutch.

and the railway station. It nevertheless remains as much a landmark site as it was when, as home to the Dutch East India Company, it stood guard over the bay. Its designer, French engineer Vauban, also worked for Louis XIV; a moat and five bastions – named Buren, Leerdam, Oranje, Catzenellenbogen and Nassau, after the various titles of the Prince of Orange – are its outstanding features. Each day, as the noon gun is fired from Signal Hill, a military band plays in the lawned inner quadrangle.

The old stone-walled fort retains its military tradition by serving as headquarters for the Western Province Military Command. It also houses a military museum and a gallery displaying part of the William Fehr Art Collection. The gallery and the museum are open to the public, as are the dungeons that once confined slaves.

Adjacent to the Castle is the Grand Parade, Cape Town's oldest square, created in 1697 as a parade ground for the Castle garrison. Today the Grand Parade is an outdoor marketplace – most notably for flowers, fresh produce and fabrics – and a popular starting point for marathons and car rallies.

Mother of mountains

The 350 million-year-old massif of sandstone and shale, visible on a clear day from 150 kilometres out to sea, is an extraordinary natural feature. But it is more than that: Table Mountain is the very backbone of the Mother City, and is synonymous with the spirit of Cape Town.

ABOVE: CAPE TOWN CITY *nestles in a 'bowl' rimmed by the distinctively flat-topped mountain and its flanking peaks. Devil's Peak is on the left.*
BELOW: A BREATHTAKING *panorama unfolds on the cable-car ascent to the mountain's summit 1 000 metres above sea and city.*
OPPOSITE BELOW: LOOKING DOWN *on Lion's Head, the suburb of Sea Point and, beyond, Robben Island.*

For the early seafaring explorers, men weary from months at sea, its well-defined bulk was a welcome landfall. Its magnetism, it seems, is as strong for 20th-century visitors, many thousands of whom, every year, ascend the 1 086 metres to its summit by cable car.

Records show that 4 000 years ago, when the Khoisan (Bushman and Hottentot) people roamed alone in the Western Cape, the lower slopes of Table Mountain glittered with groves of indigenous silver trees (*Leucadendron argenteum*). The trees, largest and arguably loveliest members of the protea family, were brought to near-extinction by the Dutch settlers, whose slaves felled them for domestic firewood. After the slaves were emancipated in 1834, many of them continued to chop and sell the wood for a living.

More than a century later, another threat to the mountain's ecological balance was posed by the ever-increasing number of town houses which were creeping up its slopes in answer to the need for further accommodation. When the mountain was declared a protected natural environment and a national monument in 1957, it was none too soon.

Today numerous organizations protect its welfare, and five mounted conservation officers regularly patrol large areas, on the lookout for forbidden barbecues, unauthorized vehicles and illegal picking of protected indigenous species. If the South African Nature Foundation succeeds in the aims of its wide-ranging 25th anniversary campaign, Table Mountain, which is recognized as one of South Africa's most ecologically sensitive national assets, will be declared a World Heritage site.

The abundance of flora on Table Mountain is remarkable; within its 60 square-kilometre area are found 1 470 plant species – more than in all the British Isles. Most of these are classified as fynbos. The silver trees have

Some include a tour of historic sites, such as the romantic ruins of early Cape socialite Lady Anne Barnard's 200-year-old cottage in Newlands Forest, Cecil John Rhodes' carriage track to Constantia Nek from his former residence at Groote Schuur, and General Smuts' path to Maclear's Beacon.

Options for the adventurous include a 'hands-on' scramble up Lion's Head or a winding six-kilometre ascent up Devil's Peak.

Platteklip Gorge, a deep cleft on the north face, was the first recorded route up the mountain and is still regarded as the safest. The National Botanical Garden at Kirstenbosch is the starting point for two popular and relatively easy ascents to the Table – up Skeleton Gorge or through the steeper Nursery Ravine. From Cecilia Forest another path leads you to the top, where there are several picturesque reservoirs and the Waterworks Museum which houses the equipment used to build Cape Town's first major water storage dams in 1893.

Maps at the upper cableway station illustrate a series of well-marked, short and level walks on the summit, that present spectacular views of Lion's Head, Signal Hill, the City and the whole of the southern Peninsula. Besides offering the inexperienced tourist safe and accessible routes, these paths minimize trampling and erosion, and help to ensure the continued preservation of the natural environment.

PRIDE OF TABLE MOUNTAIN

The 'Pride of Table Mountain' is the showy red disa (*Disa uniflora*), an orchid that generally flowers between February and March. Once thought to be exclusive to Table Mountain, it is in fact fairly widely distributed in the peaks of the Western Cape, growing in damp, mossy places beside streams and waterfalls.

The red disa has been the emblem of the Mountain Club of South Africa since its founding in 1891, and it is also the flower of the Cape Province.

Multiflowered stems are also common; where the plants grow in clusters, the massed flowers are a breathtaking sight. The red disa is the largest of all South African orchids but is just one of 80 species in a genus whose flowers occur in a multitude of shapes, sizes and colours. The red disa itself varies in colour on Table Mountain, often occurring in a reddish-orange shade; a yellow form is also occasionally found.

been re-established in high groves (most notably on the slopes of Lion's Head) and are well protected by strict regulations. The mountain is also home to a wide variety of local fauna. There are baboons, porcupines and tortoises. Flocks of raucous guineafowl roam freely, occasionally wandering into the backyards of mountainside homes, and pushy rock rabbits (known locally as dassies), blatantly beg scraps from sightseers at the restaurant on the summit.

Pathways of pleasure

The most rewarding exploration of Table Mountain is on foot – for novices, preferably with an experienced guide, because the heights have their hazards. Walks are well chronicled in numerous books and are carefully graded in terms of suitability, ranging from easy rambles for the positively unfit to challenging expeditions for the superfit.

Walking through history

When Jan van Riebeeck arrived in Cape Town in 1652, he did not foresee that

the town he founded would soon overflow its allotted space; even by the late-

18th century the city was straining at the seams.

The rapid expansion resulted in a certain lack of formal urban planning in this nevertheless beautiful city.

One notable exception is St George's Mall, which has the impressive St George's Cathedral as a focal point at its southern limit. Entirely pedestrianized in recent years, it makes the ideal starting point for a meander through a city renowned for the architectural beauty of its oldest buildings. St George's Church is built on a site which was consecrat-

ed by the Bishop of Calcutta in 1827; it only became a cathedral in 1848. It is one of Cape Town's landmarks, having been, on many occasions, a haven of refuge and a site of political protest. Designed by Sir Herbert Baker in Edwardian Gothic style, it is built of golden Table Mountain sandstone, and has been extended and renovated a number of times over the years. Its rose window is worth more than a passing glance, and its choir sings like a flight of angels.

Diagonally across from it stands the Cultural History Museum, which traces the development of the social and cultural life of all South Africa's peoples. Previously used as the Supreme Court, it was originally built as a lodge to house up to 500 slaves of the Dutch East India Company. The upper floor was added in 1751 to provide offices.

Across the road from the museum, and crushed between an art deco office block and a busy street, is the Dutch Reformed Groote Kerk, which stands on the earliest consecrated site in South Africa. First inaugurated in 1704, it has been entirely rebuilt over the years but for its soaring steeple. The present structure was consecrated in 1841, and is notable for its pulpit, resting on a pedestal of lions, which was designed by Anton Anreith, the renowned German sculptor who left a legacy of superb architecture and craftsmanship in the Cape.

A few streets away one finds cobbled Greenmarket Square, once the venue for a farmers' fresh produce market, and now host to a bustling open-air craft market. The square has been dominated since 1755 by the Old Burgher Wacht Huis (Watch House), which, as its name implies, originally housed the Burghers' Watch, Cape Town's first constabulary. It subsequently served as the Burgher Senate and then as the Magistrates' Court. In 1840 it became Cape Town's first City Hall, until the new one was built in 1905 on its present location overlooking the Parade. None of the Wacht Huis's original interior remains, but it has been restored in the style of an old Dutch Guild Hall. The façade, however, has not changed since 1811, and still bears the City's coat-of-arms and plaster mouldings above the windows.

Palms and pilasters

In nearby Long Street attractively restored Victorian shops sell a bit of everything, from old books and antiques to second-hand clothing; a pair of leaning palm trees marks the site of a mosque built in 1777 by a freed Malay slave, Jan Buykies.

Other buildings of note can be seen a short walk away in Strand Street, where the recently restored Lutheran Church is flanked by Martin Melck House on one side and a beautifully proportioned building, now housing the Netherlands Consulate, on the other. The church, built by the wealthy merchant Martin Melck in 1774, masqueraded as a winestore until Lutherans were granted freedom of worship by the Dutch Reformed Church in 1780. Only then could Anton Anreith's magnificent

THE COMPANY'S GARDEN

The Company's Garden is a serene, six-hectare space in the historic heart of Cape Town. Well loved by the people of the city, it draws lunchtime strollers, amateur artists and soapbox orators. Its most popular meeting place is broad, shady Government Avenue, lined with 157 oak trees; some of those still standing today were planted in the late-17th century by former Cape governor Simon van der Stel, as part of his plan to stock South Africa with forests for timber.

Van der Stel's rows of oak saplings replaced the original avenue of apple and orange trees planted by Jan van Riebeeck, first commander of the Cape. On orders from the Dutch East India Company, Van Riebeeck, on arrival, had created an 18-hectare garden to supply fresh produce to passing ships. Within a year or two, large quantities of tobacco, maize, every imaginable vegetable and many kinds of fruit became readily available; one of Van Riebeeck's saffron pear trees, now more than 300 years old, still bears fruit each year.

Over the years the Garden lost 12 hectares to the expansion of thè city. Some of the buildings which stand on that land are: the Houses of Parliament; the State President's town residence, Tuynhuys; the South African Library; the National Gallery; the National Jewish Museum; and the South African Museum and Planetarium. The first to be erected was Tuynhuys, originally built in 1701 for Cape Governor Willem Adriaan van der Stel as a single-storeyed guest house. When Lord Charles Somerset used it as his main residence he closed the garden for his private use, causing an uproar in the town. He also made some ruinous alterations to the house. An exception was his grand white-and-gold ballroom which provided the venue for the coming-of-age ball in 1947 of Princess Elizabeth, now Her Majesty Queen Elizabeth II of England.

LEFT: RUST-EN-VREUGD, *a graceful 18th-century townhouse, contains part of the valuable William Fehr collection of rare prints and South African watercolours.*

pulpit be installed. The tower with three bells was also a subsequent addition, as were the pilasters on the church façade, designed by Louis Thibault.

Further down Strand Street is the magnificent 18th-century Koopmans-De Wet House, which, like most older Cape architecture, was originally single-storeyed. Thibault introduced the fluted pilasters when, at the end of the 18th century, the house was remodelled in Louis XVI style.

Buitenkant Street boasts the old Government Granary built in 1814, with Thibault and Anreith once more collaborating on the lion and unicorn embellishments on the façade, and the lovely old Cape Dutch town house Rust-en-Vreugd. The only example of Rococo style architecture surviving in South Africa, it flaunts Anreith's most exuberant entrance in a frieze of carved figures.

Victorian charm and modern glamour

The Victoria and Alfred Waterfront development in the historic Alfred Basin is

much more than a great tourist drawcard and money-spinner for Cape Town;

it has helped restore the city's links with the sea.

In the last 50 years, huge areas of land between Table Mountain and Table Bay have been reclaimed from the sea, increasingly separating the city from its harbour. The Waterfront has gone some way towards reversing this process; it has taken the first step on the way to re-establishing Cape Town as 'the Tavern of the Seas'.

What distinguishes the Waterfront from 350 similar developments throughout the world is that it is the only working leisure port where traditional harbour activities take place alongside quayside entertainments. By its expected completion in the year 2001, the development will cover 80 hectares of land, and will have cost an estimated R3,2 billion. Its initial expansion has focused on entertainment, retail and leisure facilities – there are almost 40 restaurants, three hotels and 100 shops. Future projects include office accommodation, residential apartments and loft studios, a 300-room international hotel, an aquarium, a further 12 000 square metres of retail space and extra parking.

Carnival air

Sensitive planning has ensured that new structures are architecturally integrated with the predominantly Victorian style of the original harbour buildings, many of which have been converted for commercial use. The infamous Breakwater Prison now houses the University of Cape Town's Graduate School of Business, and the old North Quay Warehouse is a luxury hotel, with soft furnishings offset by a framework of industrial beams and bulkheads.

The Waterfront attracted six million visitors in its first year, 1991. This figure almost doubled – to more than 10 million people a year – within two years. The crowds are drawn by the perpetual carnival feeling and

CAPE TOWN'S VICTORIA AND ALFRED WATERFRONT *redevelopment scheme has transformed the 19th-century dockland into a highly imaginative fantasia of hotels and bistros, pubs and nightclubs, theatres, cinemas, markets, museums and marinas, promenades, walkways and waterways.*

the variety of entertainments on offer. Street artists and buskers add to the holiday mood, while more formal theatrical events are staged at the popular Dock Road Theatre, the V & A Waterfront Theatre and a small open-air amphitheatre.

Rich and varied aromas emanating from colourful cafés and restaurants beckon passersby to cool, shady interiors or to inviting quayside tables, with magnificent views overlooking the harbour.

Trips and flips

The Waterfront is a consumers' mecca, with speciality shops at one end of the spectrum and fascinating indoor arts and crafts markets displaying exotic wares at the other.

Visitors can enjoy a helicopter ride, or take a trip on a catamaran, a luxury yacht, or a harbour cruiser. They can also experience a short voyage back in history on the 'penny

FORGOTTEN FEATURES

Less prominent than the SA Maritime Museum or the *Victoria* museum ship are several reminders of less sophisticated times. One of these, the Robinson Dry Dock, built in 1870, has the distinction of being the oldest working dry dock in the world. Another relic is the elegant clock tower that features on so many postcards. A part of the Port Captain's former office buildings, it has a magnificent mirrored room from which the port captain could survey his domain from all angles. The clock tower and the nearby time-ball tower on Portswood Ridge were important aids to accurate timekeeping for early mariners. The latter, built in 1894 and one of the few of its kind remaining in the world, had to be elevated several times over the years, as new buildings threatened to obscure it.

Near the tower stands a dragon tree (*Dracaena draco*) which bleeds red resin. Although over 100 years old, this specimen is a mere sapling compared to those in Tenerife, its native country, which are reported to live for over 1 000 years.

TOP: MANY OF THE WATERFRONT'S *speciality shops have found a home in converted dockyard buildings.* ABOVE: THE WATERFRONT *functions as a worked-in, lived-in area as well as a fun place; fishing boats mingle with leisure craft along the quaysides.*

ferry'. The ferry first came into service in 1871 to transport harbour staff across the Cut, the original entrance to Alfred Basin. For those with nautical interests, there is the SA Maritime Museum, and the beautifully restored ship *Victoria*, where varied artefacts from ships wrecked on the treacherous Cape coast are displayed.

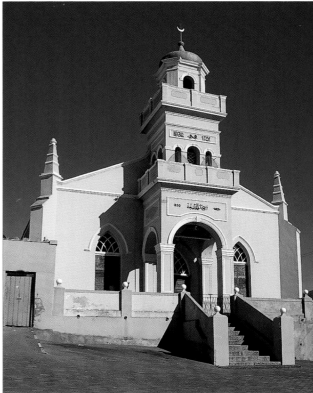

ABOVE LEFT: CAPE ARCHITECTURE *of the 18th and 19th centuries is preserved along a cobbled Bo-Kaap street.*
ABOVE: MOSQUES AND MINARETS *in the Bo-Kaap; the faithful are summoned to prayers five times a day.*
OPPOSITE PAGE: SARTORIAL SPLENDOUR *distinguishes these painted minstrels. The annual New Year's parade is a vibrant mix of music, dance and colours.*

Bo-Kaap and beyond

The Bo-Kaap ('upper Cape Town') is a living showcase of the traditions

of the city's Muslim community, whose skills, customs and religious beliefs are

woven into the social, cultural and economic fabric of South Africa.

The first members of this close-knit community were slaves, often talented craftsmen imported from Java and other Indonesian islands by early settlers. They were later joined by high-born political exiles, who were banished to the Cape by the Dutch after their conquest of Java and Sumatra in 1694. Their numbers continued to increase over the years, and they became increasingly valued for their fine craftmanship, which were making a solid contribution to the development of the young country. There was relatively little intermarriage with other groups over the centuries, and the present community has maintained a strong sense of identity, which, however, owes less to a common 'Malay' heritage than to the unifying force of Islam.

A corner of the East

Once enabled by the abolition of slavery in 1834 to own property, many of Cape Town's early Malay residents settled in a tiny district a short walk from the Heerengracht (Gentlemen's Walk), now Adderley Street. They bought the little flat-roofed terraced houses built in the 18th and early-19th centuries, which until then had been occupied by European artisans, and began to erect their own mosques. In due course the area became known as the Malay Quarter. They set up small businesses as carpenters, cabinet-makers, fishermen, tailors, spice merchants, coopers and retailers. Many passed on their homes and stores to their children; some Bo-Kaap properties have been occupied by the same family for generations.

There is a strong sense of community in this district; the narrow, cobbled streets, the picturesque, pastel-painted houses, and the cries of the *bilal* summoning the faithful to prayer from the minarets are typical everyday images here, all bringing to mind some distant corner of the East.

Not all Malay people settled in the Bo-Kaap. Many bought properties in other areas of the Peninsula and some went even further afield. Not all the moves were voluntary, however; under the former apartheid regime, in the name of 'urban renewal', a large number of Cape Town's longest-standing citizens were relocated from their homes in District Six on the lower slopes of Table Mountain to bleak new Cape Flats settlements.

Desolate for many years, District Six is at last being redeveloped with affordable housing and will once again become a natural extension of the suburbs of Salt River and Woodstock, where generations of Malay people have lived and worked.

Adding spice

Of all the fine culinary traditions to have come to South Africa through history, none has exerted a stronger and more lasting influence as that inherited from the Malay settlers.

In fact, what is generally referred to as 'traditional Cape' cuisine has borrowed liberally from the Eastern use of spices and exotic blends of ingredients. It includes dishes such as bobotie and breyani, curries and bredies, served with traditional Malay accompaniments: atjars, sambals and blatjangs.

Truly authentic Malay cuisine can only be found at a few restaurants. One such is Biesmillah, in the Bo-Kaap, where, according to Islamic tradition, no alcohol is served, and the delicious food more than justifies a visit.

Holy circle

Just above the Bo-Kaap, on Signal Hill, sits one of a series of six kramats that surround Cape Town in a 'holy circle of Islam'; the others are at Faure on the Cape Flats, on Robben Island, at Macassar, Oudekraal and Constantia. Each is the burial ground of a Muslim holy man, although the Signal Hill kramat also enshrines several *tuans*, or men of rank. The Faure kramat is the resting place of Sheik Yusuf, founder of the South African Muslim community – an imam, a prince and one of the most important of the political exiles banished to the Cape by the Dutch.

It is believed that Muslims who live within this sacred circle will be protected from natural disasters. However, should the kramats be destroyed or moved, evil will befall the entire community.

COON CARNIVAL

New Year celebrations in Cape Town would be incomplete without the rowdy, gaudy Coon Carnival. The carnival, a singular Cape tradition, starts on New Year's Eve, when troupes congregate in Adderley and Wale streets and march in procession through the city until 'Tweede Nuwejaarsdag' (second New Year's Day, 2 January). At the height of the festivities, streets are cleared and thousands of supporters line the routes to shout encouragement above the din of the bands, as the colourfully clad Coons make music, dance and sing in an exuberant display of sheer exhibitionism.

After several preliminary rounds, a final judging of songs and costumes takes place at two large sports stadiums.

Each troupe has its own identity, and carnival preparations begin months in advance; new songs, dances and costumes have to be devised. The latter have only one objective – to dazzle. Trousers are made of silk or satin and are trimmed with vertical stripes. Jackets are often sequined in silver or gold; brightly trimmed straw hats or brollies – or both – complete the costumes. Indispensable troupe mascots – small, beaming boys bursting with pride – are dressed identically to the rest of their troupe. In traditional style, all faces are painted with multi-coloured masks which tend to melt and slip by the end of the day's frenetic activity.

Beautiful coastline

The Cape Peninsula, only 70 kilometres long as the crow flies, features about

150 kilometres of scenic coastline sculpted into a myriad bays, bights and

beaches, each with a distinct character.

Some are almost deserted but for fishermen and divers; others are famed for surfing, skiing and sailing. There is a beach for nudists; there are family beaches, singles beaches, cold-water beaches and warm-water beaches; beaches for horse-riding and ones for dog-walking.

Clifton, Camps Bay, Llandudno, Sandy Bay and Hout Bay all lie on the western coast of the Peninsula, where sea temperatures are distinctly chilly. This is partly due to the prevailing summer south-easter, a wind that blows the surface water away, causing much colder water to well up from the depths of the ocean. Generally speaking, these beaches are renowned for their turbulent seas and breathtaking sunsets. By contrast, the waters off the eastern side are considerably warmer. This is the reason why most of the beaches in False Bay, including Fish Hoek, St James and

Boulders – where Jackass penguins strut about freely – are popular family beaches. Miller's Point, Seaforth, Glencairn – they all offer safe, warm-water swimming, as well as spectacular sunrises.

In summer these qualities attract thousands of sun-seekers to Muizenberg, where many of the old stately seafront mansions and hotels have been converted into holiday flats in recent years. The beach, so beloved by Rudyard Kipling ('White as the sands of Muizenberg, spun before the gale'), attracts surfers and swimmers.

Atlantic splendour

The coastal drive which heads for Clifton from the city meanders along the beachfront to Sea Point, a densely populated area with a Riviera-style promenade overlooked by high-

ABOVE: SEA POINT'S HIGH-RISE *ocean frontage is a popular venue for Capetonian promenaders.* BELOW: SUN, SEA, SAND *and boulders entice the quieter holidaymaker to secluded Llandudno.*

rise apartments. Here a large public swimming pool is frequented by bathers who don't want to be bothered with sand between their toes. Just a block from the beachfront is a buzzing shopping area crowded with boutiques, fast-food kiosks and restaurants of every ethnic variety. At the far end of Sea Point, the drive winds along the coast, past some of the most expensive real estate in the country. The closer one gets to Clifton, South Africa's St Tropez and shrine to the body beautiful, the more lavish the apartment blocks and houses become. In high summer, the narrow road is jammed with cars, and the 'famous four' beaches of Clifton are crammed with trendy sun-worshippers; private yachts lie anchored nearby.

The palm-lined beach at Camps Bay is a better choice for the claustrophobic. Lying at the foot of the Twelve Apostles (a chain of distinctive buttresses running at right angles

RIGHT, ABOVE: HUNDREDS OF SPECTATORS *converge on Camps Bay beach to watch rubber duck racing.*
RIGHT, BELOW: CLIFTON'S FOUR *famous beaches, much favoured by the beautiful people.*

to Table Mountain), it has a Florida feel emphasized by the beachfront architecture.

Camps Bay runs into Bakoven, where building development comes to an abrupt halt and the drive opens up to an unspoilt coastline of extraordinary beauty. At the crest of a long hill a sudden side-road leads down to exclusive Llandudno, where the seriously wealthy reside in luxurious homes, set among huge smooth boulders, with uninterrupted views of the Atlantic. The beach below, although not large, is often wind-free and is a good choice for sunset picnics.

The Llandudno car park is the starting point of the one-kilometre walk through spectacular fynbos to the nudist beach of Sandy Bay. Although the Bay has attracted some less-than-favourable publicity in its time, devotees proclaim it a fine stretch of sand, untainted by commercialism, with good swimming and plenty of space for everyone.

The spectacular Chapman's Peak Drive starts at Hout Bay and continues past the Peninsula's longest and most windswept beach – Noordhoek's Long Beach, hangout of

Back on the coastal drive, a final twist reveals Hout Bay lying below, with its fishing-village atmosphere and beautiful bay. Ever-popular with yachties and board sailors, the town has boomed considerably in the last few years, reflecting the ever-increasing demand for coastal accommodation in a scenically magnificent setting.

surfers. The road then continues to Kommetjie, with its pretty tidal pool and outlying beds of kelp that offer rewarding crayfishing.

Further on, the Cape of Good Hope Nature Reserve has no shortage of spots for swimming and fishing beneath its craggy cliffs, but broad, beautiful Buffels Bay is probably the most popular family beach.

A living from the sea

Kalk Bay in the east, Hout Bay in the west and Table Bay itself have one thing

in common: each is a lively commercial harbour and the base of a thriving

community of fishermen who put fresh fish on restaurant tables.

The three bays each provide shelter to a fleet of fishing vessels, which every day set out to catch the silvery haul on which they rely for their continued existence.

The Kalk Bay way

The superb local linefish served in the majority of Cape restaurants is landed at Kalk Bay, a picturesque little harbour on the False Bay side of the Peninsula. When the catch comes in, Cape Town's chefs and restaurateurs, savvy housewives and Kalk Bay villagers line up to buy, and, depending on the season,

they go home with one or more of a dozen varieties of fresh linefish. Around June and July for instance, snoek are landed here in large quantities.

Time has moved so slowly in Kalk Bay that some locals still conduct their transactions in 'bobs', 30 years after the introduction of decimalization in South Africa.

On the beach and at nearby Fish Hoek, other fishermen land their catches with 'trek' nets. They secure one end on shore, and row out to sea with the other – following signals given by a lookout on the hill behind – to capture shoals of mullet (haarders), horse

mackerel (maasbankers), and sometimes yellowtail. There is never a shortage of hands when it's time to drag the weighty haul back onto the beach, and then every available container is filled and immediately carted off to the roadside or to the nearest marketplace.

Kalk Bay (lime bay) was so-named because locals produced lime for painting buildings here, by excavating seashell quarries and burning the shells in kilns. The ruins of the kilns can still be seen on the hill above the village. The bay was also a whaling station for a short while, and recent excavations for a new jetty have exposed whale ribs and other artefacts, recalling a time when the mammals were harpooned from long boats.

Spirit of independence

Hout Bay lies in a deep inlet on the west coast of the Cape Peninsula, guarded by a towering peak in the east and a brooding rock formation, known as the Sentinel, in the west. The Sentinel is among Cape Town's most impressive natural attractions, best admired from vantage points along the breathtaking 10-kilometre coastal drive round Chapman's Peak, or, better still, from the deck of a launch out at sea.

ABOVE: COMMERCIAL FISHING *boats in Hout Bay.*
RIGHT: KALK BAY'S *usually colourful quaysides on a wild winter's day.*

CATCH OF THE DAY

Delicious local linefish is a speciality of the Cape; when fresh it needs little more than a brief spell under the grill and a lemon wedge to raise it to unsurpassed heights of gastronomic excellence. As it constitutes a best-selling menu item, chefs compete fiercely for the pick from the 'catch of the day' and locals begrudge the large quantities flown to Johannesburg daily. A few major Cape hotels and restaurants go as far as chartering their own fishing boats to secure fresh supplies.

Depending on the season, 'catch of the day' may be red roman, yellowtail, red or white steenbras, Cape salmon (geelbek), elf, kob (kabeljou), musselcracker, hottentot, silver fish, snoek, stumpnose or tuna.

Although South Africa's national fish, the galjoen, is classified as a linefish, it is seldom seen on restaurant menus. Once abundant in South African coastal waters, the galjoen (named after the stately Spanish sailing vessel, which it resembles) is now rigorously protected by strict size limitations, and a season which is closed from early October to the end of February. There are those who consider its distinctive, slightly gamey flavour and marbled, black-veined flesh gourmet fare, and those who dislike it, but all anglers agree that fishing or spearfishing for galjoen provides a fine sport. The fish feeds close inshore, particularly in white water around wave-smashed rocks, where a rich supply of titbits is stirred up from the ocean floor.

rub shoulders with charter boats that take visitors on seal-spotting trips to Duiker Island. Last but not least there is the minesweeper of the Hout Bay 'navy'. In a tongue-in-cheek publicity stunt a few years ago, Hout Bay declared itself an independent 'republic' and issued its own passports.

A la Portuguese

In a small corner of busy Table Bay Harbour, about 80 brightly coloured, diesel-driven, wooden fishing boats lie at Collier Jetty in the Alfred Basin. Their owners are Portuguese fishermen who came to Cape Town from Madeira 30 to 40 years ago. Some of them pull up only rock lobster, for just three weeks a year; others chase whatever is running – tuna, swordfish and snoek – and stop only in winter. A fish run, communicated by radio through an elaborate system of coded messages, brings an urgently assembled crew to the quayside; minutes later the boats chug out into the wide waters of the bay, bound for Cape Point and St Helena Bay, following the birds who, like the predatory snoek, are in pursuit of surface shoals. The catches are off-loaded at Fish Quay and are then distributed to markets in the Victoria and Alfred Waterfront and to city wholesalers. In recent years many of the sons and grandsons of these elderly Portuguese fishermen have abandoned commercial fishing for more sophisticated pursuits, and the future of this little fleet is by no means assured.

ABOVE RIGHT: THE SPECTACULAR SENTINEL *massif guards the entrance to Hout Bay.*
BELOW: THIS BRONZE LEOPARD *has overlooked Hout Bay beach for more than 30 years.*

Although Hout Bay is a major commercial fishing centre, especially for snoek and rock lobster, it retains a village air. Colonies of writers and artists have settled here, drawn by its tranquillity and natural beauty. A flourishing tourist industry has developed around its fishing activities, and harbourside curio shops and boutiques, seafood restaurants and fresh fish and lobster outlets are a mecca for weekend trippers. The harbour is crowded with vessels of all shapes, sizes and vintages: old wooden fishing boats painted in bold primary colours are moored next to trawlers; rows of expensive yachts

Kirstenbosch National Botanical Garden

In 1895 Cecil John Rhodes bought Kirstenbosch, a 152-hectare farm, as a first step towards his dream of preserving Devil's Peak and the eastern slopes of Table Mountain as a national park. On his death in 1902, he left the land to 'the united peoples of South Africa'.

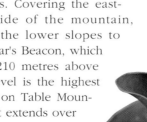

Today what has become Kirstenbosch National Botanical Garden is enjoyed by people from all over the world. The site draws more than 400 000 visitors a year, vying with Table Mountain for first place as Cape Town's premier natural attraction. Lying at the foot of the towering Castle Buttress, in the main catchment area of the Liesbeeck River, the garden has a plentiful water supply, derived from the streams that flow from Window, Skeleton and Nursery gorges. Covering the eastern side of the mountain, from the lower slopes to Maclear's Beacon, which at 1 210 metres above sea level is the highest point on Table Mountain, it extends over an area of 528 hectares – only 36 of which are under cultivation. The best known of South Africa's eight national botanical gardens, it was the first in the world to showcase only indigenous plants, and today boasts more than 6 000 different species.

Botanical research

Kirstenbosch was selected for its present role in 1913, when it was officially declared the first National Botanic Garden of South Africa. Its aims were to promote the study, preservation and cultivation of indigenous flora. Initially, scientific research was confined to the Compton Herbarium, which now contains more than 250 000 specimens. Extensive

nurseries, glasshouses and research laboratories have since been added. There is a comprehensive botanical library and a lecture and exhibition hall. The offices of the Botanical Society of South Africa are also based here.

The continuous work and research that is carried out at Kirstenbosch is critical to the maintenance of the fragile ecological balance of South Africa's environment; in addition, scientists are doing valuable exploratory work in the field of the curative properties of many indigenous plants and flowers.

At the same time, the garden remains a place to be enjoyed by everyone. Although it is delightful in any season, it offers particularly spectacular floral displays in springtime. There are a variety of walks, carefully

ABOVE: THE GARDEN, *with its woodlands and 9 000 different kinds of flowering plant, is a much-favoured venue for school outings.*

planned to suit all tastes and needs. The Stinkwood Trail caters for the very young or the not-so-fit; the Yellowwood and Silvertree trails are ideal for those wanting to explore the mountain slopes. A Fynbos Walk was opened in 1993, as part of the garden's 80th birthday celebrations.

A fragrance garden and a Braille trail have been laid out for the sight-impaired.

Crafts and concerts

A further point of interest is provided by the shady Dell, where a natural spring is encircled by an attractive, bird-shaped sunken bath, built in the early 19th century by a Colonel Bird, and popularly but incorrectly known as Lady Anne Barnard's bath.

Kirstenbosch's annual calendar of events includes regular craft markets, flower shows, varied educational programmes, November's early evening 'Firefly Walks' and the four-month-long summer season of Sunday sunset concerts. The concerts are attended by large appreciative audiences who sit on the lawns with picnics and enjoy a wide range of local musical talent in the glorious natural surroundings. There is a sale of indigenous seeds and plants every March, and a small nursery is open all year round. Customs certificates are provided for purchases which are to be taken abroad.

FYNBOS: FLORA EXTRAORDINAIRE

The Cape Floral Kingdom, richest of the world's six floral kingdoms, yet smallest in area, is of enduring interest to botanists worldwide and a conservation priority for South Africa. Supporting 8 500 species of plants – of which 7 300 are classified as fynbos – this tiny plant principality is of vital significance.

Fynbos, literally meaning 'fine bush' (a reference to the fine-leaved form of many of the shrubs), includes proteas, restios (reeds) and ericas (heaths), as well as irises, daisies and lilies. In the daisy family alone, there are 1 000 species. To survive climatic hazards – notably summertime drought – the plants have adapted to their habitat by developing leathery leaves, thick bark and underground bulbs or rootstocks. Although fynbos is dependent on fire every 15 or 20 years for regeneration, more frequent mountain blazes have threatened many species with extinction. Urbanization, alien plant invasions and encroaching agriculture are other menaces.

Much of the Western Cape's fynbos is in full flower during the region's 'Green Season' (April to October), and one can admire it in the numerous reserves and parks that lie just an hour's drive away from the centre of metropolitan Cape Town.

This is also a splendid season for ornithologists, as the colourful blooms attract a kaleidoscopic array of birds.

Hiking trails through fynbos territory take visitors into historic country villages, private reserves and farmlands. Many reserves have picnic and camping sites; some offer more permanent accommodation.

The Helderberg Nature Reserve at Somerset West, the Harold Porter Botanical Garden near Betty's Bay, the Fernkloof Nature Reserve at Hermanus, the Villiersdorp and Hottentots Holland nature reserves, the Caledon Nature Reserve and Wild Flower Garden – as well as the Kirstenbosch National Botanical Garden – are just some of the ideal destinations for viewing this fynbos wonderland.

Historic suburbs

The Cape Peninsula's southern suburbs, linked by a series of scenic highways, were once a string of villages sprawled along the foothills of the Table Mountain range. Several display legacies of one of the Cape's most influential men: the financier, politician and visionary Cecil John Rhodes.

The road follows the folds of the mountain around the bulge of Devil's Peak to meet the northern boundary of the magnificent Groote Schuur Estate, once the property of Cecil Rhodes. Below it sits the vast complex of the Groote Schuur Hospital, where the pioneering surgeon, Professor Christiaan Barnard, performed the world's first human heart transplant.

A few kilometres further on, the late-18th-century Mostert's Mill stands proudly on the corner of Rhodes Avenue. Originally built for grinding wheat, it was restored in 1936.

Dominating Rhodes Drive from the slopes of Devil's Peak is the imposing Rhodes Memorial. Cecil Rhodes loved to walk and ride here, and perhaps the many contour paths which start from this point follow the same routes he took on horseback. The memorial, built in 1912, ten years after his death, was designed by his great friend, the architect Sir Herbert Baker. It is an impressive

monument built of granite hewn out of Table Mountain rock. Eight bronze lions guard a flight of steps leading to an imposing neoclassical temple which contains a bronze bust of Rhodes. A towering equestrian statue by the British sculptor GF Watts, entitled 'Physical Energy', stands in front of the building. Overlooked by Rhodes Memorial are

TOP: ONE OF WYNBERG VILLAGE'S *many charmingly restored Victorian cottages.*
ABOVE: THE IVY-MANTLED CAMPUS *of the 12 000-student University of Cape Town, South Africa's oldest tertiary seat of learning. The backing heights are part of the magnificent Table Mountain complex.*
LEFT: WATTS' IMPOSING EQUESTRIAN FIGURE, *titled 'Phyical Energy', surveys the fashionable suburb of Rondebosch from Rhodes Memorial.*

some of the ivy-covered sandstone buildings of the upper campus of the University of Cape Town. Built on a commanding site set aside by Rhodes for the purpose, they form part of the country's oldest university.

A kilometre or two further east, a lone sentry guards the entrance to the grounds of the Groote Schuur manor house. The mansion was Rhodes' former home, and today serves as the official residence to South African heads of state. It contains valuable manuscripts, artworks, tapestries and *objets d'art* bequeathed by Rhodes to the nation.

To the east of the Groote Schuur Estate is the 'village' of Newlands, which has the reputation of being one of the wettest districts in Cape Town. It is also the home of a cricket stadium and of a rugby stadium, where major national and international sporting battles are waged. Standing at the entrance of the rugby grounds, surrounded by beautiful old oak trees, is Josephine Mill, built in 1848 and

Cape Town's last surviving watermill. Besides housing a fascinating rugby museum, a shrine to 'white' South Africa's national game and its heroes, the mill is also the headquarters of the Cape Town Historical Society.

Adjacent suburbs, such as Mowbray and Rondebosch, having developed as they did from open rural areas, are the natural locations for excellent golf courses, while

Kenilworth is home to a racetrack, venue for 'The Met', the Cape's premier racing event.

Further east, Wynberg's 'Little Chelsea' area retains a village atmosphere with its streets of exquisitely preserved and restored Cape vernacular and Victorian buildings. Another

prime attraction of this charming suburb is Maynardville, a public park where a colourful charity community carnival takes place every year. In the park there is also an open-air theatre where Shakespearean productions are staged in the summer.

GROOT CONSTANTIA

The grandest and oldest of the Cape's wine estates, Groot Constantia lies no more than a 20-minute drive from the heart of Cape Town.

The land on which it stands was granted to Cape governor Simon van der Stel in 1685. He made the 770 hectares his retirement estate, living there for 13 years until his death in 1712. In the intervening years he created an idyllic farm in the shelter of the Constantia mountain, with large areas of land under vine. The deep, cool soil produced abundant harvests which, combined with meticulous methods of harvesting, pressing and general hygiene, resulted in a much-sought-after 'Governor's wine'. The wine was exported to Europe, where it found its way to the tables of royalty. In Batavia the only criticism it received was that there was too little of it.

On his death the original Van der Stel estate was divided into three independent wine-producing farms: Groot Constantia, Klein Constantia and Buitenverwachting. Today each has a magnificent Cape Dutch homestead and produces a distinctive cellar of exclusive world-renowned wines.

Groot Constantia had an eventful history after 1712. It was bought by Hendrik Cloete in 1778, who employed the Cape's leading architect, Louis Thibault, to design a fine cellar, and commissioned Anton Anreith to add some finishing touches to the homestead – exuberant bacchanalian reliefs, which drew criticism for their 'prurience' from the prudes of the day.

Some 90 years later the vines in Groot Constantia fell prey to the tragic phylloxera epidemic which decimated vineyards throughout the world, and the Cloete family were forced to sell the estate to the

Colonial government. For almost 50 years after that, Groot Constantia was an educational and experimental wine farm.

In 1925 a massive fire all but destroyed the property. The magnificent homestead, one of the finest examples of early Cape Dutch architecture, was quickly rebuilt, and the priceless period furniture replaced, largely through gifts and donations, to re-open as a public museum in 1927.

Once described as an 'architectural phoenix', Groot Constantia has risen from the ashes of relative obscurity to bask in glory as one of the country's greatest treasures and national monuments.

Cape of Good Hope Nature Reserve

The widely held belief that Cape Point is the meeting place of the Indian and

Atlantic oceans is a myth. The real rendezvous, oceanographers contend, takes

place at desolate Cape Agulhas, the southernmost tip of Africa.

Knowing this in no way diminishes the impact of one of the Peninsula's most spectacular natural features. A lookout site at the very tip of Cape Point, perched on the highest sea cliffs in the country, offers unforgettable views of the turbulent sea far below; a 'dividing line' of foam is also clearly visible from here, lending strong credibility to the theory of it being the meeting point of the two oceans. In fact, this line of foam is created by the notorious Cape south-easter, the wind which, on its way to the Equator, howls towards and hits the mainland, whipping up the water in its wake.

Such is the magical attraction of these waters that yet another tale is connected to them at this point: the curse of the *Flying Dutchman*, according to which a sea captain is destined to haunt them with his vessel until the end of time.

Natural abundance

The massively imposing promontory of Cape Point constitutes the southern boundary of the 7 750-hectare Cape of Good Hope Nature Reserve. The reserve is a triangular piece of land defined by Schuster's Bay on the western coast, and Smitswinkel Bay, an inlet on False Bay, on the east. It has about 40 kilometres of ruggedly dramatic coastline, and close inspection shows it to be a conservation site of great ecological importance.

The interior offers interesting topographical features. There are few trees, but enormous floral diversity: the local fynbos includes over 1 114 varieties of plants, of which the restio (reed) species predominate. In September and October the spring flowers are a delight.

Reptiles such as snakes (a few of them poisonous) and tortoises live among the shrubbery, and the rare Cape platanna (*Xenopis*

gilli) is safeguarded in this protected habitat. Many of the larger animals in the reserve – antelope and mountain zebra – are not easily seen except by patient observers prepared to wait. In any case, this is not strictly antelope country: fynbos has too low a nutritional value to support large herds. Other mammals, notably the inquisitive and sociable chacma baboon, have always roamed the area, and are often seen combing the beaches. Most importantly, nearly 250 species of land- and seabirds have been recorded here, ranging from land-bound ostriches, to cormorants to minuscule sunbirds.

TOP: A LESSER DOUBLECOLLARED SUNBIRD *probes for nectar among the fynbos vegetation of the nature reserve.*
ABOVE: CAPE POINT *(foreground) and the backing nature reserve are among the region's prime tourist attractions.*

On the north-western coast of the reserve – in one of the few areas out of bounds to the public – a breeding sanctuary for black oystercatchers has been established, to safeguard future generations of this shy species.

Cape of storms

The Cape of Good Hope Nature Reserve is open throughout the year and has generous areas allocated to fishing, picnics and barbecues. In spite of the fact that a large number of tourists visit it in the summer, there is always enough space for everyone. Safe bathing can be enjoyed in the tidal pools at Buffels Bay and Bordjiesrif, two beautiful inlets on the False Bay side. Excellent fishing – for snoek and yellowtail among others – is to be had at Rooikrans.

Walking trails and picnic sites have been developed, and whale-watching points and viewsites are well signposted. A little field museum and an information centre are housed in one of the few remaining old farm cottages of the area, built from blocks of local sandstone held together with lime.

ABOVE: TOWERING CLIFFS RISE *up from the chilly and often storm-tossed Atlantic Ocean at the tip of the Cape Peninsula. It is off Cape Point that The Flying Dutchman, the ghost ship of seafaring legend, has occasionally been sighted, most notably by a future King of England.*

CHACMA CHARACTERS

The chacma baboons found throughout southern Africa are the largest of the baboon species. With their very long, narrow muzzles and dark, heavily browed eyes, they have a serious and intelligent air.

Despite being valued by conservationists, who regard them as integral to the natural environment, and by the promoters of ecotourism, the numbers of chacma baboons of the southern Peninsula are dwindling. Regional conservation groups identify feeding by humans as the greatest threat to their survival.

Encroachment by building development has put tremendous pressure on the baboons' habitat, reducing it to a core area on the Table Mountain chain, which includes the Cape of Good Hope Nature Reserve. Unfortunately, it is here that they are fed by well-meaning visitors.

Hand feeding disturbs the animals' natural feeding patterns. Once accustomed to human contact, and tempted by the proximity of easily obtained food, the baboons sometimes boldly venture into residential areas bordering the reserve, to forage in backyards and kitchens. Many are shot. The fortunate ones are trapped by conservationists and relocated on the reserve. While baboons are naturally adaptable in their feeding patterns, the reserve's population is thought to be unique within the primate world for its foraging habits: crustaceans, molluscs, sea snails and other intertidal organisms supplement their otherwise largely vegetarian diet.

Scattered around the reserve are monuments erected in honour of early seafarers. One in particular is dedicated to Bartolomeu Dias, who, in 1488, made the first recorded rounding of Cape Point. Dias's apt name for the Point was 'Cabo Tormentosa' (Cape of Storms), and yet, although the eight-metre-high waves, gale force winds and submerged reefs have claimed many lives over the centuries, it also often shows a serene face.

An intrepid early visitor, on reaching Cape Point by oxwagon more than a century ago, was so profoundly moved by its majesty that she wrote, 'The outlook over sea and land was glorious ... the many-coloured mountainous cliffs, with every depth of shadow on their faces, the foam-flecked sea, the land barren but beautiful ... one's sense of freedom and intoxication, the result of the loveliness of the scenes and God's glorious oxygen, fresh and pure.'

LEFT: SEAFORTH BEACH *at Simon's Town is lapped by the blue and inviting waters of False Bay. The town and its dockyards have been intimately associated with both the Royal and the South African navies for nearly two centuries.*
BELOW: A REGAL FIGUREHEAD *surveys the tranquil gardens of Admiralty House.*

preserved old buildings that line the main street and serve as naval offices and lodgings.

A concentrated taste of the social and naval history and architecture of Simon's Town can be enjoyed by ambling along the 'historic mile' from the station to the east dockyard gates. Some 40 landmarks, many of them gracious buildings dating back to the mid-18th century, line the route. One of the most important is Admiralty House, which has been the headquarters of British and South African naval leaders since 1809; it stands on the site of the first land grant made in Simon's Town in 1743.

Safe anchorage

Another house of note is The Residency in Court Road, which has a history of inappropriate additions and alterations that only ended when it was taken over by the Simon's Town Museum. It was built in 1777 as a winter residence for the Governor of the Verenigde Oostenryke Companje at the Cape, Simon van der Stel. Van der Stel had first surveyed the protected bay in 1687 and had declared it a safe winter anchorage for ships of the Dutch fleet. In accordance with his habit of naming places after himself, he had called it Simon's Bay. However, it was only when ship repair and victualling facilities were established in 1743 that Simon's Town began to grow in earnest to become the Cape's third official settlement. The storehouse is one of the oldest buildings in the town. One of the

Naval traditions

A morning hooter summons dockyard workers, and practice shots blast from the

Lower North Battery – they are the regular reminders of Simon's Town's status

as base of the South African Navy and important naval training centre.

Simon's Town has a special flavour, a salty blend of Victorian seaside village and bustling naval base. Comfortably nestled between two protective buttresses of the southern Peninsula mountain chain, the town occupies a small world of its own just 36 kilometres south of Cape Town.

The business of the town and the navy proceed in happy proximity. From the yacht club and town pier, flanked by naval dockyards, private yachts and fishing boats freely come and go; in the docks or out in the bay, naval frigates lie at anchor amid surfaced submarines and commercial tankers. For security reasons, however, 'happy snaps' are forbidden: none of the naval buildings, vessels or dockyard areas may be photographed. Unfortunately this includes many of the well-most curious landmarks is probably Bay View House, built around 1803. The house has been occupied by a succession of Simon's Town's harbour masters, but it was once also a post office. This probably explains why whole walls of the first-floor rooms have been papered with postage stamps, individually applied and varnished over for posterity.

ABLE SEAMAN JUST NUISANCE

A life-sized bronze statue of Simon's Town's greatest celebrity, Able Seaman Just Nuisance, occupies pride of place in Jubilee Square.

He stands on a rock in typical Great Dane pose, relaxed but alert, ears slightly pricked, eyes intently scanning the bay. His naval cap, which by Admiralty orders he was excused from wearing, lies between his front paws.

In the 50 years since his death, the life and times of this great black dog – the only canine ever to be officially enlisted in the ranks of the Royal Navy – have been documented in a television series and in countless articles and books.

When his owners, Mr and Mrs Benjamin Chaney, were transferred to Simon's Town in 1939, the two-year-old Nuisance took to the navy like – a dog to water. He and his brother Bats nosed round the ships and the shore base, making friends with all they met. While Bats did voluntary service as a guard dog at the Royal Navy Hospital, Nuisance rode the suburban trains – he insisted on accompanying the ratings on trips to and from Cape Town, never leaving the city station until the last young 'square rig' had safely boarded.

South African Railways officials, enraged that he travelled free of charge, regularly threw him off the train and, after a battle lasting several months, threatened to put him down, at which point there was such a public outcry that the Admiralty intervened, and made sure the dog was equipped with a permanent, complimentary railway ticket. They also officially enlisted him in the Royal Navy: on August 25 1939 he became Able Seaman Just Nuisance.

From the time he first arrived in Simon's Town, until he died in April 1944, Just Nuisance travelled thousands of kilometres with the naval ratings of wartime Simon's Town. In many ways, this pedigreed Great Dane was a giant among dogs.

TOP: PANORAMA OF BAY AND HARBOUR. *Simon's Town is a mecca for yachtsmen and watersports enthusiasts, and for sun-worshippers drawn to its broad white sands.*
ABOVE: SIMON'S TOWN MUSEUM *is housed in the two-centuries-old Residency.*

For many of the visitors who come to Simon's Town, history matters not a jot as they head for its glorious beaches. During the summer months the little town, with its quaint atmosphere and Riviera climate, is subjected to at least as much tourist pressure as the rest of the Cape, but it is well equipped to cope. Its real distinction, say residents, lies in the fact that the local pub is the southernmost watering hole in the Peninsula.

Stellenbosch, heart of the winelands

When Simon van der Stel, in the late-17th century, instructed the newly settled burghers to plant vines in the Eerste River Valley, he laid the foundations for an industry which has brought world renown to all of South Africa.

On his arrival as commander at the Cape in 1679, Van der Stel decided that emergency measures were needed to save the settlement at Table Bay. The climate wreaked havoc with crops in the Company's Garden, and food was constantly in short supply; increasing numbers of dispir-ited settlers were returning home. It was with the primary aim of raising stock and boosting supplies of wheat that Van der Stel granted the burghers farms in the valley of the Eerste River; the vines were almost an afterthought.

More than three hundred years later, Stellenbosch lies at the heart of a region that produces 280 individual wines. The region has a number of micro-climates, and has contrasting growth environments: granitic soils on the mountain slopes and sandy soils in the lower areas. It is therefore ideal for the production of both red and white wines from the very best grape varieties.

Many mansions

The town itself is one of the most beautifully preserved in the country, with magnificent examples of Cape Dutch architecture. The old village centre contains 60 buildings that are declared national monuments. Four of these are carefully restored homes, with cool rooms redolent of lavender and linseed; they have been furnished to various levels of sophistication to reflect the town's development, and together they make up the Village Museum.

The Stellenryck Wine Museum in Dorp Street is another stop that should be on everyone's tour agenda, whereas the Van Ryn Brandy Cellar at Vlottenburg and the Oude Meester Brandy Museum on the Old Strand Road are interesting for their collections of

ABOVE: STELLENBOSCH'S *Dorp Street, lined by stately oaks and beautifully restored historic houses, ranks among the country's loveliest thoroughfares.*
RIGHT: ONE OF THE MORE ELEGANT *of the Cape's country houses is Libertas, outside Stellenbosch. Privately owned, it is noted for its fine furnishings and wall paintings. The medallions here depict the seasons.*

GLORIOUS GABLES

The Cape gable displays extraordinary levels of versatility, creativity and craftsmanship. The earliest surviving example, with its simple, curvilinear shape, dates from 1756, and is found at Joostenburg near Stellenbosch.

Later Cape gables became ever more bold and elaborate, with complex coils, splits, scrolls and powerful knots. Simple edge mouldings evolved into elaborate volutes; triangular and semi-circular caps put in an appearance, and urns adorned the top of pilasters.

All these embellishments create a constantly changing interplay of light and shade across the gable face – they were seen as a status symbol which reflected the prosperity of the home's owners.

In the late-18th century the Dutch Renaissance gable gave way to an Italian Renaissance-style gable with distinctly Baroque elements. The enduring 'halsgewel', of which the Groot Constantia gable, c.1793, is an excellent example, was developed during this period. A similar gable frames the entrance to the 'dakkamer' (room on the roof) of the Lutheran Parsonage in Cape Town.

In the interior of the Cape, charming regional variations bear witness to unskilled labourers' interpretation of city fashions. A case in point is the 'holbol' or Prince Albert gable which appears throughout the Karoo. It has convex-concave outlines topped with round or pointed caps and sometimes has horizontal 'string courses' which divide the gable face into upper and lower sections.

There are also the gables of Swellendam, which are straight-winged, and those in Worcester and Ceres that have short, simplified wings with square corners.

provide convenient bicycle-props for the 13 000 or so students of the town's university. The campus has overflowed into all aspects of village life, and the façades of many of the oldest buildings display numerous advertisements for student accommodation alongside their bronze plaque of the National Monuments Council.

Enduring estates

There are 18 wine estates and five big co-operatives, all open to the public, within a 12-kilometre radius of the town. It was in this area, in 1971, that South Africa's first wine route was established. Since then, many of the beautiful old Cape Dutch homesteads on historic wine estates have been restored and converted for commercial use, thereby ensuring their preservation for future generations. Some of them have been purchased by wealthy international buyers. One such estate is Neethlingshof, first farmed in 1692. The estate has benefited from the input of vast resources: vineyards have been replanted with noble varieties, and a restaurant has been developed in the restored homestead.

Twelve years after his arrival in the Cape, and in recognition of his services to an ailing colony, Simon van der Stel was promoted to the rank of Governor. If he could only see Stellenbosch now!

BELOW: TAKING TIME OUT *to enjoy country-town hospitality in one of Stellenbosch's pavement cafés. Among the most historic, and most charming, of the venues is D'Ouwe Werf, a hotel that started life in 1710.*

brandy stills, bottles and glasses. Oude Libertas, an open-air theatre and wine centre on the outskirts of town, is a popular gathering place which offers a varied season of ballet, opera, drama and music in the summer, as well as wine tastings and cellar tours throughout the year.

Oaks of old

Stellenbosch is an orderly town, as is pleasingly evident in the formal layout, generous open spaces and serene, oak-shaded avenues. Many of the European oaks are still the original ones planted under the direction of Simon van der Stel or his son Willem in the 17th century; the beautiful avenue formed by the trees in Dorp Street is one of the best preserved in the country.

It therefore seems appropriate that the country's oldest European oak should stand on nearby Vergelegen, the former estate of Willem Adriaan van der Stel. Successive owners of the property have gone to great lengths to preserve the ailing tree: its heart has been hollowed out, lined and reinforced with steel struts, allowing a dozen people to stand upright within its cool interior.

The generously proportioned boles of the oaks that line so many Stellenbosch streets

The Cape winelands

In the last few decades, the South African wine industry has greatly expanded and has seen many innovations. Burgeoning wine routes in the manner of the French Routes du Vin and German Weinstrassen have increased the general public's awareness of this great national asset.

TOP: VINEYARDS STRETCH *to the far hills of the Drakenstein range in the fertile Paarl-Franschhoek segment of the winelands.*
ABOVE: THE FAMED WINES *of Nederburg mature in elaborately carved oak casks.*

The Cape's winelands are well patronized, and not only by foreign guests. Capetonians themselves are regular and enthusiastic visitors, and for many the arrival of an out-of-towner is often excuse enough to take off yet again for one or more of the nearby wine routes. The great pleasure of buying wine at a favourite estate or remote co-operative, preferably after having sampled a few vintages, is further enhanced by the obligatory stop for a leisurely lunch under the oaks of one of the magnificent estates or beneath the vines of a country restaurant.

There are five wine-growing regions in the Cape Province, and 10 districts fall within these regions, spanning a very wide area. Vineyards thrive in the cool coastal regions of the south-west Cape; in the blazing, dry heat of the Little Karoo interior; up the West Coast and across the Swartland; at Piketberg in the Sandveld and along the banks of the Olifants River. However, the oldest wine-growing region of the country, Constantia, lies just 20 minutes' drive from Cape Town.

Scenic routes meander through most of the winelands, and excellent accommodation is available in all these districts, where comfortable bed-and-breakfast establishments vie for custom with elegant restored manor houses where fine cuisine is the order of the day.

As one would expect, the dramatically diverse climatic and soil conditions in which South African grape varieties are grown yield a correspondingly wide range of wines. The Stellenbosch, Paarl and Constantia regions are the most versatile, producing an astonishing variety of vintages that encompasses rich, fortified wines, racy dry whites, very drinkable rosés and some of the country's greatest reds. The estates around Stellenbosch in particular are renowned for producing many famed wines. The town hosts the headquarters of the Stellenbosch Farmers' Winery (SFW), the country's largest wine co-operative, which produces a multitude of popular labels.

However, it is Paarl, a picturesque town overlooked by three great granite domes and embracing the Berg River, that is regarded as the headquarters of the South African wine industry. It hosts the Koöperatiewe Wynbouers Vereeniging (KWV), the world's largest cellar complex. Brandies as well as fortified and natural wines are produced in the vast vats of this co-operative.

An annual wine auction, first held at the Nederburg estate in 1975, has become the premier event of the South African wine calendar. It attracts almost 3 000 local and international wine-buyers. To add to the region's prominence, in recent years Paarl wines made from the chardonnay, sauvignon blanc and cabernet sauvignon varietals have won several top awards.

Some distance north of Paarl lies the beautiful valley of Tulbagh, where summer daytime temperatures approach 40˚C. To safeguard the fruity aroma and flavour of the grapes grown in this region, the innovative winemakers at the local Twee Jongegezellen estate have taken to harvesting in the cool of the night, by torchlight.

The town of Tulbagh, restored to its pristine perfection after being shaken by a severe earthquake in 1969, possesses the country's highest concentration of national monuments

ABOVE: A RUSSET CARPET *of autumnal vines covers the lush basin of the Hex River Valley.*

THE FRENCH CONNECTION

About 200 French Huguenots, fleeing religious persecution and civil war in their own country, arrived at the Cape between 1688 and 1690. Simon van der Stel, who was governor at the time, settled them in the Groot Drakenstein and Franschhoek valleys.

Some of these immigrants were familiar with general wine-making methods and procedures, and they brought refinements to the viticultural practices of the Free Burghers. Within a few generations, the Huguenots were socially and culturally integrated into their new homeland, and little

trace of their origin remained except for their wine-growing skills and the names of the estates in the valley: L'Ormarins, La Motte, La Provence and others.

Today, the Huguenot Museum at Franschhoek (shown below) is visited by remote descendants from far and wide, anxious to trace their genealogy.

French wine-growing traditions are proudly upheld by the Vignerons de Franschhoek, a society formed by the area's 14 producers, that includes such famed estates as Boschendal, Plaisir de Merle, and Bellingham.

– gabled and thatched Cape Dutch houses, surrounded by lush, immaculate gardens, sedately line the delightful Church Street.

South of Paarl, near Hermanus, lie Africa's most southerly vineyards. Their grapes benefit from fresh coastal breezes, yielding a fine pinot noir and other elegant red wines in the Burgundian style.

East of Paarl, the Breede (or Breë) River area around Worcester is recognized for its superior brandy and is responsible for having popularized colombard table wines. Rain is scarce this far inland, and it becomes even scarcer as one travels further east into the Little Karoo. This hot region of low rainfall (though it is well watered by rivers) is fast gaining a reputation for its ports, which have been likened in quality to those produced in Portugal's Douro Valley.

Finally, cheerful, everyday table wines are produced in the warm, dry West Coast area. They are as unpretentious as the region's hospitable people.

Although it was Simon van der Stel who formalized and expanded the wine industry in the late 17th century, it was the ever-resourceful Jan van Riebeeck who made the first Cape wine in 1659. His diary records thanks to God for the first pressing: 'muscadel and white round grapes – with a very good taste.'

Hermanus: the whale trail

It is a rare sight anywhere, and one least expected on this sunny coast of Africa, where holiday homes tumble all the way down to the shore. It is a close view of whales just beyond the ocean's breakers.

It's surprising how many trails seem to lead to Hermanus. This little coastal town, close to Africa's most southerly point, draws its visitors from all over the world, visitors who return time and again to savour its delights. And among the most regular of callers, journeying thousands of miles from the far, frozen south, are the mighty whales.

It may be as early in the year as May or June that the whale crier sounds his trumpet of dried seaweed to announce to the town that the whales have returned. His billboard displays the best viewsites and recommends certain times of the day, and soon tourists and townsfolk alike line the cliffs that overlook the blue arc of Walker Bay.

The first sighting they have of these large visitors is often the column of vapour and expelled air that a whale blows on surfacing, up to a height of five metres, or perhaps it is

ABOVE: THE ROCKY SHORES *of Walker Bay.*
BELOW: THE TOWN WHALE CRIER *alerts whale-watchers with a billboard and a horn of kelp.*
BELOW LEFT: THE OLD HARBOUR, *once a thriving fishing port and now a 'living museum'.*

the lazy wave of a fluke, majestic in its massiveness and grace. It is the southern right whale, recognizable by its great black bulk sprinkled with white markings along its back and underside. Individual animals weigh as much as 100 tons and measure up to 18 metres in length, but, supported by the sea, they move with delicate ease. Whales may be seen all the way round this southernmost tip of the continent, most often from Die Kelders in the east to as far as Saldanha on the west coast. But it is Walker Bay that has the distinction of being one of the 13 prime whale-spotting sites in the world, and one of the very few in the southern hemisphere. In Hermanus, southern right whales come in close, in pairs and in

small family groups, to court and to mate, to calve and to raise their young. Sometimes there are humpbacks, too, distinguished by the dorsal fin, absent on the southern right whale, and their long, tapering flippers, which are usually whitish underneath. The humpback is smaller than the southern right whale, and is black or grey in colour, with a lighter underside. Both species have been classed as 'vulnerable', and are protected by

an international treaty. South African legislation confers further protection on them: to approach a whale closer than 300 metres is against the law, and if one should surface next to your boat, the onus is on you to remove yourself. Locals have also thrown their weight behind the conservation effort by vociferously opposing attempts to offer visitors close-up whale-watching trips.

It's all a far cry from the days when boats put out, not to watch whales, but to kill them. The old whaling stations and whale-catchers, at nearby Betty's Bay and at Donkergat, are rusting and derelict. Although the hunting has stopped, whales still have considerable commercial value: their presence gives Hermanus a winter tourist season that almost extends to the summer holidays.

Fynbos finery

The town's other attractions include its setting of sandy beaches, low cliffs and a coastal mountain range covered with the immensely varied vegetation of the Cape floral kingdom. Fernkloof Nature Reserve is among the prides of Hermanus. Rising in elevation from around 60 metres to more than 840 metres, it has a wealth of flora that includes 50 species of erica as well as surviving pockets of the old indigenous forests hidden in cool, moist ravines. At least 40 kilometres of footpaths can bring visitors close to it all.

In the mailship era that ended in the 1970s, every disembarkation at Cape Town included its complement of wealthy travellers headed towards Hermanus. They were known as 'swallows', these visitors who pursued summer in its course up and down the latitudes. Even today, a walk through the centre of the town in the south-of-France-atmosphere of high season is likely to show a famous face or two. An off-season stroll through the residential areas, though, will reveal the surprising fact that more than one-third of the properties are holiday homes, occupied for perhaps no more than a month every year.

Most of their owners hope to retire to Hermanus, and perhaps to take daily pleasure in a walk along the cliff path. The path runs from the new harbour in the west, through the town and past the old harbour — now a picturesquely evocative, and informative, open-air museum.

WHALE TALK

The southern right whales return every year between the end of May and early July to the friendly waters of Walker Bay to mate and give birth to a single calf, after a gestation period of about a year.

These great mammals of the sea are the largest creatures on earth – and among the least aggressive.

Their exuberant behaviour has been classified into component gestures which form the basics of whale 'language'.

- *Breaching*: leaping from the water in an arching back-flip and falling back again; indicates play and communication.
- *Grunting*: like a whale 'roar' that can be heard up to two kilometres away.
- *Lobtailing*: slapping the tail flukes on the surface.
- *Spyhopping*: 'standing'

vertically with head and body, as far as the flipper, above the surface; allows the whale to obtain a clear view of its surroundings.

- *Blowing*: exhaling through the blowholes on surfacing; the southern right blow a V-shaped stream. They can remain under water for up to 90 minutes before returning to the surface to 'blow'.

Abakwetha (male initiation ritual), 105
Abel Erasmus Pass, 60
Addo Elephant National Park, 113
African National Congress (ANC) 24
  reconstruction and development plan, 32
  resistance, 25
African people
  main groups, 27
  traditions, 26
Agriculture, 31
Agulhas Current, 13
Albasini, João, 54
Amabutho regimental system, 94
Anreith, Anton, 150-1
Apartheid, 25
Arniston, 126
Atlantic Ocean, 12-3
Augrabies Falls National Park, 136-7
Australopithecus africanus, 44

Bain, Thomas, 132
Baker, Sir Herbert, 40, 150, 162
Barber, Graham, 65
Barberton, 61, 65
Barnato, Barney, 135
Bathurst, 113
Battles
  Blood River, (1838), 23, 78,
  Colenso, (1899), 79
  Isandlwana (1879), 79
  Magersfontein, (1899), 135
  Majuba, (1881), 79
  Rorke's Drift, (1879), 79
  Spioenkop, (1899), 79
  Talana Hill, (1899), 79
  Tugela River, (1879), 79
  Ulundi, (1879), 23, 79
  Vaalkrans, (1899), 79
Benguela Current, 12, 15
Berg-en-Dal restcamp, 57
Bhaca people, 77
Bushmen, 21, 26
  rock art, 73

Big Hole, Kimberley, 135
Birds, 20, 101
  Wilderness area, 121
Bisho, 106
Bloukrans massacre, 78
Blyde River, 64
Blyde River Canyon, 60
Blydepoort Trail, 62
Boeresport, 29
Bontebok National Park, 127
Bourke's Luck Potholes, 61
Bo-Kaap, 154-5
Bredasdorp, 127
British Kaffraria, 106
British Occupation, 22
British settlers, 77
Anglo-Zulu conflict, 1879, 79
Buffalo, 57
Bulawayo (Zulu royal kraal), 95
Bushveld vegetation, 11
Button, Edward, 64

Cango Caves, 123
Canoeing, 83

Orange River, 137
Cape Agulhas, 13, 126
Cape gable, 169
Cape Malay people, 154-5
  culinary tradition, 155
Cape of Good Hope
Nature Reserve, 157, 164-5
Cape Padrone, 13
Cape Peninsula, 144
  beaches, 156
  southern suburbs, 162
Cape Town, 144, 147
  historic buildings, 146, 150-1
  historic sites, 151
Castle of Good Hope, 146-7
Cathedral Peak, 70
Cathkin Peak, 70
Cedarberg, 15
Cetshwayo, (Zulu king), 79
Chacma baboons, 165
Chapman's Peak Drive, 157
Chromium, 30
Church of England, 81
Ciskei, 106
  see also Eastern Cape
Climate, 10
Coal, 30
Coelacanth, 107
Colenso, 79
Company's Garden, Cape Town, 151
Comrades Marathon, 83
Coastal reserves, 13
Coon Carnival, 155
Cradock Kloof Pass, 125
Crayfish, *see* Rock lobster
Cricket, 29
Crocodile, 19
Crocodile Bridge restcamp, 57
Cullinan, Sir Thomas, 44
Cycads, giant, 60

Da Gama, Vasco, 88
Da Saldanha, Antonio, 146
De Hoop Nature Reserve, 127
De Kaap Valley, 61
De Kuiper, François, 54
Desert vegetation, 11
Diamonds, 23, 30, 44, 134-5, 141
Dingane, (Zulu king), 23, 78, 81, 95
Dingiswayo, Nguni king, 94
Dinosaurs, 69, 72
Disa uniflora, 149
Discriminatory legislation, 24-5
Dolphins, 91, 93, 111
Donkin, Sir Rufane, 111
Double Drift Game Reserve, 109
Drakensberg, 14, 60, 66, 70, 82
  geological history, 72-3
  passes, 71
  rock art, 73
Drakensberg Boys' Choir, 70
Duiwelskloof, 60
Dunn, John, 86
Durban, 79, 84, 87
  aquarium, 91
  port, 88-9
  seafront, 90-1
Dutch East India Company, 22

Dutch settlement, 22
Eastern Cape, 106, 112
  territorial conflict, 23
  see also Ciskei, Hogsback, Transkei
Eastern Transvaal, 50-65
  see also Lowveld
Echo Caves, 61
Eckstein, Hermann, 41
Economy, 30-3
  informal sector, 32
Election (1994), 25
Elephant, 18, 57
Elizabeth II, Queen of England, 71
English immigrants, 102
Eskom, 30-1
Eureka City, 65

Farewell, Francis, 86
Fernkloof Nature Reserve, 173
Fishing industry, 159
Fish kraals, Kosi Bay, 101
Fitzpatrick, Sir Percy, 55
Forest Falls Hike, 63
Forestry, 50, 119
Forest vegetation, 11
Fortuna Mine Trail, 63
Funduzi Lake, 60, 62
Fynbos, 11, 161
Fynn, Henry Francis, 86, 89

Game animals, 17-8, 52, 101, 137-8
  'Big Five', 57
  extermination programme, 96
Game parks/reserves, 17
  Addo Elephant National Park, 113
  Augrabies Falls National Park, 136-7
  Bontebok National Park, 127
  Double Drift Game Reserve, 109
  Hluhluwe-Umfolozi Game
  Reserve, 18, 96-7
  Giant's Castle Game Reserve, 70-1
  Golden Gate Highlands National
  Park, 66, 69
  Greater St Lucia Wetland Park 98-9
  Inyati Game Park, 53
  Itala Game Reserve, 97
  Kalahari Gemsbok National
  Park, 138-9
  Karoo National Park, 17
  Londolozi Game Reserve, 53
  Makuya National Park, 62
  Mala Mala Game Reserve, 53
  M'Bali Game Reserve, 53
  Mkuzi Game Reserve, 97
  Motswari Game Reserve, 53
  Natal Drakensberg Park, 74
  Ndumu Game Reserve, 101
  Phinda Resource Reserve, 97
  Pilanesberg National Park, 45, 49
  Royal Natal National Park, 71, 74
  Sabi Sabi Game Reserve, 53
  Sabie Game Reserve, 55
  Tembe Elephant Park, 101
  Timbavati Reserve, 19
  Tsolwana Game Reserve, 109
  Ulusaba Game Reserve, 53
  West Coast National Park, 142
  Wilderness National Park, 121

Gandhi, Mohandas, 87
Garden Route, 114-20
Gardens
  Kirstenbosch National Botanical
  Garden, 160-1
  Margaret Roberts Herb Centre, 45
  National Botanical Garden,
  Nelspruit, 63
Gardiner, Allen, 86
Geology, 14, 72
George, 124
German immigrants, 102
Giant's Castle Game Reserve, 70-1
Giraffe, 19
God's Window, 61
Goegap Nature Reserve, 141
Gold, 23-4, 30, 36, 50, 64-5
Golden Gate Highlands National
Park, 66, 69
Gold Nugget Trail, 63
Gold Reef City (museum), 39
Gondwana, 10, 72
Grahamstown, 112
Great Escarpment, 10, 14, 50, 60, 66
Great Trek, 23
Greater St Lucia Wetland Park, 97-9
Groot Constantia, 163
Groote Schuur, 163
Grosvenor (shipwreck), 104

H.F. Verwoerd Dam, 69
Hager, Carl Otto, 123
Harris, William Cornwallis, 40, 44
Hartbeespoort Dam, 44
Herb Centre, Margaret Roberts, 45
Herbalists, 47
Hermanus, 13, 172-3
Heuningberg Trail, 127
Hiking trails
  Drakensberg area, 74-5
  Eastern Transvaal area, 62-3
  Fanie Botha Trail, 62
  Fortuna Mine Trail, 63
  Gold Nugget Trail, 63
  Heritage Trail, 110
  Heuningberg Trail, 127
  Jock of the Bushveld Trail, 63
  Johannesburg area, 40-1
  Kaapse Hoop Trail, 63
  Klipspringer Hiking Trail, 137
  Lekgalameetse Trail, 63
  Mabunda-Shango Hike, 62
  Magaliesberg area, 44
  Magoebaskloof Trail, 63
  Mapulaneng Trail, 63
  Otter Trail, 117
  Pretoria area, 42
  Shipwreck Route, 107
  Strandloper Trail, 106
  Table Mountain area, 149
  Tugela Gorge Trail, 75
  Whale Trail, 172
  Wild Coast area, 104-5
Hluhluwe-Umfolozi Game
Reserve, 18, 96-7
Hogsback, 108-9
Hottentots, 21, 26
  impact of white settlers, 22

Hout Bay, 158-9
Huguenots, 27, 171
Huis River Pass, 133

Immigrant groups
  Dutch speaking, 22
  English speaking, 77, 102
  German speaking, 102
  Indians, 27, 87
  Portuguese speaking, 27
India, 10, 72
Indian immigrants, 27, 87
Indian Ocean, 12-3
Industry, 31
Injasuti Dome, 70
Inyangas, 47
Inyati Game Park, 53
Islam, 27, 154
Itala Game Reserve, 97
Ixopo, 76

Jameson, Leander Starr, 135
Jock of the Bushveld, 55
Jock of the Bushveld camp, 56
Jock of the Bushveld Trail, 63
Johannesburg, 34, 36-41
  domestic architecture, 40
  historic sites, 40
  recreational areas, 41
  suburbs, 40
Joubert, Piet, 79
Jukskei, 29
Just Nuisance (dog mascot), 167

Kaapschehoop, 61, 65
Kaapse Hoop Trail, 63
Kakamas, 136
Kalahari Desert, 138-9
  vegetation, 11
Kalahari Gemsbok National
Park, 17, 138-9
Kalk Bay, 158
Kanniedood Dam, 58
Karoo, 128, 130
  succulent vegetation, 11
Karoo National Park, 18
Kerkenberg, 68
Khoikhoi, *see* Hottentots
Kimberley, 128, 134-5
  Big Hole, 135
  McGregor Museum, 135
  Mine Museum, 135
King, Dick, 89
King William's Town, 106
Kirstenbosch National Botanical
Garden, 160-1
Klipspringer Hiking Trail, 137
Knersvlakte, 16
Knysna, 118
Knysna forests, 119
Komsberg, 15
Kosi Bay
  fish kraals, 101
  lake system, 100
Kraal museums
  Lotlamoreng Cultural Village, 45
  Phumangena uMuzi (Zulu), 45
  Shakaland, 95

Kruger National Park, 50, 54-6, 58-9
Kruger, Paul, 43, 48
Kwazulu-Natal
  coastal areas, 92-3
  early settlers, 86
  game reserves, 97
  Midlands region, 76-7
  Northern region, 78-9, 100-1
  subtropical region, 84
  tourist attractions, 92-3
  water resources, 82-3

Lake Bangazi, 100
Lake Sibaya, 100-1
Lake St Lucia, 98
Lammergeier, 71
Langeberg, 15
Langenhoven, CJ, 123
Le Vaillant, François, 114
Lebombo Mountains, 18, 101
Lekgalameetse Trail, 63
Leopard, 57
Lesotho, 14, 66
Letaba restcamp, 58
Leydsdorp, 65
Lion, 19, 57
  white lion, 19
Lippizaner horses, 41
Londolozi Game Reserve, 53
Lost City, 48-9
Lotlamoreng Cultural Village, 45
Lower Sabie restcamp, 57
Lowveld, 19, 54
  waterfalls, 61
  see also Eastern Transvaal
Luvuvhu River, 58-9
Lydenburg, 50

Mabunda-Shango hike, 62
Mac Mac camp, 50, 64
Madagascar, 72
Magaliesberg, 44
Magoebaskloof, 60
Magoebaskloof Trail, 63
Mahlangu, Esther, 47
Makhonjwa Mountains, 61
Makuya National Park, 62
Mala Mala Game Reserve, 53
Malay Quarter, 154
Maluti Mountains, 66, 68
Mandela, Nelson, 25, 147
Mapulaneng Trail, 63
Maputaland, 100
  turtle breeding beaches, 101
Margaret Roberts Herbal Centre, 45
Maritz, Gert, 81
Market Theatre, 39
Marks, Sammy, 43
M'Bali Game Reserve, 53
McGregor Museum, Kimberley, 135
Meintjies, Lourens, 29
Meiringspoort, 14, 132-3
Mfecane, 78, 94
Mhlangana, (Zulu prince), 95
Midmar Holiday Resort, 83
Mine Museum, Kimberley, 135
Minerals, 30, 34, 61
Mining, 31, 37

Mkuzi Game Reserve, 18, 97
Modjadji Nature Reserve, 60
Montagu Pass, 125
Mont-aux-Sources amphitheatre, 70
Mooi River, 76
Mossel Bay, 124-5
Motswari Game Reserve, 53
Mozambique Current, 13
Mtunzini, 13
Muzi, Chief, 46
Mwene Mutapa (Monomatapa), 64

Namaqualand, 141
  spring flower phenomenon, 140
  vegetation, 15-6
Nama-Karoo
  vegetation, 11, 16
Nara melon, 16
Natal, see KwaZulu-Natal
Natal Drakensberg Park, 74
Natal Parks Board, 71, 97
Natal Witness (newspaper), 81
National Botanical Garden,
Nelspruit, 63
National Party, 25
Nature reserves
  Cape of Good Hope
  Nature Reserve, 157, 164-5
  De Hoop Nature Reserve, 127
  Fernkloof Nature Reserve, 173
  Goegap Nature Reserve, 141
  Modjadji Nature Reserve, 60
  Oribi Gorge Nature Reserve, 82
  Robberg Nature Reserve, 116
  Wonderkloof Nature Reserve, 63
Ndebele people, 34, 46
  women's art, 46-7
Ndibande, Francina, 47
Ndumu Game Reserve, 18, 101
Nguni people, 27
Nickel, 30
Nieu-Bethesda, 14
Nuweveldberg, 15

Ohrigstad, 50
Olifants restcamp, 57
Orange Free State, 66
Orange River, 69
Orange River Valley, 136
Organ Pipes Pass, 71
Oribi Gorge Nature Reserve, 82
Ostriches, 122-3
Otter Trail, 117
Oudtshoorn, 122
Outeniqua Choo-Tjoe, 119
Outeniqua mountain range, 15
Outeniqua people, 121

Pangaea, 10
Pansy shells, 116
Parktown and Westcliff Heritage
Trust, 40
Patterson, 'Wheelbarrow Alec', 64
Phinda Resource Reserve, 97
Phumangena uMuzi kraal, 45
Pierneef, Jacob, 43
Pietermaritzburg, 80
  British influences, 80

Voortrekker influences, 81
Pilanesberg Mountains, 48
Pilanesberg National Park, 45, 49
Pilgrim's Rest, 50, 61, 64
Pioneer Reef, 65
Platberg, 68
Platinum, 30
Plettenberg Bay, 116-7
Port Alfred, 113
Port Elizabeth, 110-11
Port Natal settlement, 79
Port Nolloth, 141
Ports, 30
Portuguese seafarers, 22, 26
Portuguese settlers, 27
Post Office Tree, 125
Pretoria, 34, 42-3
  architecture, 43
  museums and galleries, 43
  recreational areas, 43
Pretorius, Andries, 81
Pretoriuskop restcamp, 56
Private schools, 77
Property ownership, concept of, 23
Punda Maria restcamp, 58-9

Qacha's Nek, 70

Railways
  Blue Train Eastern Transvaal tour, 53
  Magaliesberg Express, 45
  Outeniqua Choo-Tjoe, 119
  Rovos Rail Eastern Transvaal tour, 53
Reconstruction and Development
plan (ANC), 32-3
Retief, Piet, 81
Rhino, 57, 97
Rhodes, Cecil John, 24, 36, 134, 160, 162
Rhodes University, 112
Richtersveld, 16, 141
Robben Island, 147
Robberg Nature Reserve, 116
Robert, Auguste 'French Bob', 65
Robinson Pass, 125
Rock art
  Drakensberg area, 73
Rock lobster, 13, 143
Rooiberg Pass, 133
Ross, John, 89
Royal Agricultural Show,
Pietermaritzburg, 76
Royal Natal National Park, 71, 74
Rugby, 29
Rustenburg, 45

Sabi Sabi Game Reserve, 53
Sabie, 61
Sabie Game Reserve, 55
San, see Bushmen
Sangomas, 47
Sani Pass, 71
Sardine run, Natal coast, 92
Sasol, 31
Satara restcamp, 57
Schreiner, Olive, 131
Seweweekspoort, 132-3
Shakaland Cultural Village, 95
Shaka, (Zulu king), 23, 78, 94

Shingwedzi restcamp, 58
Shipwreck Museum, Bredasdorp, 127
Shipwreck Route, 107
Siege of Ladysmith, 1899, 79
Simon's Town, 166-7
Sindebele, 27
Skukuza restcamp, 56
Smuts, Jan Christiaan, 39, 71
Soccer, 29
Sociable weaver (bird), 16
Sophiatown, 38
Sotho people, 21, 34
South African Native
  National Congress, 24
South African War (1899-1902), 135
Southern right whales, 173
Soutpansberg Mountains, 60
Soweto, 34, 38
Spandaukop, 14
Spitskop camp, 50, 64
Sport, 28-9
Spring flower season, 15-6, 140
Springbok (town), 141
Springbok
  national sporting emblem, 29
Stellenbosch, 168-9
Strandloper Trail, 106
Struisbaai, 126
Sudwala Caves, 61
Sugar plantations, 86, 93
  Indian labourers, 87
Sun City, 48
Swartberg, 15
Swartberg Pass, 132
Swazi people, 27

Table Bay, 146
Table Bay harbour, 152
  historic sites, 153
Table Mountain, 15, 148-9
  hikes and walks, 149
Tembe Elephant Park, 101
Thaba Nchu, 68
Thabana Ntlenyana, 70
Thathe Vondo Forest, 62
Timbavati Reserve, 19
Titanium mining question, 99
Tourism, 32
Traditional healers, 47
Transkei, 102
  see also Eastern Cape
Transvaal, 34
Trichardt, Louis, 54
Trout fishing
  Drakensberg area, 75
Tsetse fly eradication programme, 96
Tsolwana Game Reserve, 109
Tsonga people, 21
Tswana people, 34
Tugela Gorge Trail, 75
Tugela River, 83
Turtles, 101

Uitlanders, 24
Ulusaba Game Reserve, 53
Umgeni River, 82
Union, 1910, 24
University of Cape Town, 163

Upington, 136
Vaal River, 69
Valley Mountain, 15
Valley of a Thousand Hills, 77
Valley of Desolation, 15
Van der Post, Sir Lourens, 131
Van der Stel, Simon, 168-9
Van Plettenberg, Joachim, 116
Van Rensburg, Hans, 54
Van Riebeeck, Johan, 22
Vegetation, 11
VhaVenda people, 60
Waterfront (Cape Town), 146, 152-3
Vixseboxse, Johannes, 122
Voortrekkers, 23
  Anglo-Boer conflict, 79
  Voortrekker-Zulu conflict, 78
Voting rights, 24
Vulture, bearded, 71

Waenhuiskrans, 126
Walker Bay, 172-3
Waterfalls Eastern Transvaal, 61
  KwaZulu-Natal, 77
  Weenen (massacre), 78
West Coast National Park, 142
West Coast region, 12-3
  rock lobsters, 143
  seafood route, 143
  spring flower phenomenon, 142
Western Cape, 144-73
  beaches, 156-7
  Bo-Kaap, 154-5
  fauna, 164-5
  fishing, 158-9
  flora, 160-1, 164
  hikes and walks, 149
  historic sites, 146-7, 150-1, 162-3
  ports, 152-3, 166-7
  whales, 172-3
  winelands, 168-71
Whale Route, 127
Whales, 13, 172-3
  southern right, 173
Whale Trail, 172
Wild Coast, 104-5
Wild dog, 19
Wilderness National Park, 121
Wilderness (village), 120
Wine estates, 169-71
Wine routes, 170
Witteberg, 15
Witwatersrand, 65
Wolkberg Wilderness Area, 63
Wonderkloof Nature Reserve, 63
World War I, (1914-18), 24

Xhosa country see Transkei
Xhosa people, 21, 27

Yusuf, Sheik, 27, 155

Zastron, 68
Zoo Lake, 41
Zulu people, 27, 87, 94
  Anglo-Zulu conflict, 79
  Voortrekker-Zulu conflict, 78
Zwelethini, King Goodwill, 27

STRUIK PUBLISHERS (PTY) LTD

(a member of The Struik Publishing Group (Pty) Ltd)
80 McKenzie Street
Cape Town 8001

Reg. No.: 54/00965/07
First published 1994

Managing editor: Simon Atkinson
Cartographer: Loretta Chegwidden
Designer: Alix Gracie
Reproduction: Hirt & Carter, Cape Town
Printing and binding: Tien Wah Press (Pte) Ltd, Singapore

ISBN 1-86825-655-3

PHOTOGRAPHIC CREDITS